FASHIONABLE GIRLS

A COLORING BOOK FOR GIRLS

One of the Best Collection for the Beautiful Girls Out There Who Want to Paint the World with their Charm & Innocence.....!

ADULT COLORING BOOK
Vol – 4

SATYANVESHI

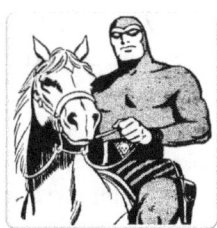

DIGITAL COMICS WORLD PUBLICATION

Published By Digital Comics World Publication
Fort, Mumbai – 400 001
digital.comics.world@gmail.com

© SATYANVESHI

Published in arrangement with
Amazon Digital Services, USA

FASHIONABLE GIRLS
ISBN-13: 978-1530007912
ISBN-10: 1530007917

I dedicate this book, with deep respect and great love, to Mother Nature.
You not only gave me the gift of life but an unrelenting passion
to live it fully. For that I am so very grateful

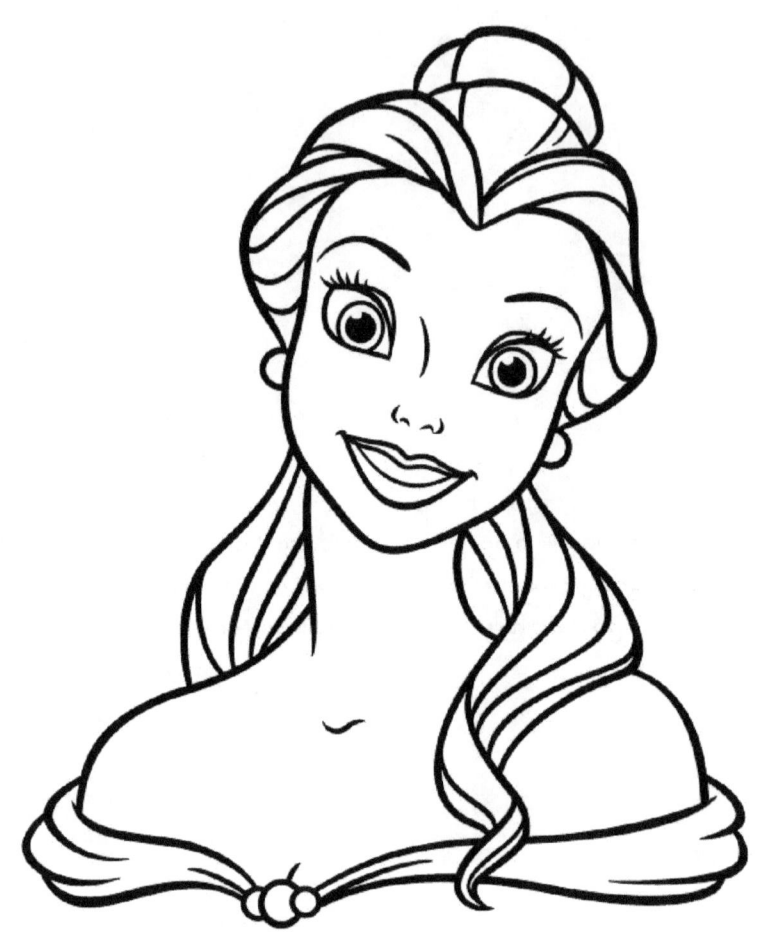

HAPPY COLORING...!

Top Ten Therapeutic Benefits of Coloring Books for Adults

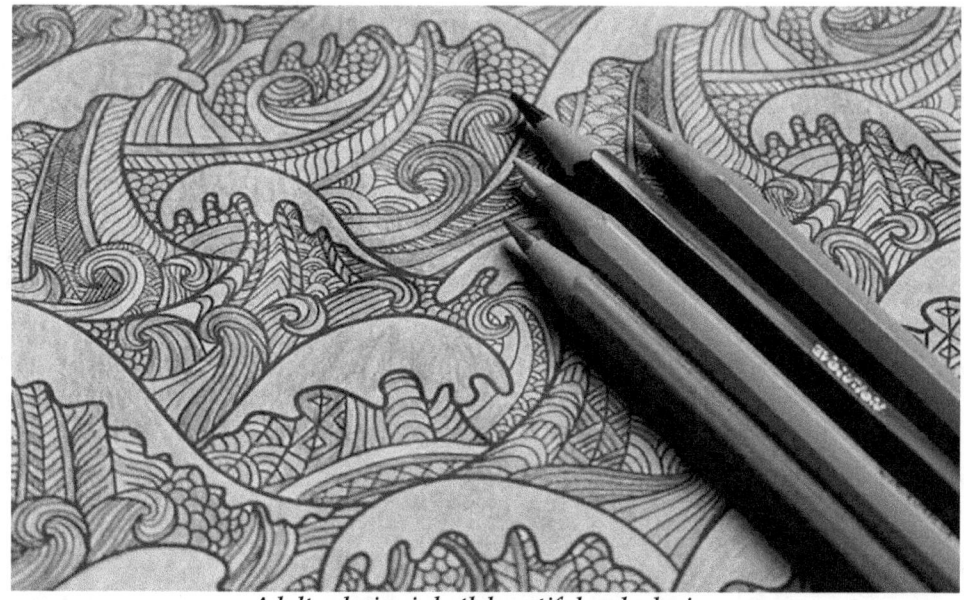

Adult coloring is both beautiful and relaxing.

Coloring is not just an activity for keeping kids occupied; we only associate it with children. In reality, coloring books and coloring pages for adults are also extremely therapeutic and can help generate wellness, quietness, mindfulness and the exact same benefits which meditation imparts on the brain. It is no wonder that, coloring books for adult are so popular these days. Such creative activities are almost like Nirvana for adults' souls. Even more popular are coloring pages with Mandalas for adults. Mandalas are symmetrical patterns and representations having their origins in India. When an adult colors these repetitive patterns, s/he actually experiences mindfulness and even reaches a meditative state. This has even been proven by several scientific studies. With so many therapeutic benefits of coloring pages for adults, it is time that every adult should make use of this book!

1. Coloring pages for adults help de-stress

One of the earliest scientists to have studied the therapeutic benefits of coloring pages for adults was Carl Jung. He studied coloring of Mandalas as early as the first half of the 20th century. He often used Mandalas (which have concentric circles and geometrical patterns in them) for his patients and found that it helped them become calmer and witness lesser stress.

2. Coloring activities activate both parts of the cerebral hemisphere

According to psychologist Gloria Martinez Ayala, the action of coloring involves both logic and creativity. When we use logic to pick up a color for a particular shape or pattern, we activate the analytical part of the brain. On the other hand, when we choose to mix and match colors, we activate the creative side of the brain. This helps incorporate both areas of the cerebral cortex which control vision and help with coordination and fine motor skills

3. Coloring pages for adults take them back to childhood

When an adult colors, s/he is transported back to the stress free days of childhood. Getting back those happy memories helps one relax and even feel optimistic and energetic for the future.

4. Coloring is like meditation

Meditation is the art of doing nothing. It is also the art of 'de-concentrating' which helps relax and reduce the chatter of a restless mind. While most people find it difficult to meditate, coloring pages and books for adults easily help induce the same meditative state. It is no wonder that many publishers in UK, France and USA have come up with coloring books just for adults. Coloring Mandalas are especially relaxing since coloring of the round and round patterns and concentric circles of these ancient designs relax the mind and make a person more mindful. It also keeps him/her focused on the present moment-just like meditation!

5. Coloring for adults helps reduce anxiety

Anxiety is a common mental condition affecting hundreds of adults. Anxiety and panic attacks cause many symptoms including: thoughts of death or dying, excessive worry, nausea, headaches, chills, fever, insomnia, etc. By using coloring pages for adults, therapists help their adult patients relax. The artistic expression helps patients go deeper into a relaxed state making other forms of therapy more effective. Research has now proven that coloring pages and books for adults can be used as prelude to regular or conventional therapy for many mental disorders.

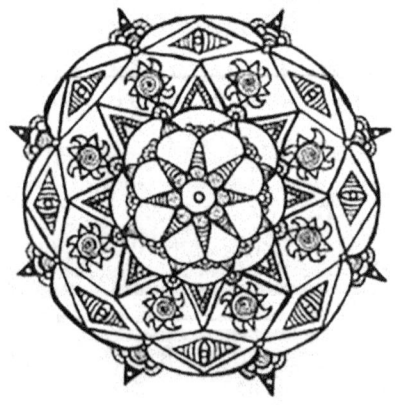

A 'MANDALA' Design

6. Coloring for adults helps them to re-discover themselves

Adults often find themselves stuck in a rut managing jobs, housework etc. Coloring pages can help one get out of this routine, making them feel more comfortable and relaxed at the end of a long day. This activity can also help one be with his/her thoughts. Many an adult has rediscovered him/herself through coloring pages for adults online and offline. You can color this book and relax with this wonderful activity at the end of a long day.

7. Coloring for adults is a perfect therapy many diseases

Coloring books for adults are ideal for patients -especially those battling health issues like epilepsy. Take the example of Cari Schofield, 38, from Stockbridge, Georgia who, due to her epilepsy, had several limitations. Since she started coloring, she finds she easily calms down and relax which, in turn, helps alleviate epileptic attacks. Due to her jerky hand movements, she used to experience difficulty holding a pen or pencil for drawing. But, by using coloring books for adults, she has started enjoying this activity again.

8. Coloring for adults helps spark creativity

One of the most important benefits of coloring books for adults is that they help ignite creativity which adults continue to experience in several other facets of their lives. Adults who color regularly find that they become great at picking colors for their clothes, their interiors etc. Coloring books and pages also help people become more creative in their jobs, analytical thinking activities and several other aspects of work and play.

9. Coloring helps adults reconnect with their Inner Child

Inner Child healing therapy is a popular therapy for disturbed adults who tend to be very harsh with themselves. As adults, we often have certain areas in our lives that need working on and all those areas are connected to certain issues which we carry forward from our past. When one reconnects with his/her inner child, a child full of innocence and love, one can actually become better as an adult. Such inner child healing especially helps break negative thinking patterns. It helps one love him/herself more-unconditionally. This, in turn, helps one become one's best self-a confidant, radiant person who is ready to take on the world without fear.

10. Coloring books for adults help transport one to a time and place faraway

If, at the end of the day, you really wish to relax and get away from it all-simply bring out your crayons and color the pages of this book. This will surely help you get out and away from it all and help you relax and unwind. It is like taking a vacation without going anywhere!

These are the 10 benefits of coloring pages for adults. ☺

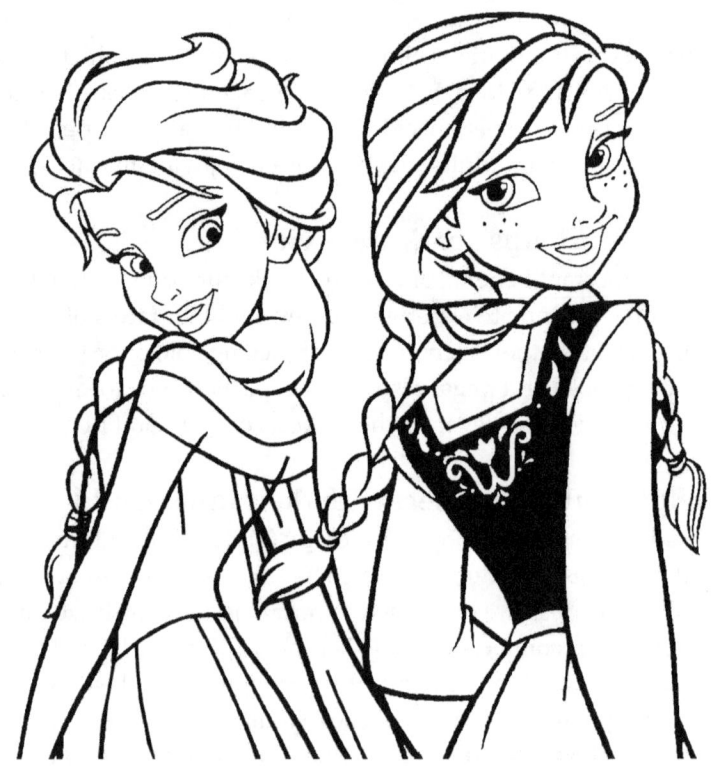

HAPPY COLORING...! ☺

How Should You Color Your New Book?

Color like a Pro:

Here are some tips from coloring-book artists.

Consider colored pencils:

"I like high-end pencils, which allow you to do shading," says Erik Siuda, tattoo artist and author of the Modern Tattoo Designs Coloring Book (Creative Haven/Dover Publications) among other titles. "I often recommend investing in Prismacolor pencils."

Keep things light:

"My top tip is not to press too hard with your pens or colored pencils," says Millie Marotta, author of Animal Kingdom. "Instead, try to build up color gradually."

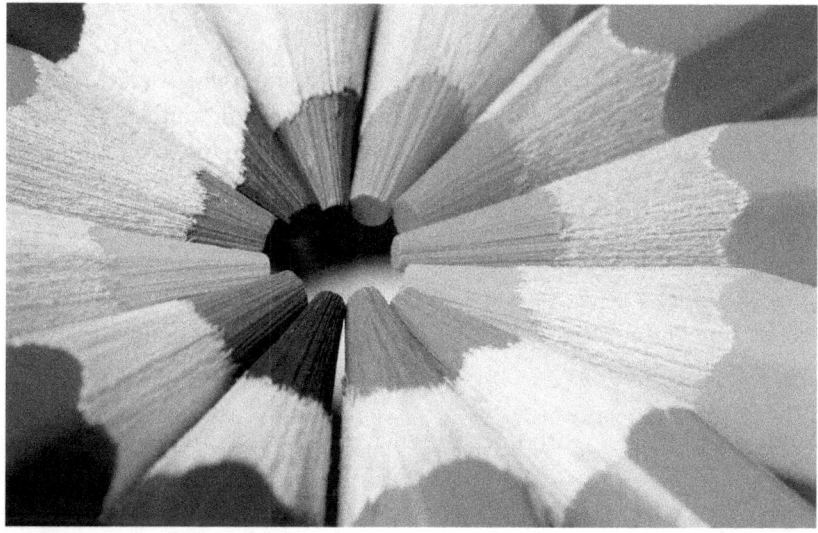

Stay sharp:

A well-sharpened pencil is the key to getting into tight spaces in intricately designed adult coloring books. Any pencil sharpener will do to keep the general edge. But "if you have trouble sharpening the softer, thicker lead without breaking it, try carefully carving the point with an X-ACTO blade," suggests mandala artist P.C. Turczyn. "You can refine the point without losing more of the wood by using sandpaper. Art supply stores sell little sandpaper blocks for this purpose."

Be a savvy Pens-man:

If pens are your thing, "try to find some that have a fine nib and are not alcohol based as these have a tendency to bleed, as do those with a heavy ink flow," says Marotta. Ask for help at your local art store.

Splash around:

Watercolor pencils offer special effects. "You can use them like regular pencils, then wash clear water over an outlined area and—presto—get a watercolor effect," says Turczyn. "Avoid applying the water with a brush that is too big for an area; if you inadvertently mix a green area and a red area, for example, you will get brown." Other techniques include wetting an area before you color it in. Or, you can try dipping the pencil in water before you draw with it, she says. "Craypas, Derwent and Prismacolor all make good-quality watercolor pencils."

Do what you like:

Or, forget all of the above and do what feels good to you. Glitter glue, Sharpie markers, Crayola, charcoal, oil pastels, tempera paint, inside the lines, outside the lines—it's all good. "One of the great things about coloring is that there are no rules," says Marotta. "And it's amazing for me to see the hundreds of variations of the same illustrations all colored in so differently. I love it."

Color Your Mood:

Colors themselves carry therapeutic qualities, according to licensed clinical professional art therapist Lacy Mucklow. Selecting colors can literally affect your mood. Here's a guide to how you can use colors to rev up or calm down—or combine them for a total mood makeover.

Cool colors like blue, green and purple have a calming effect. Use them to literally chill out.

Warm colors like red, orange and yellow are pepper-uppers. Try them when you want to brighten a bad mood.

Bright colors are energizing, so turn to them when you want a little inner lift.

Dark colors carry a relaxing energy and can be used to ratchet down an overactive mind. Pastels and light tints communicate softness and help soothe the soul.

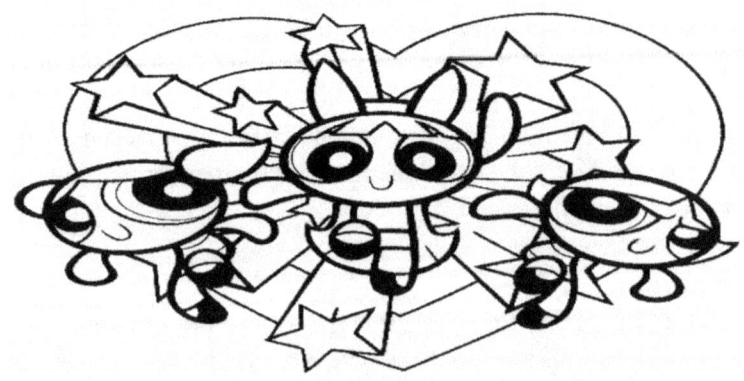

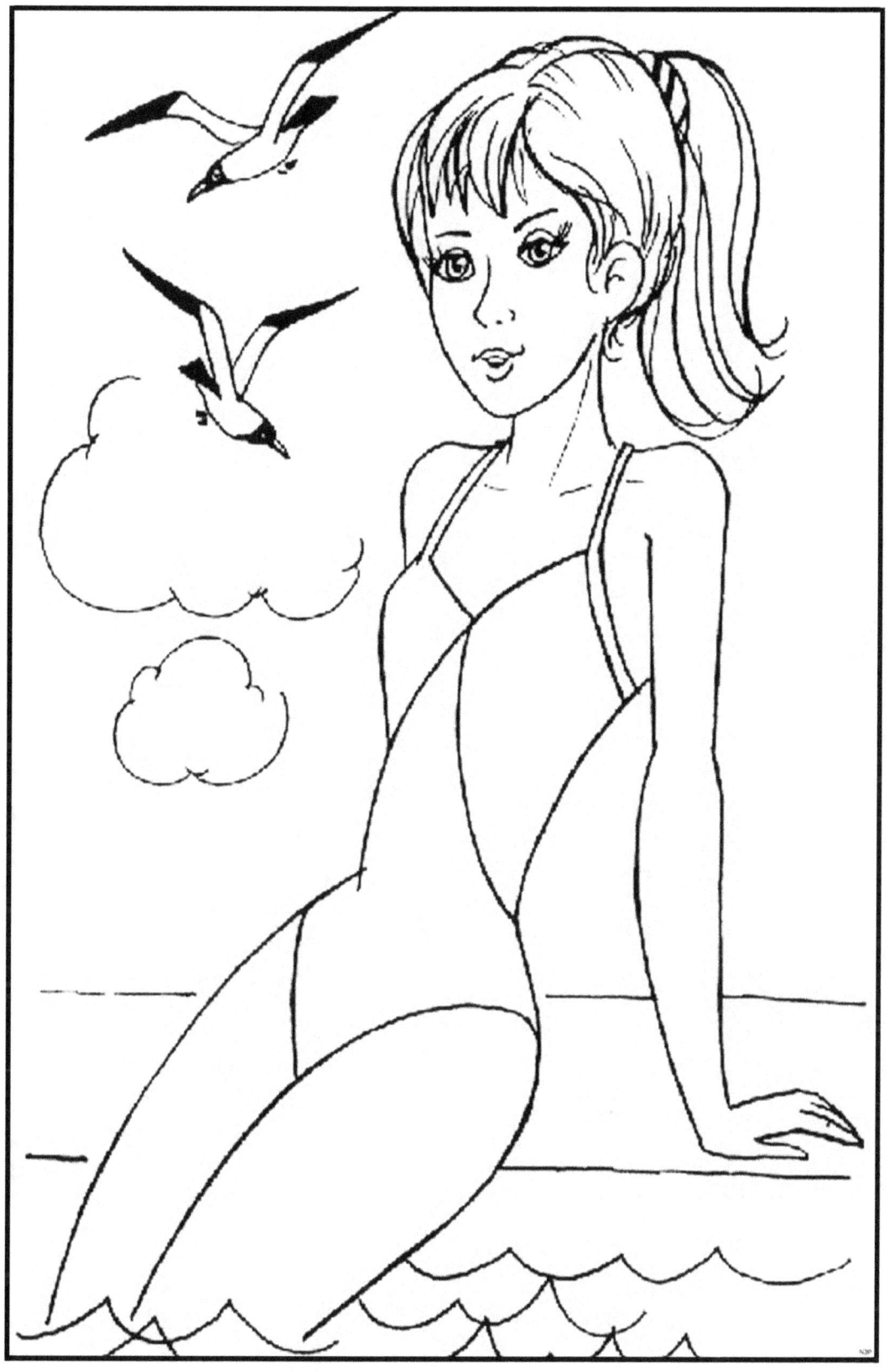

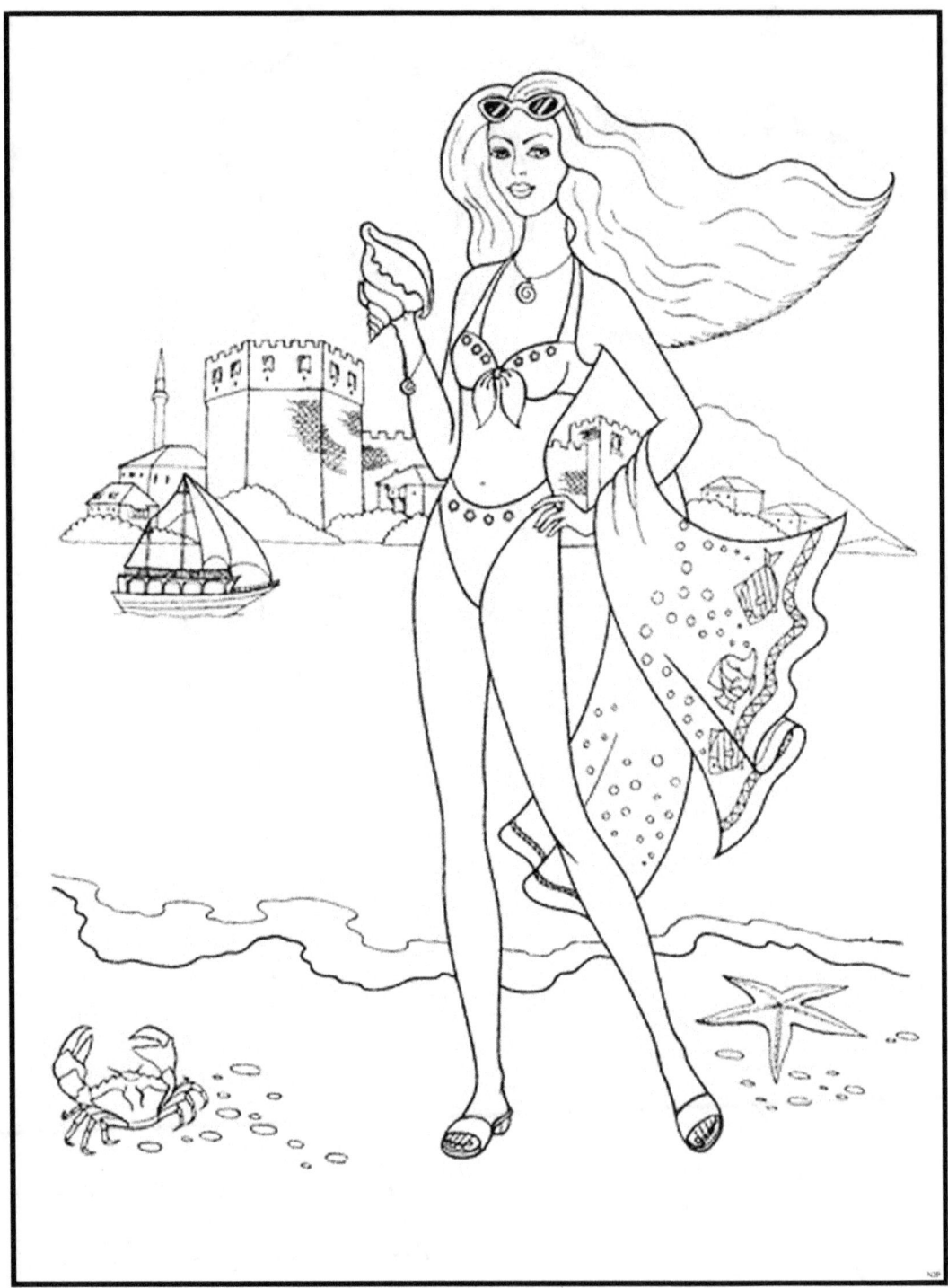

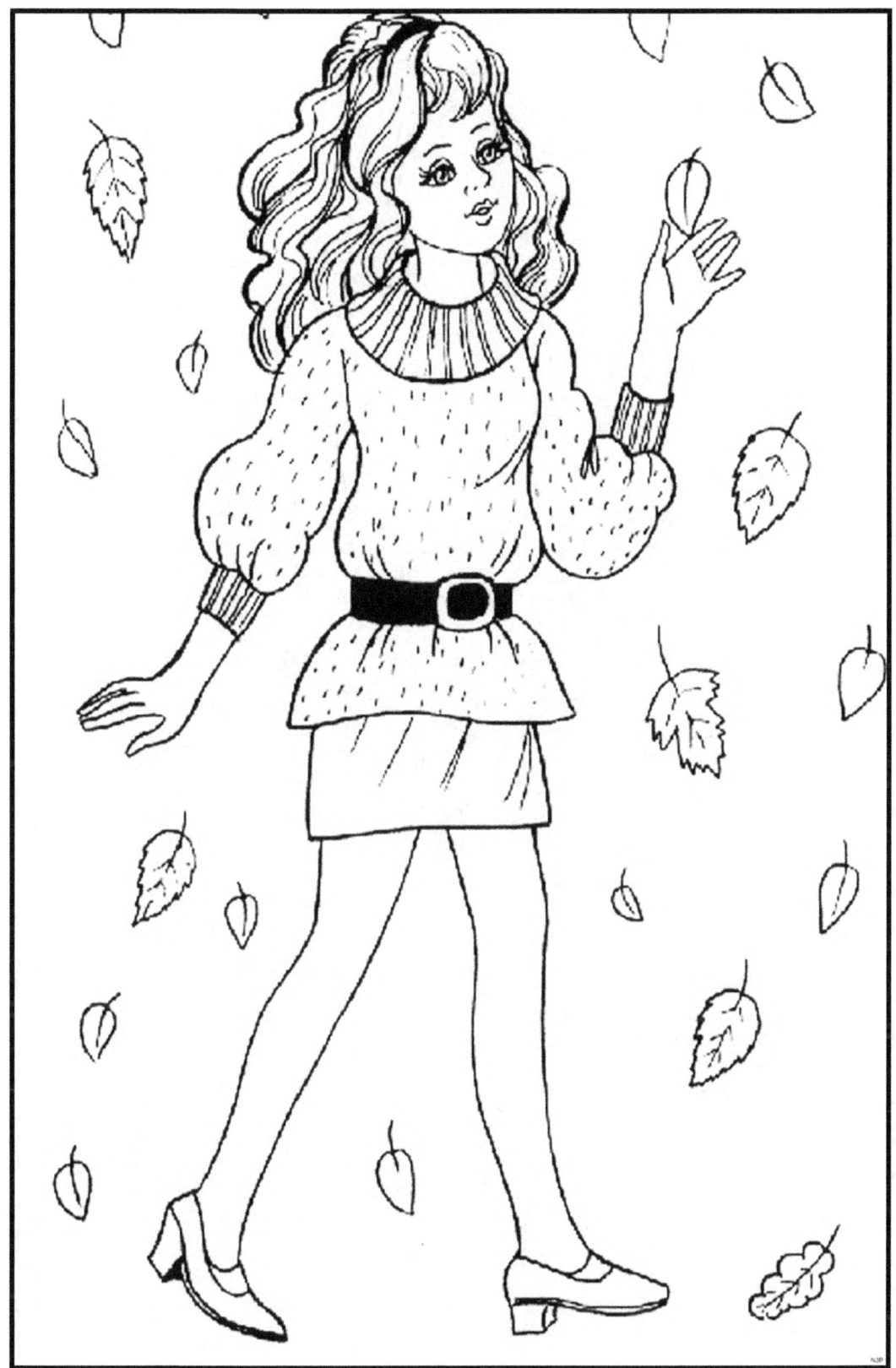

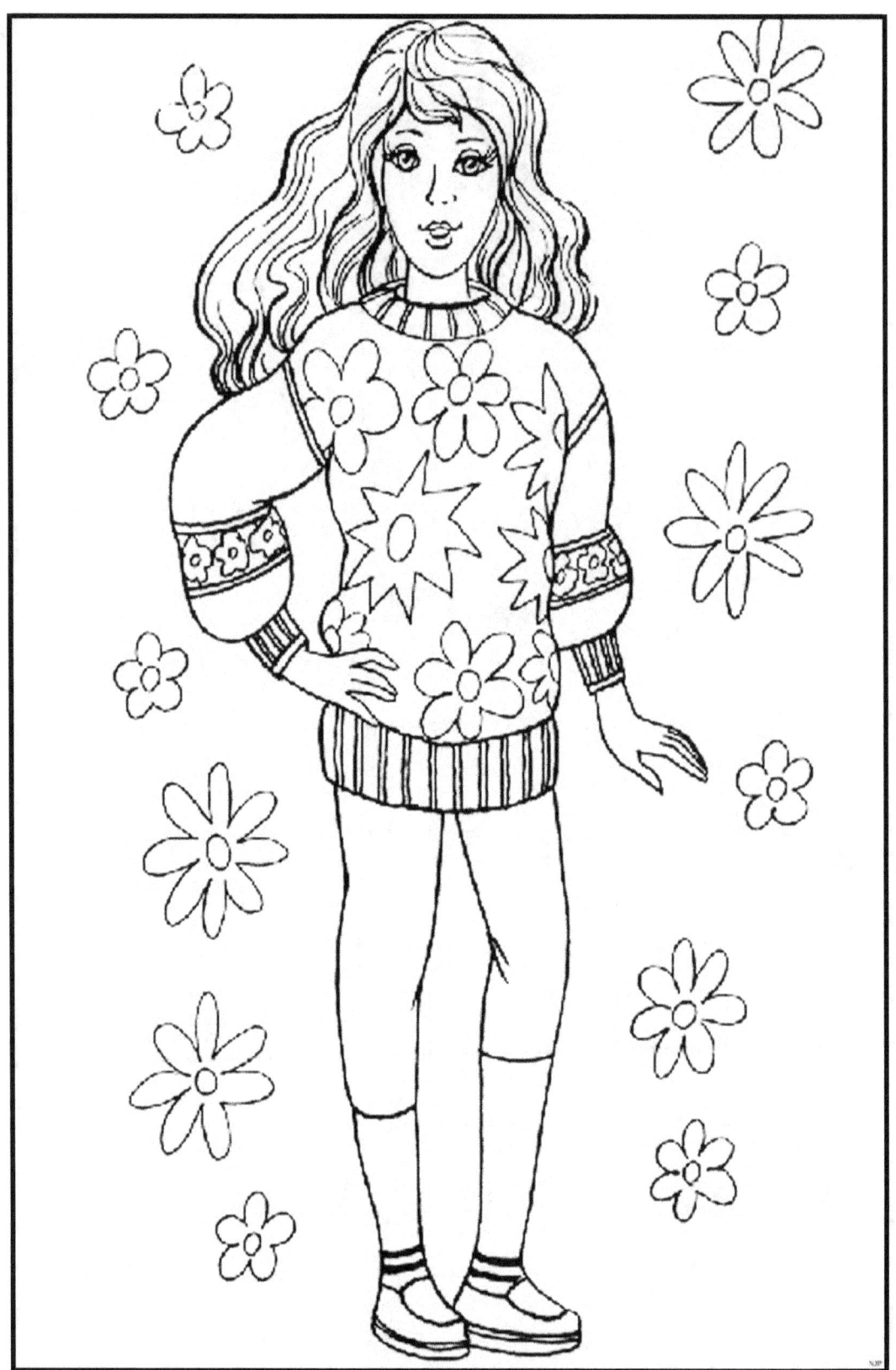

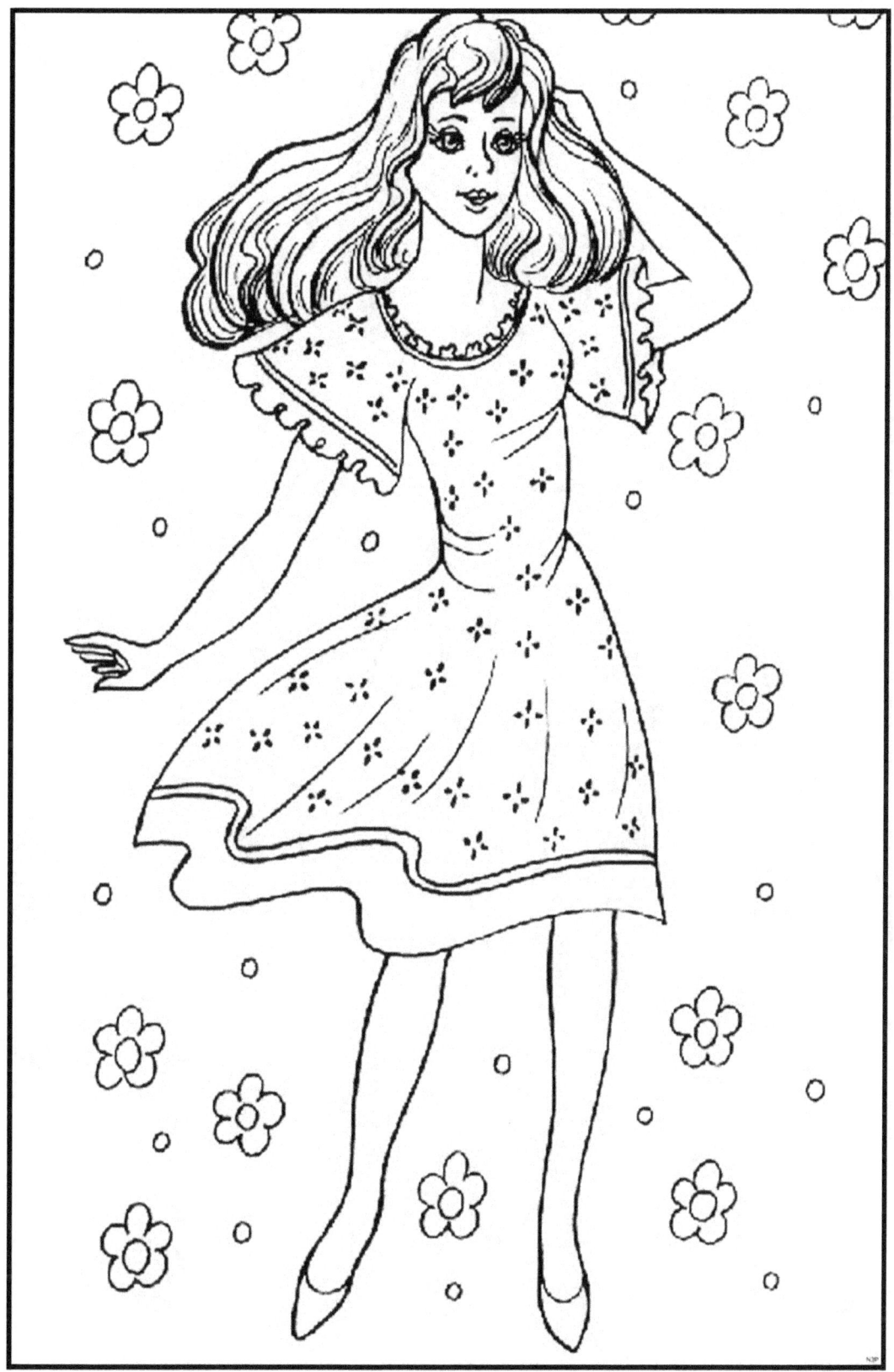

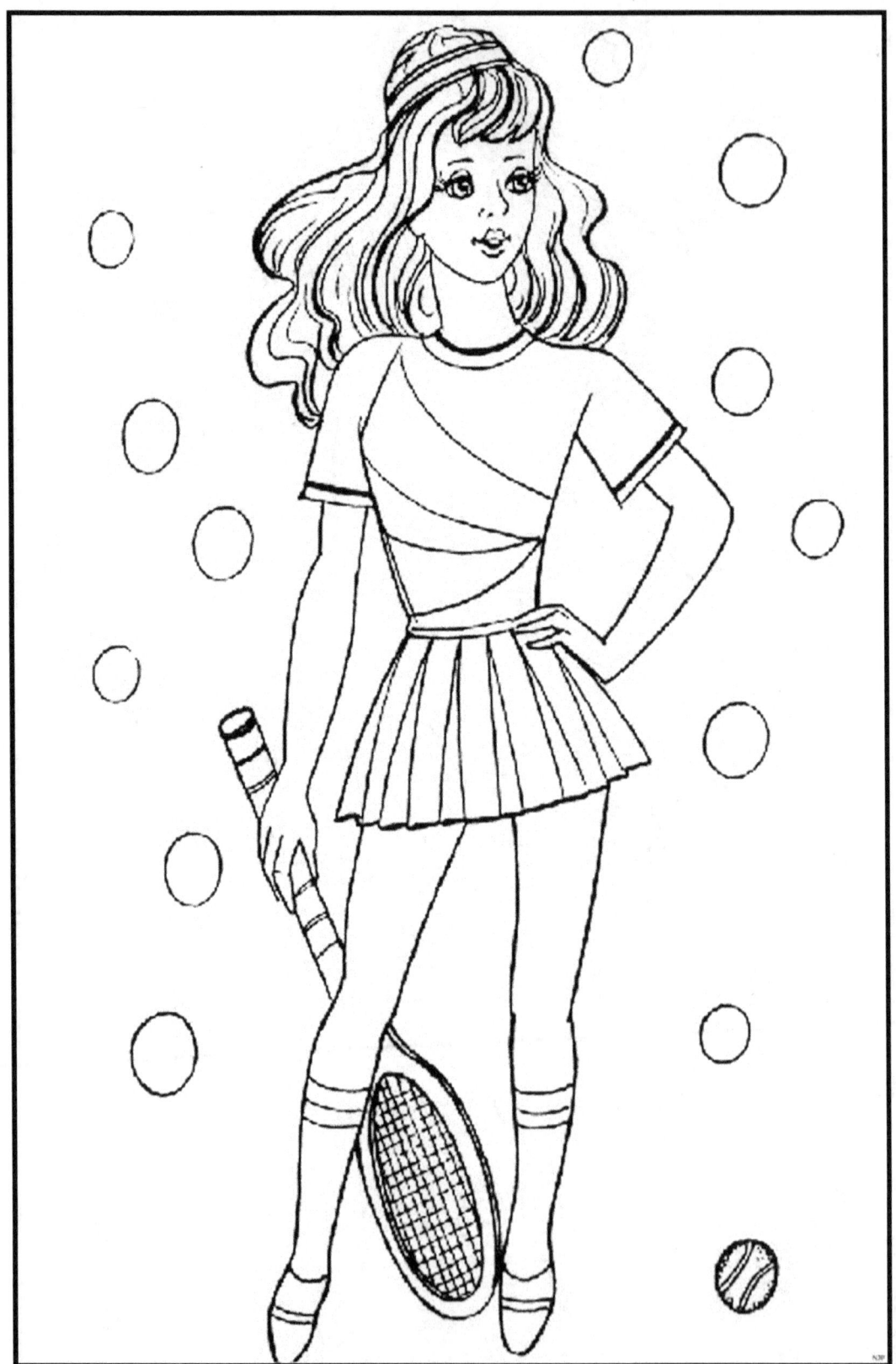

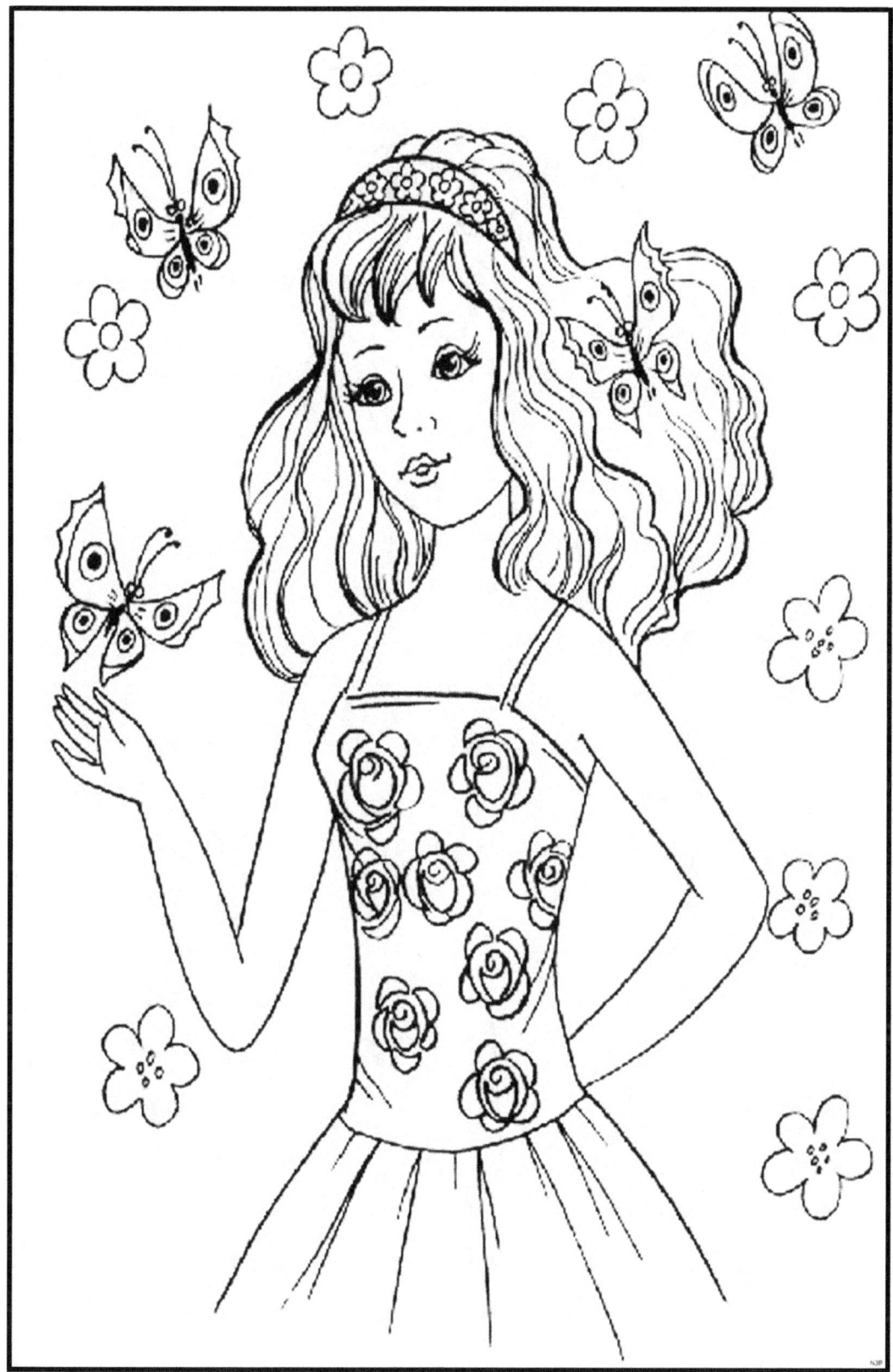

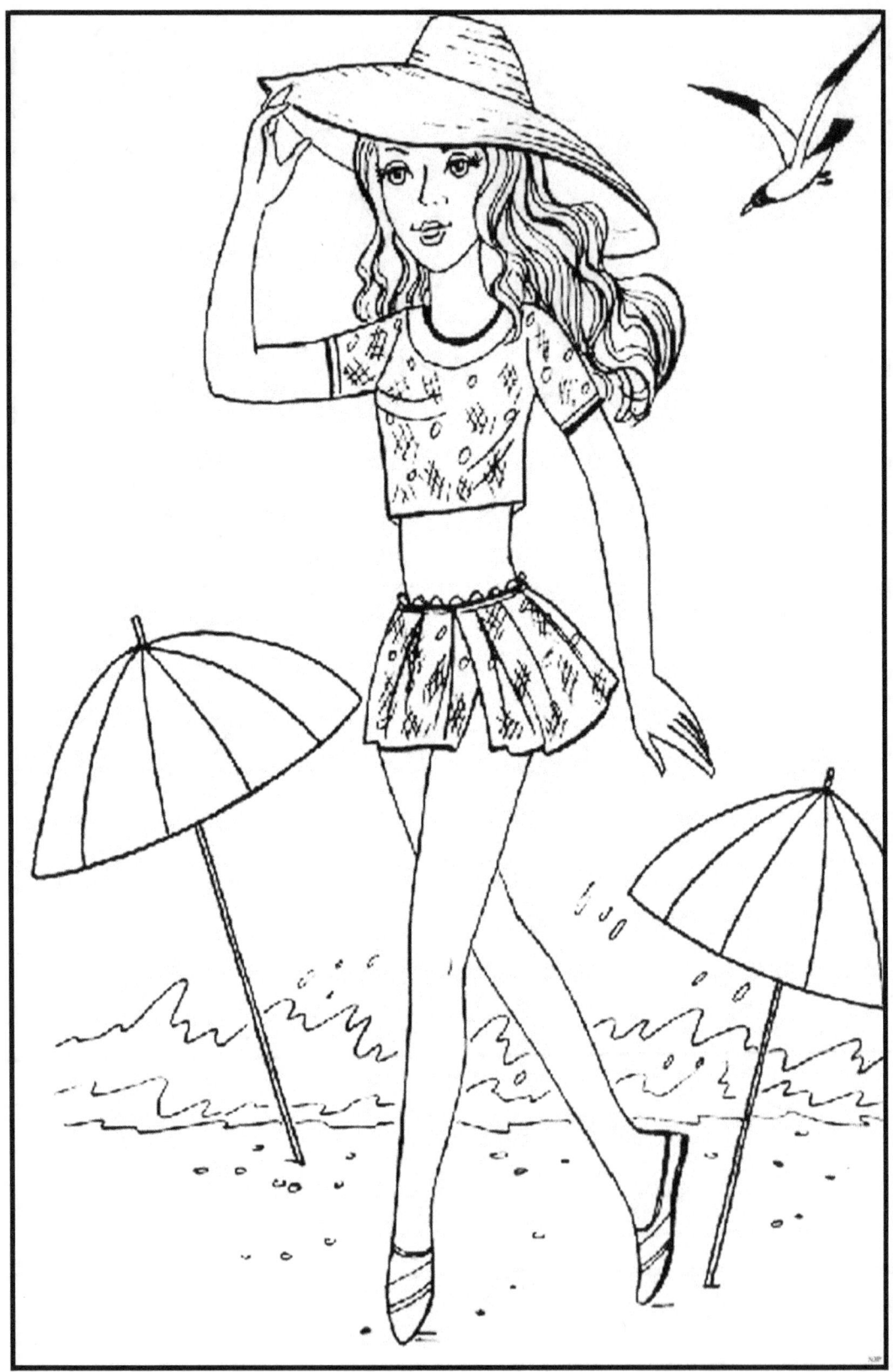

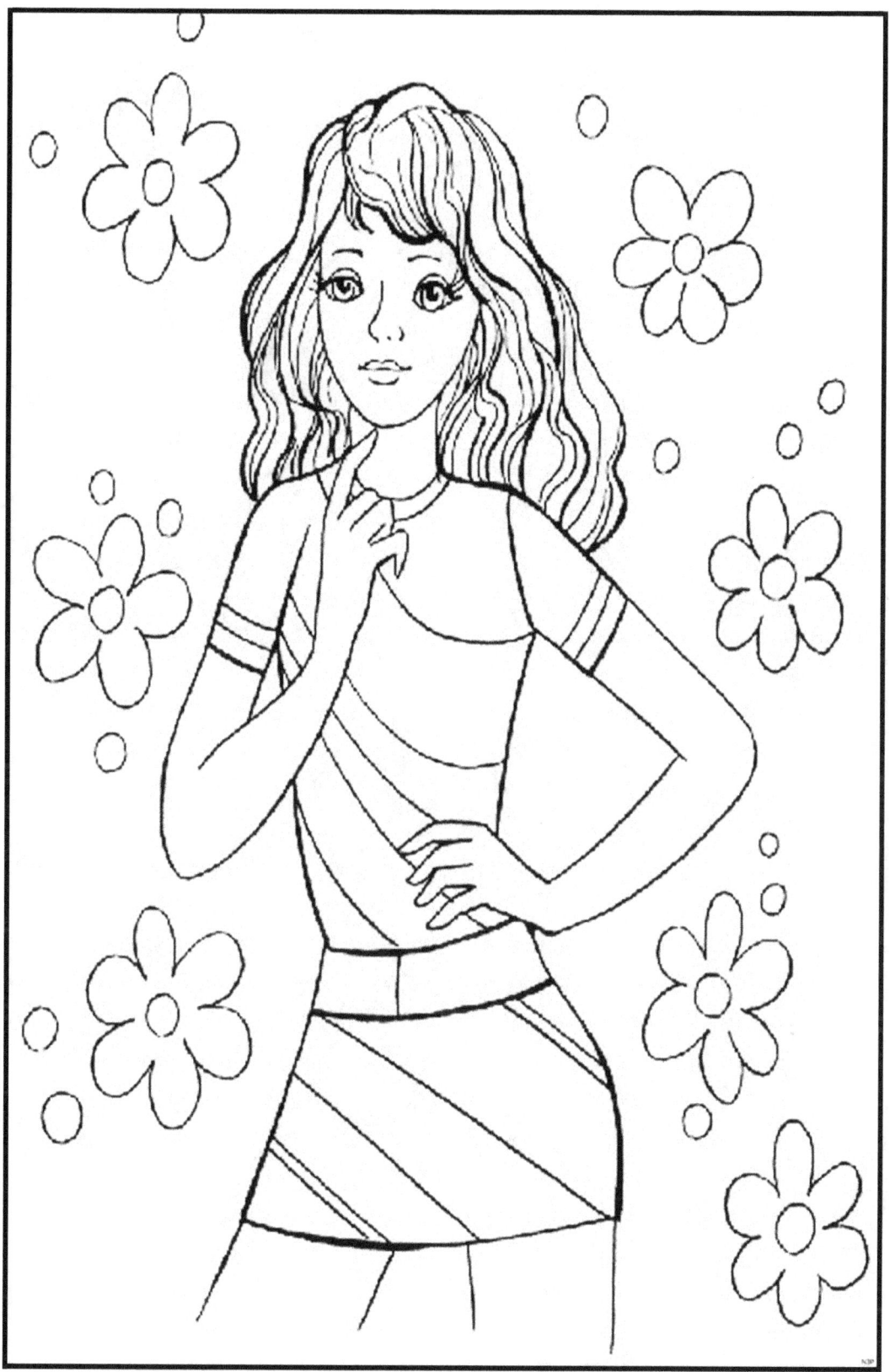

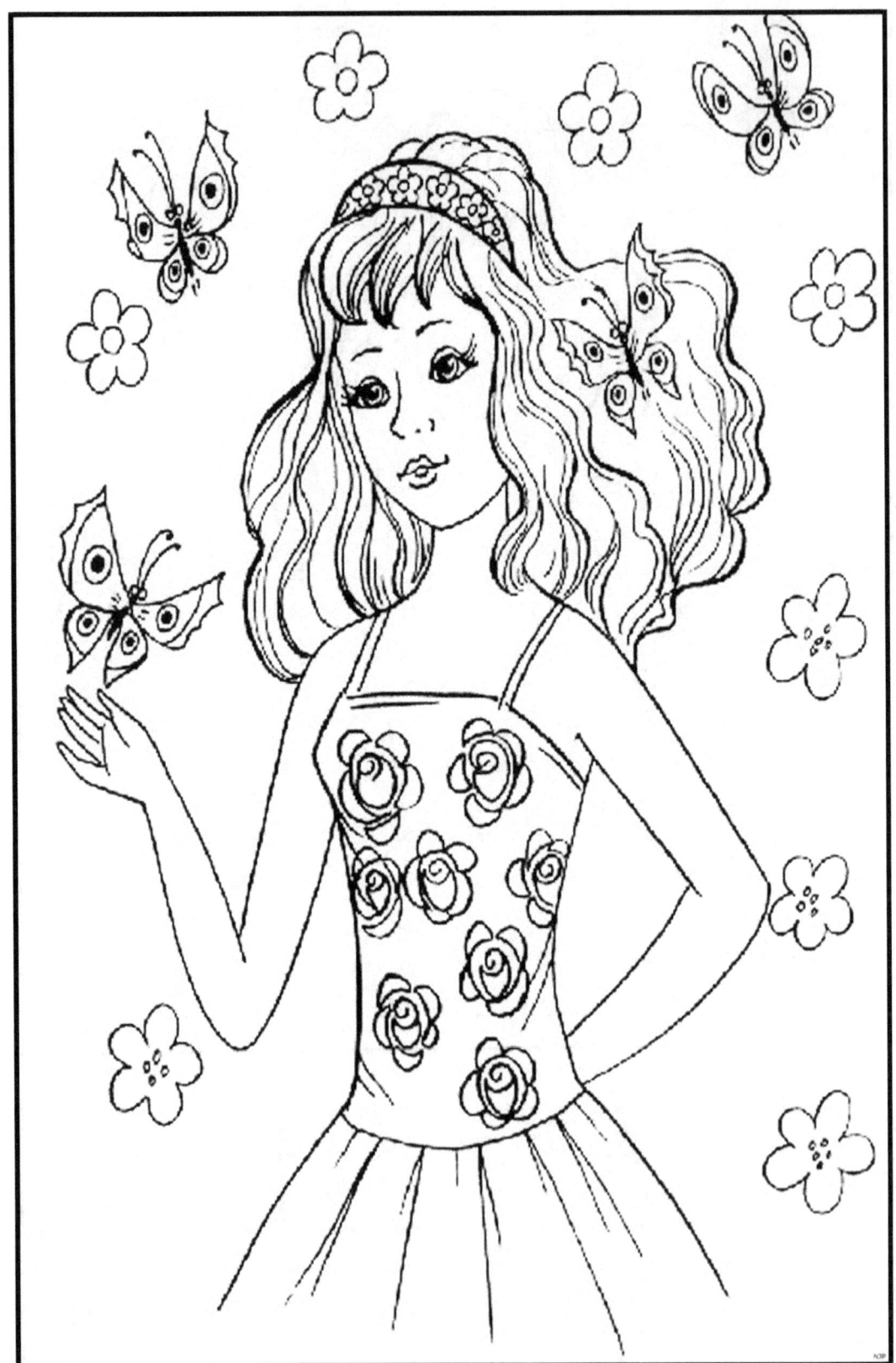

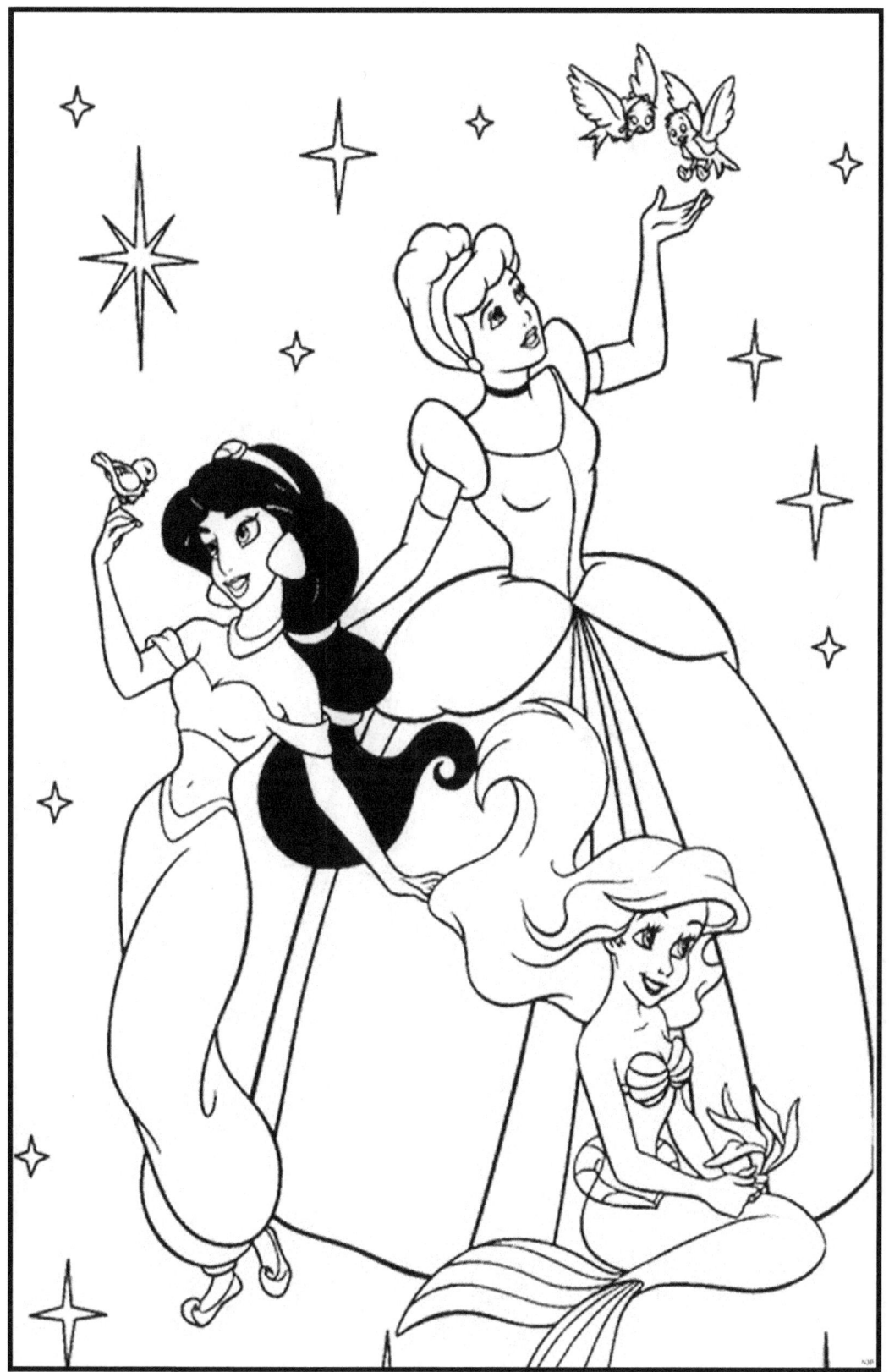

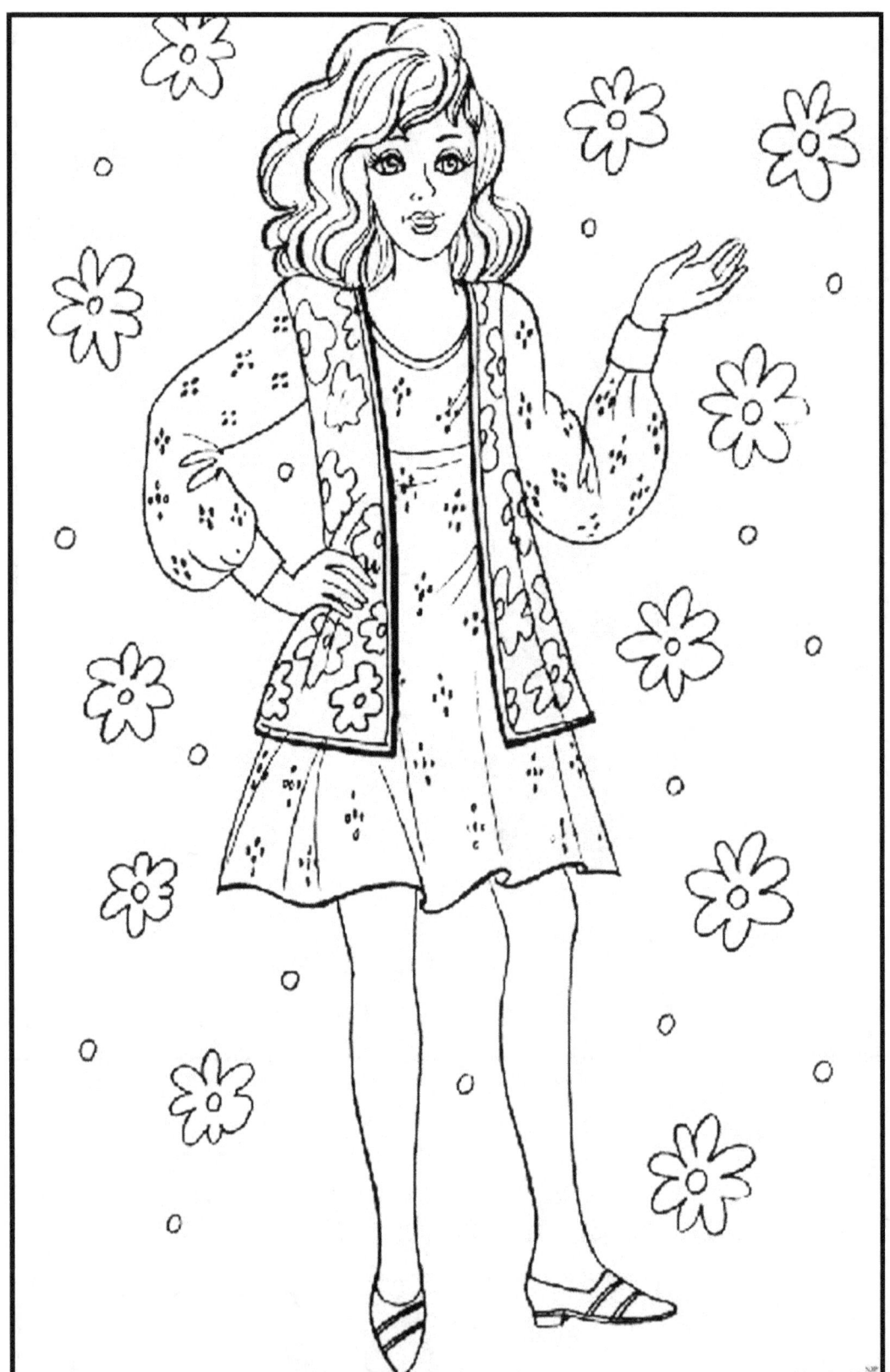

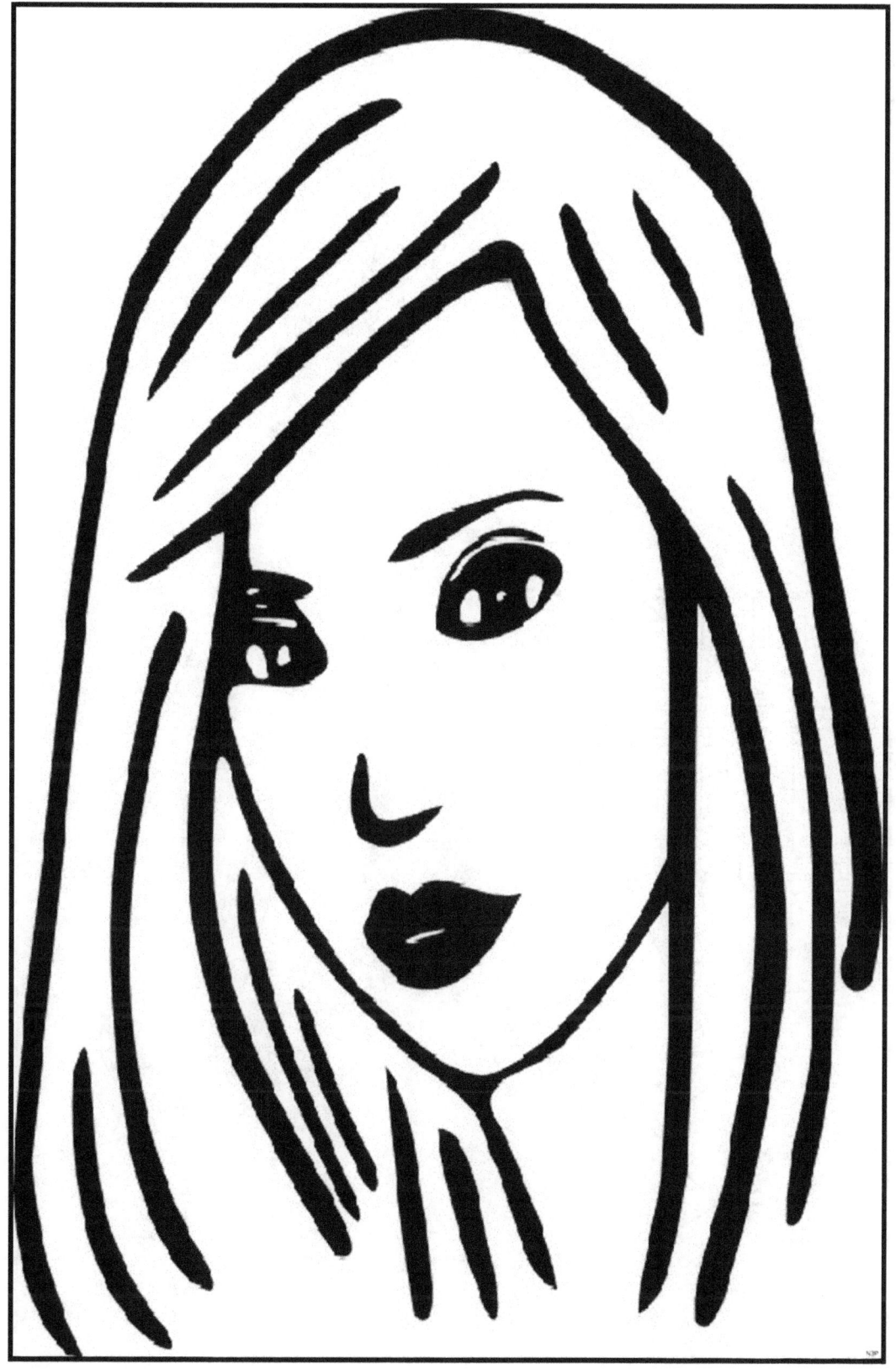

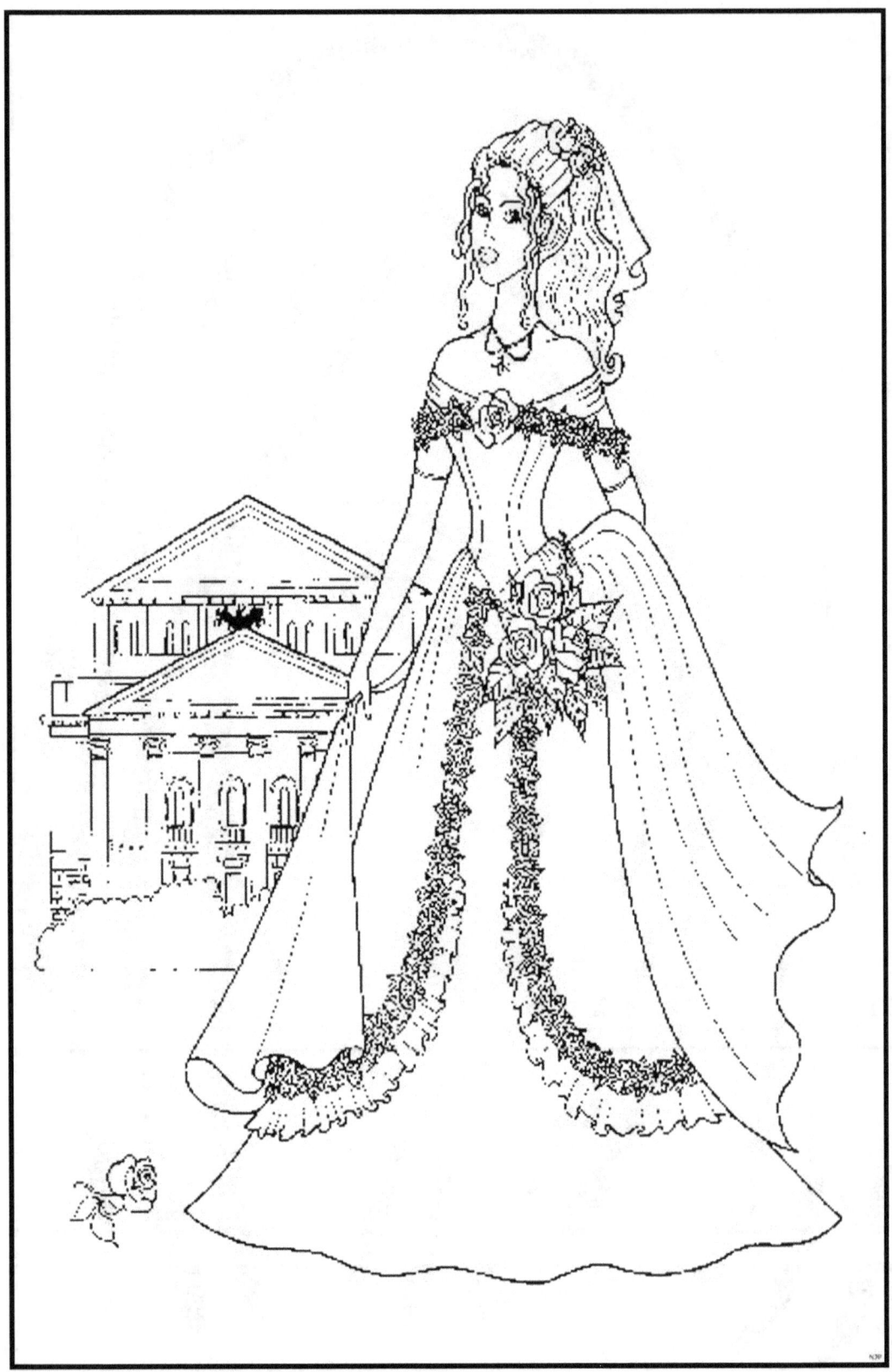

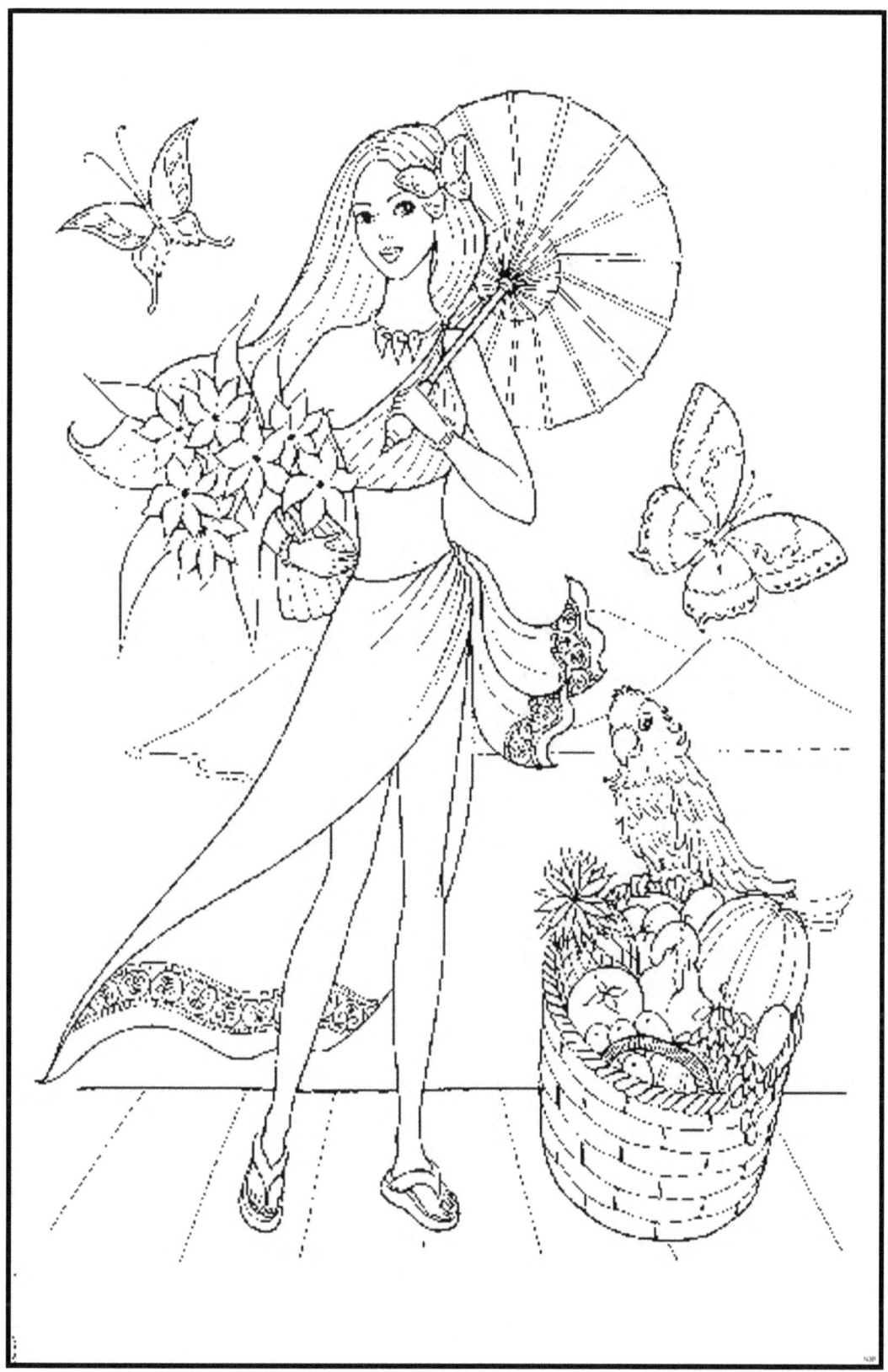

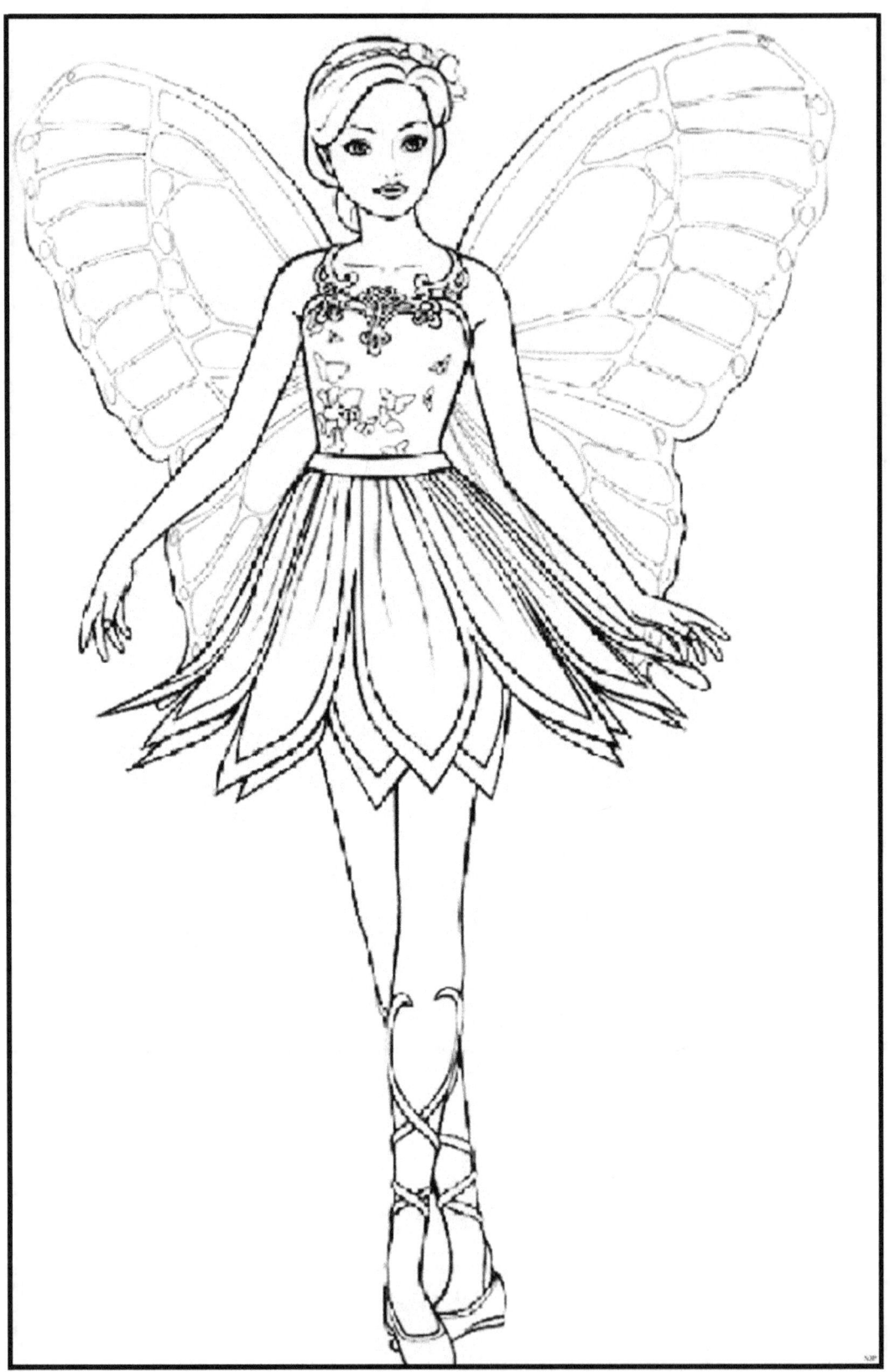

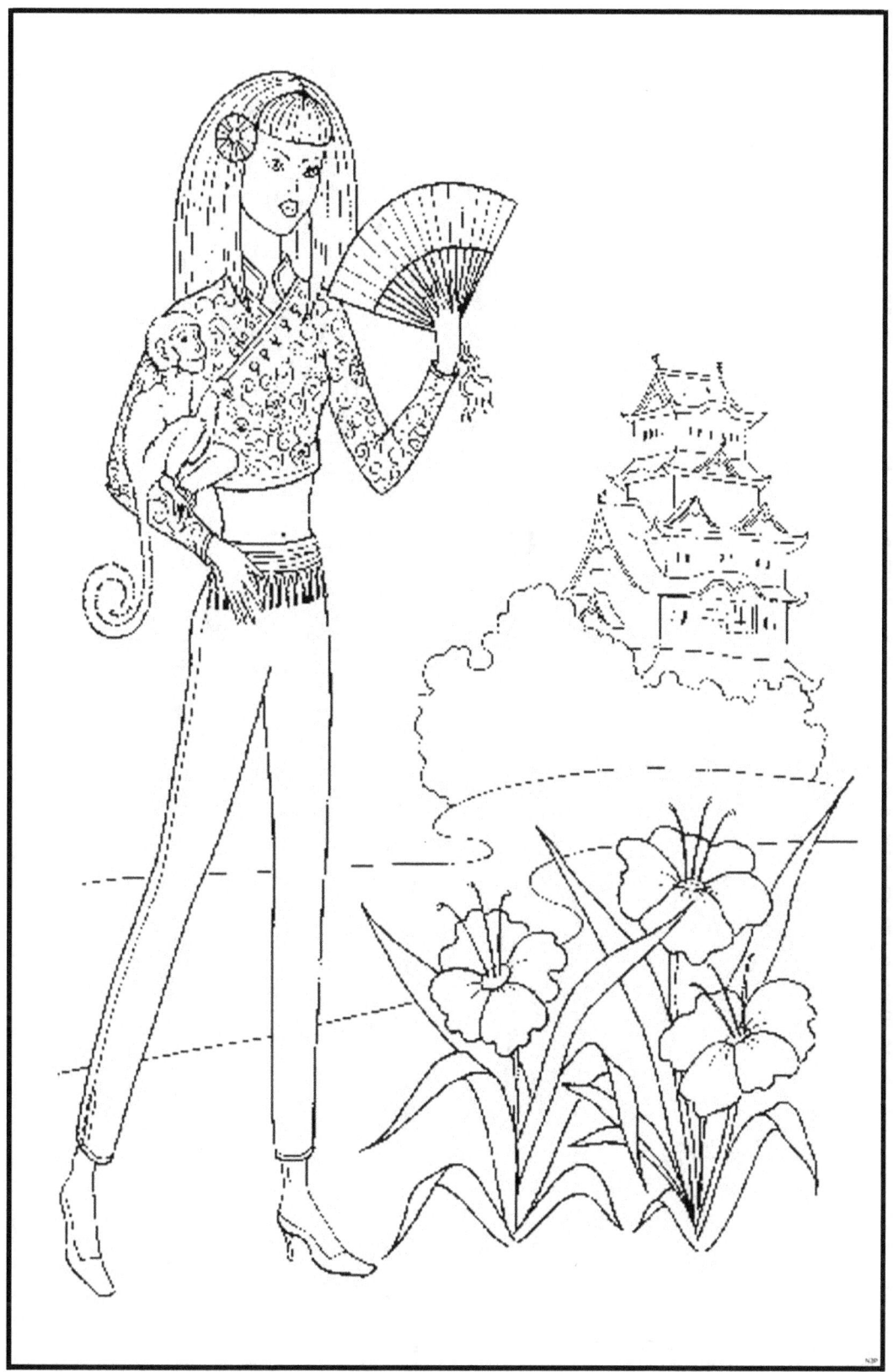

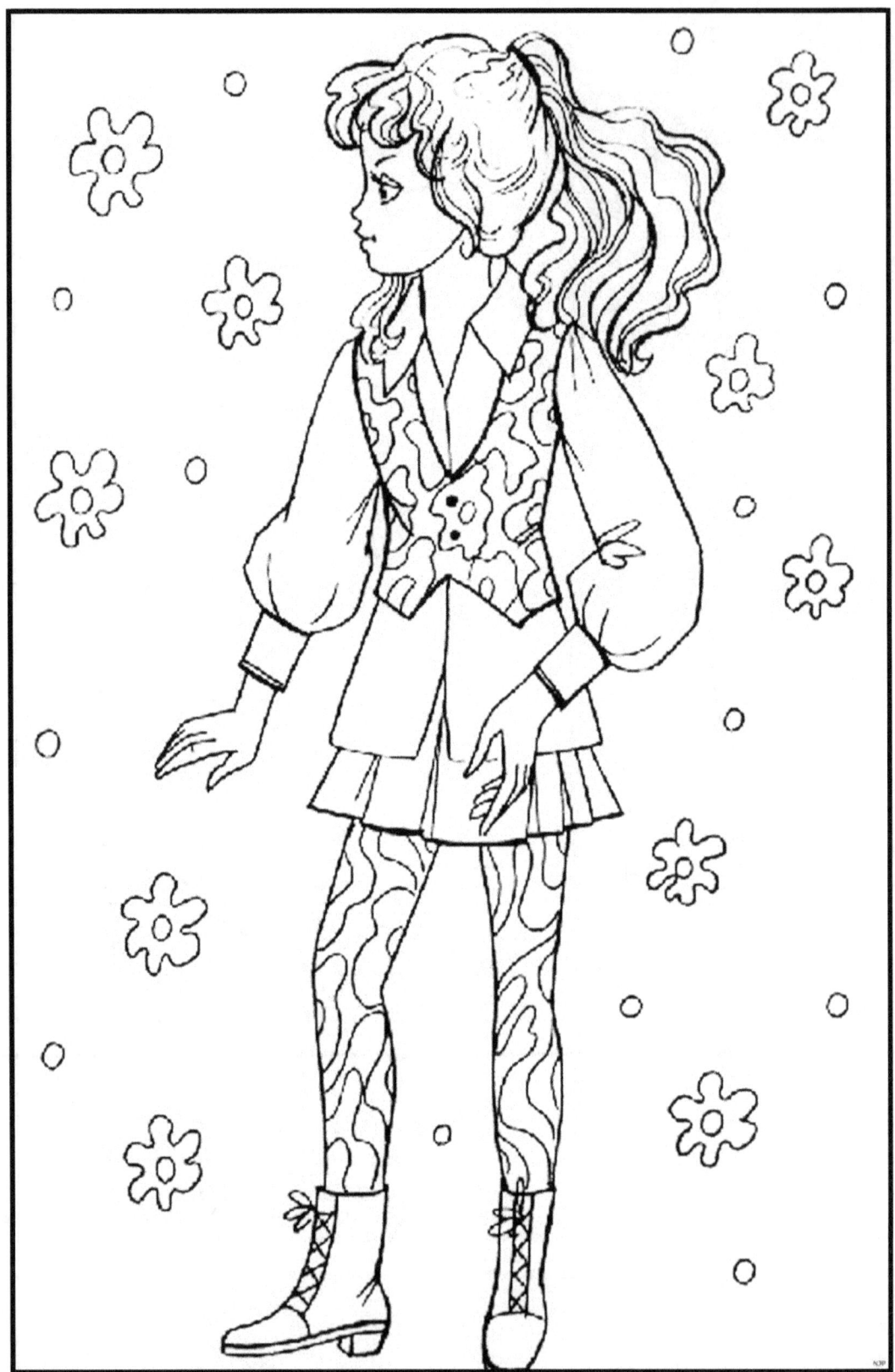

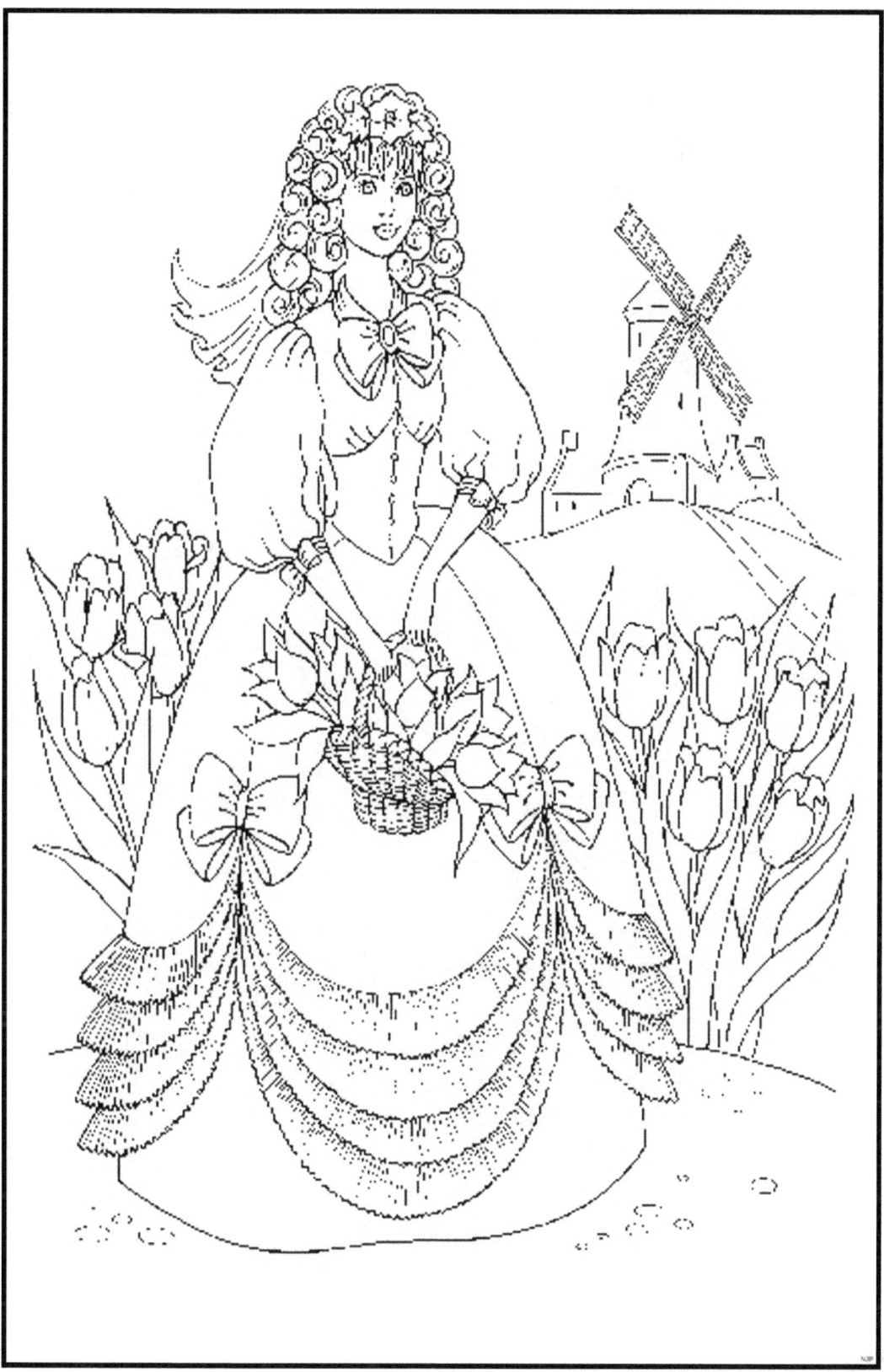

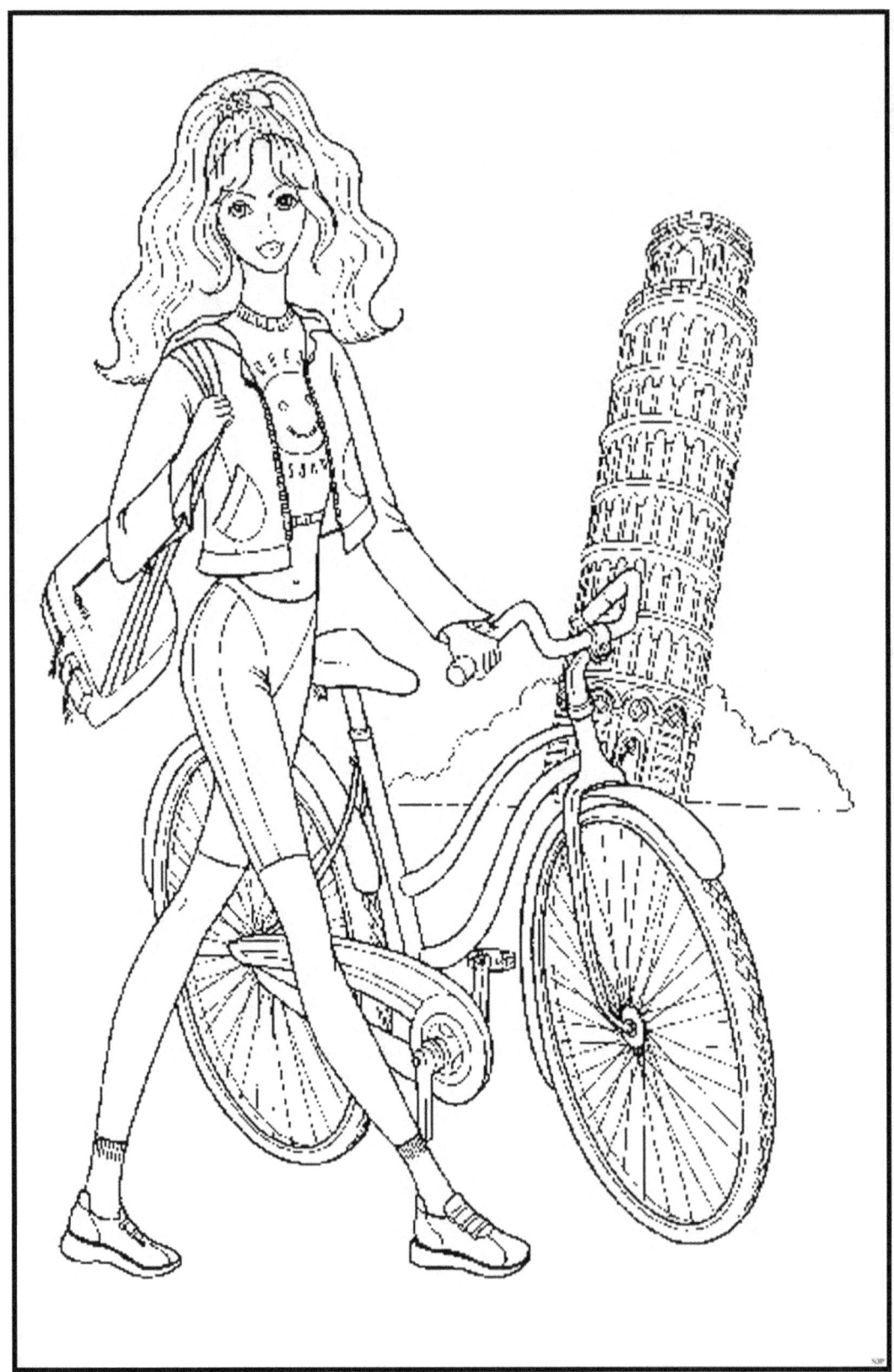

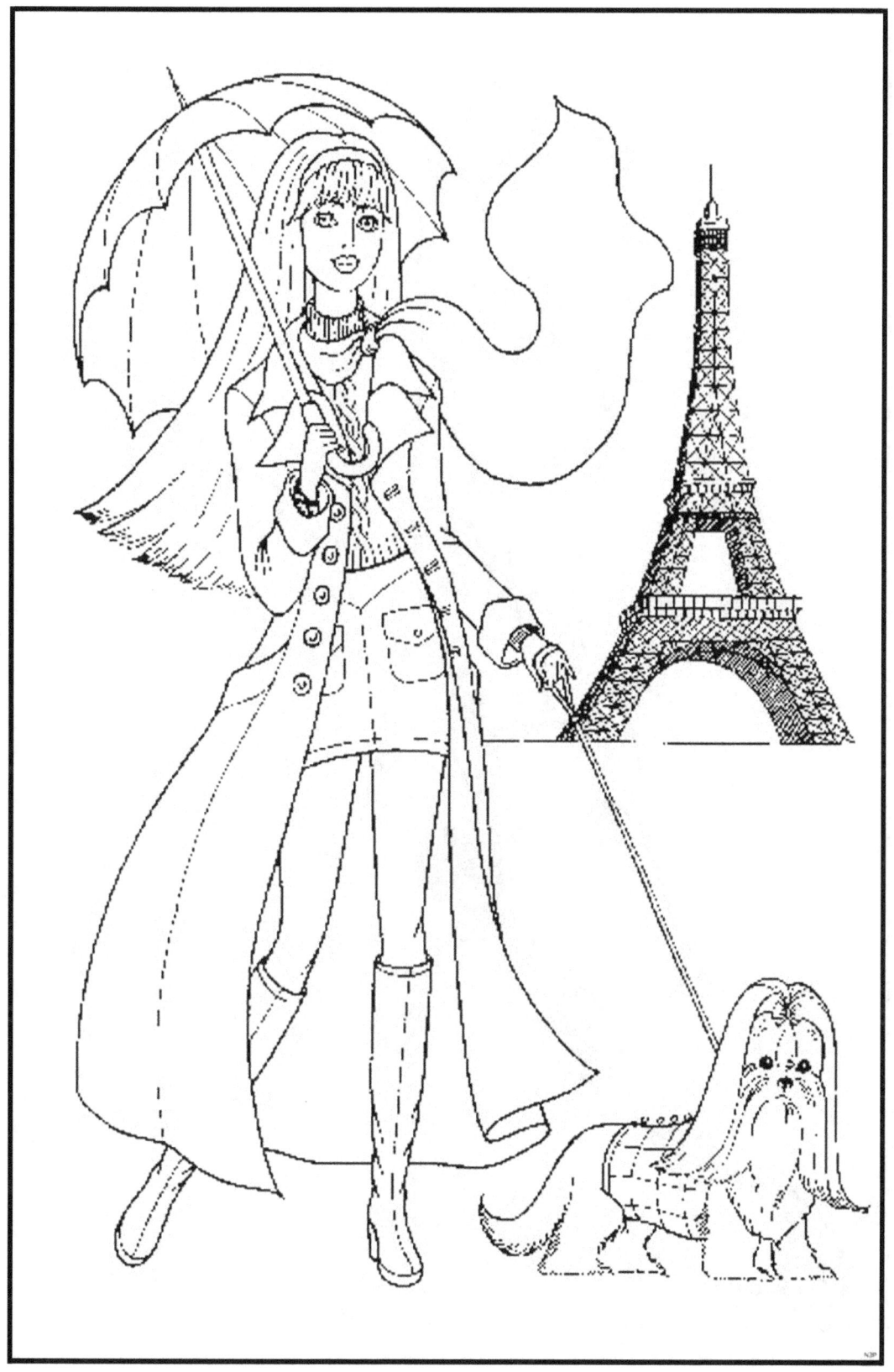

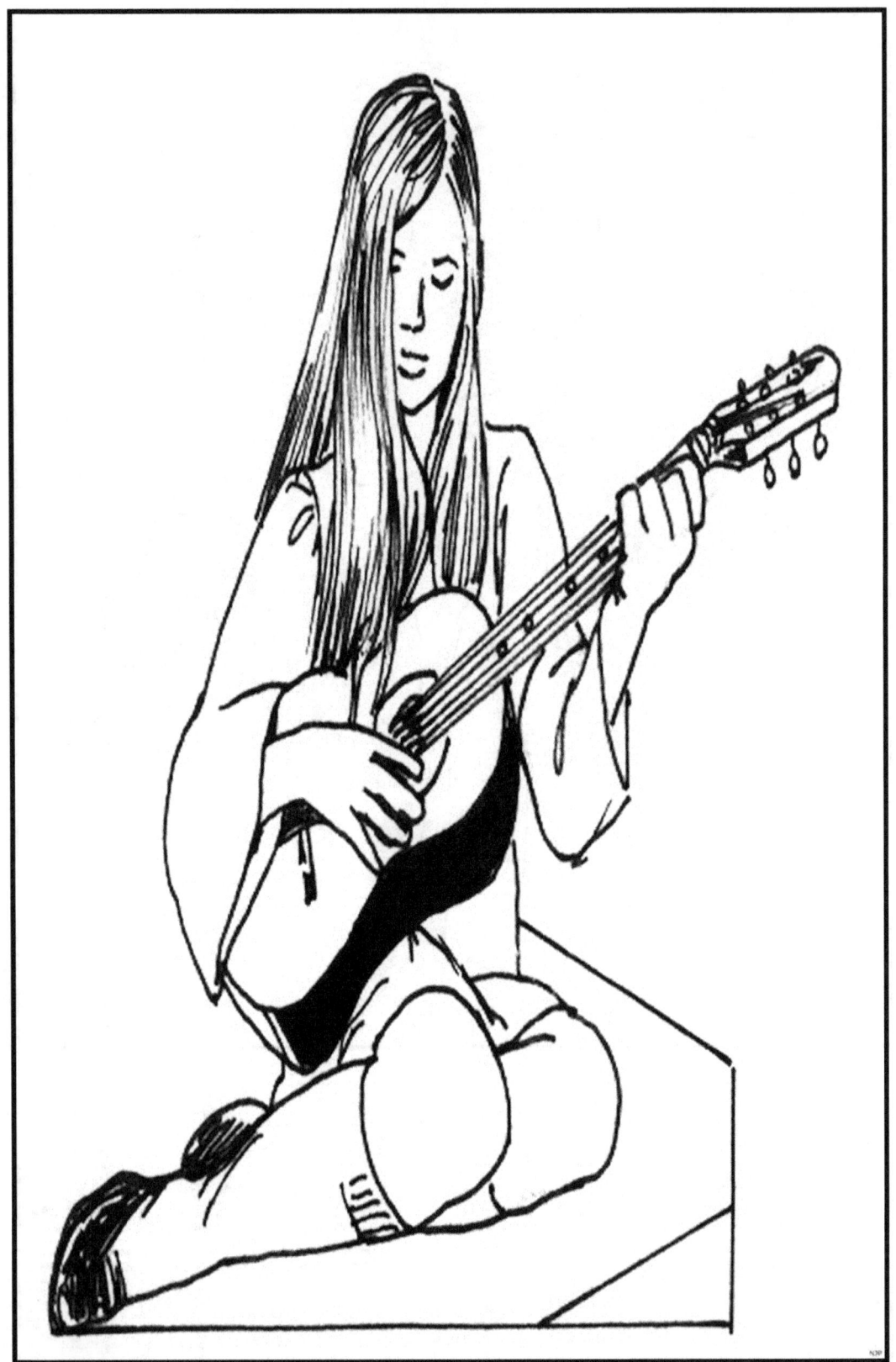

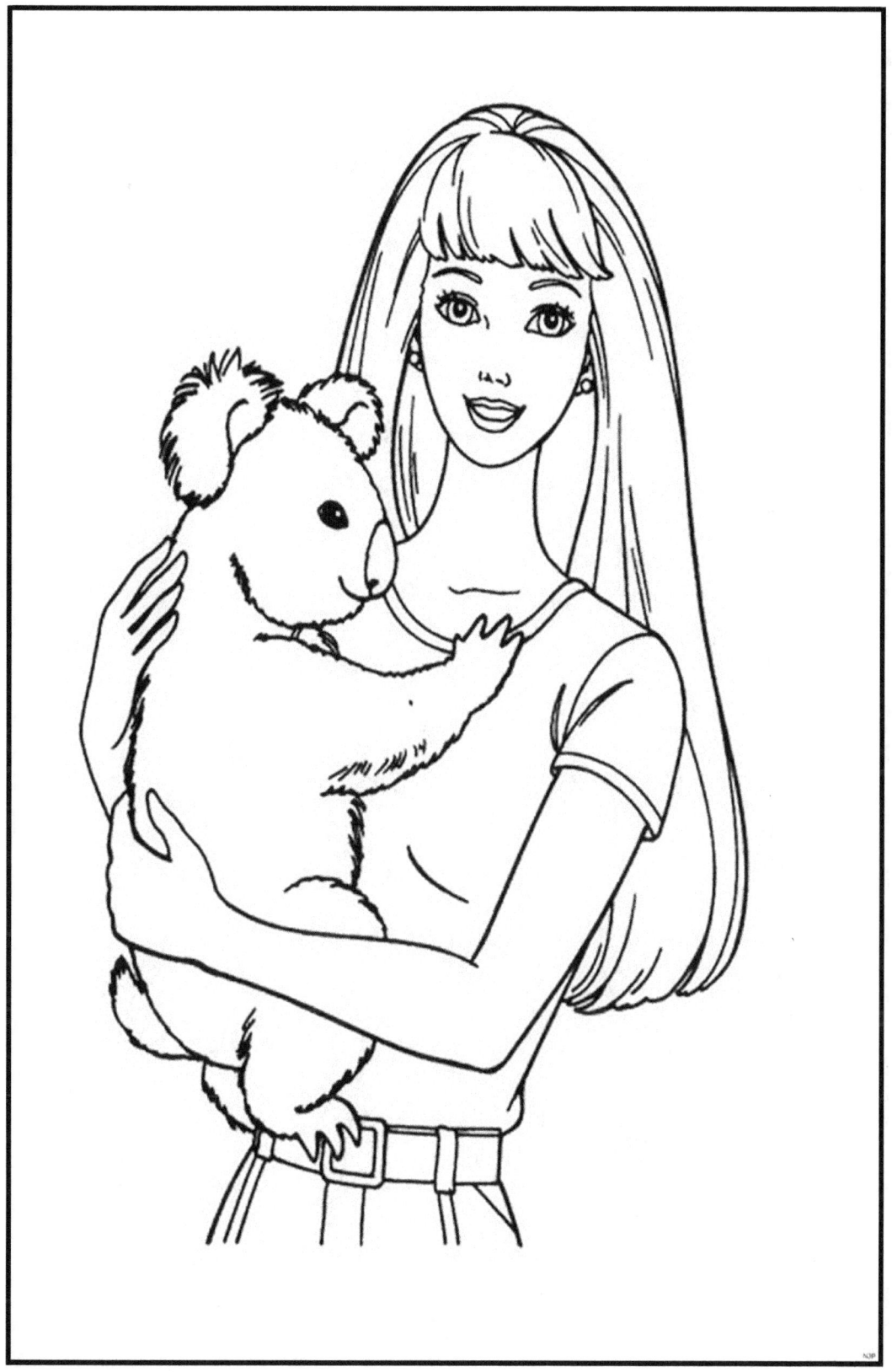

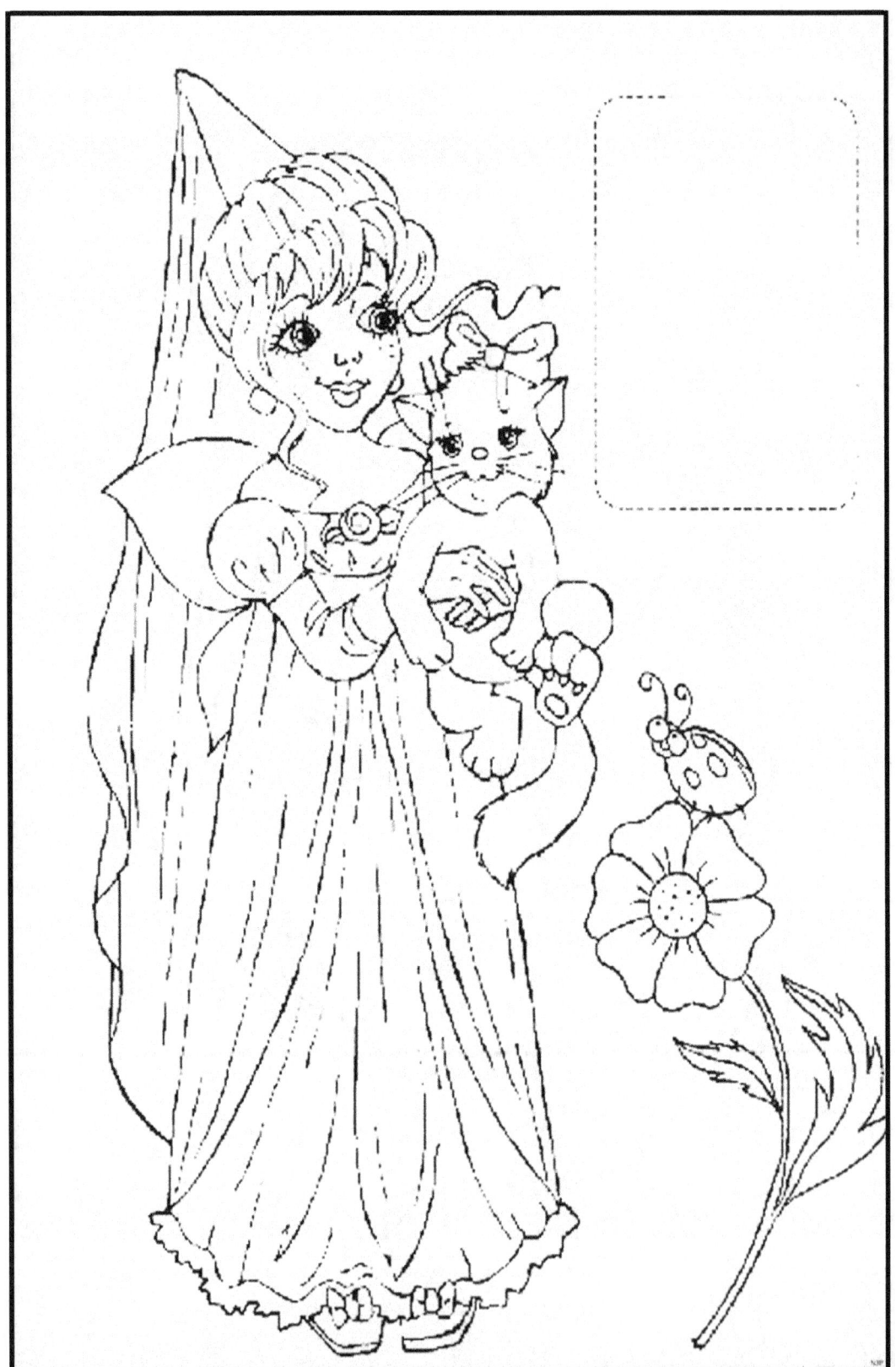

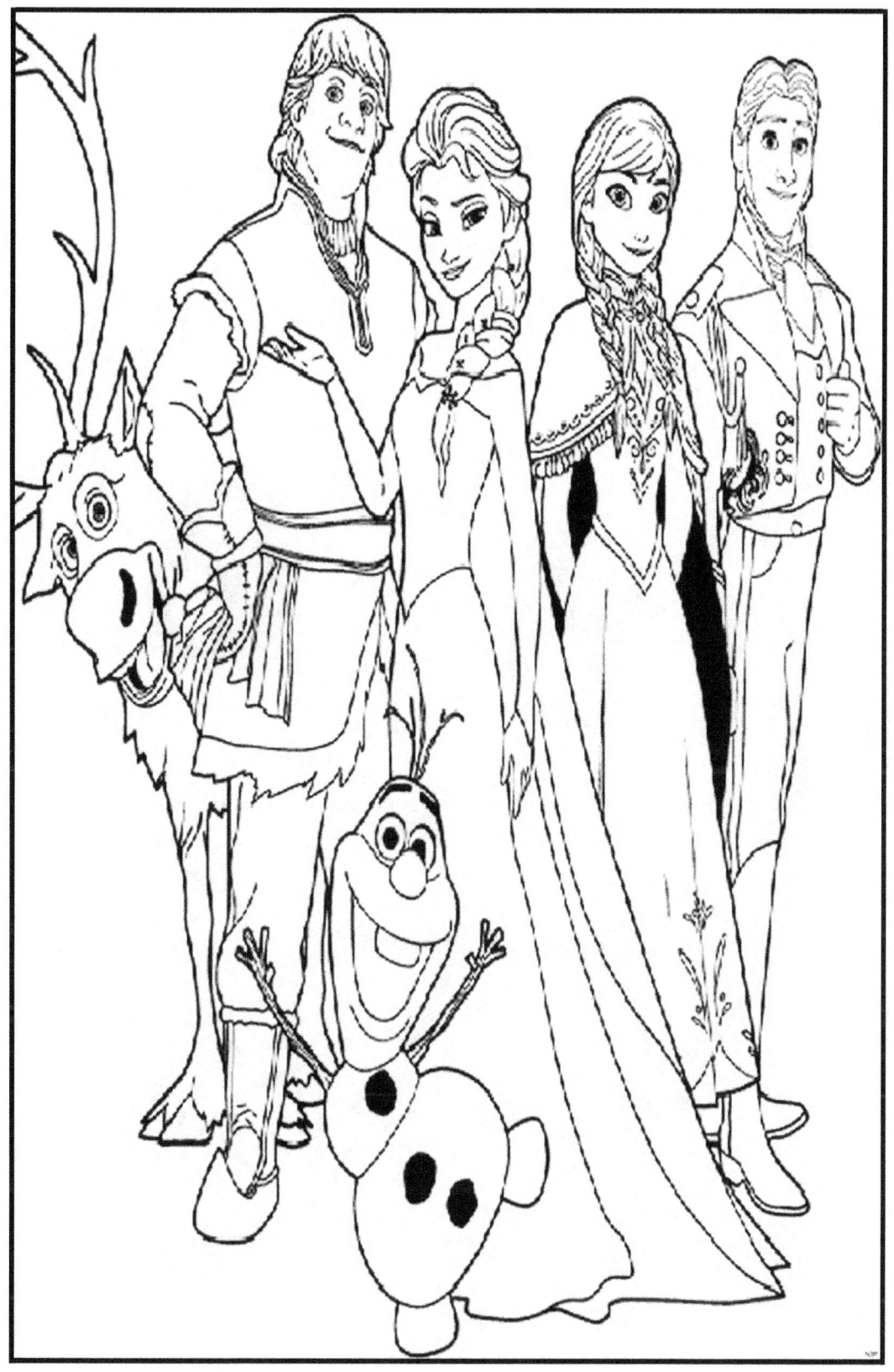

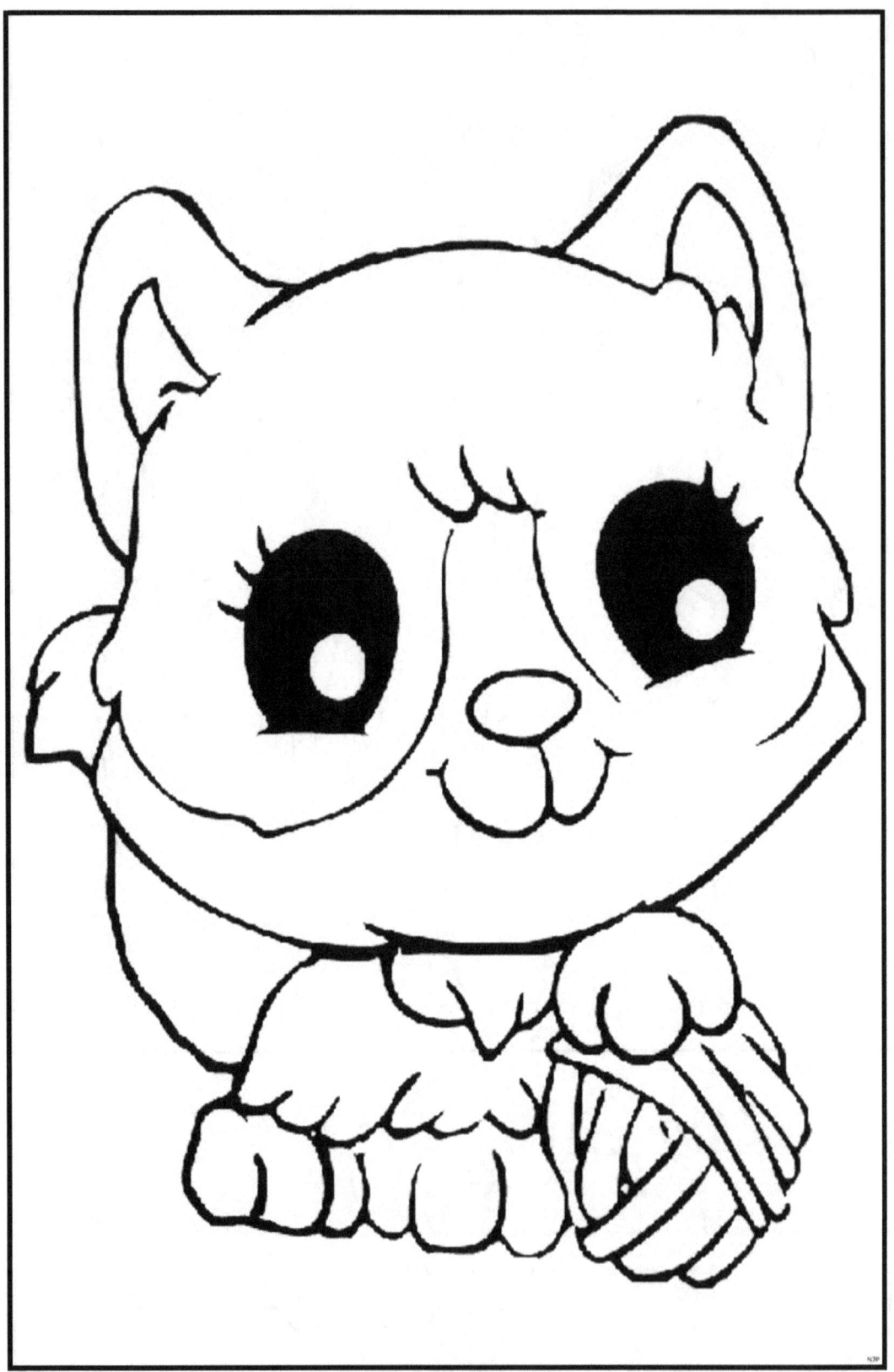

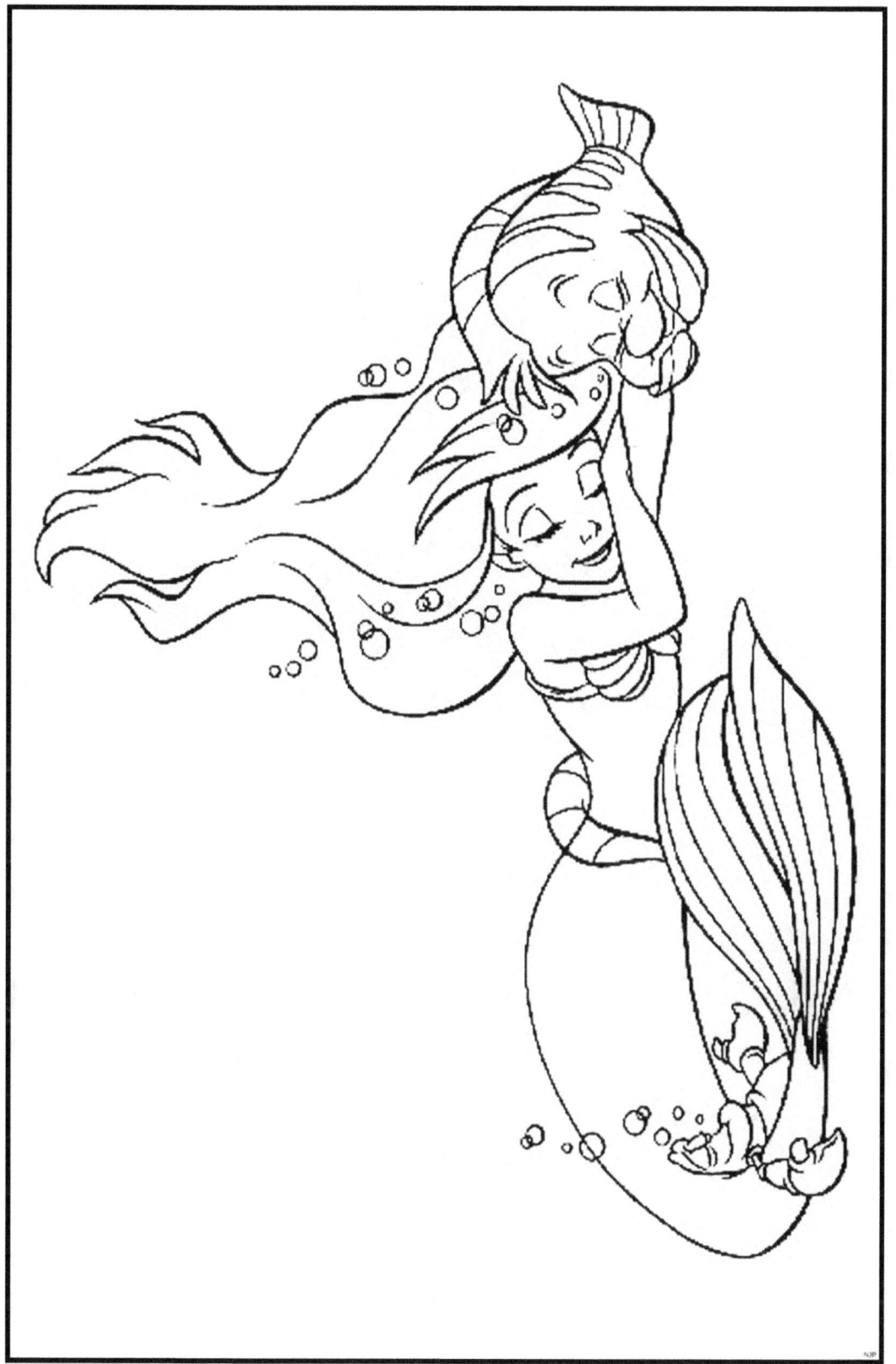

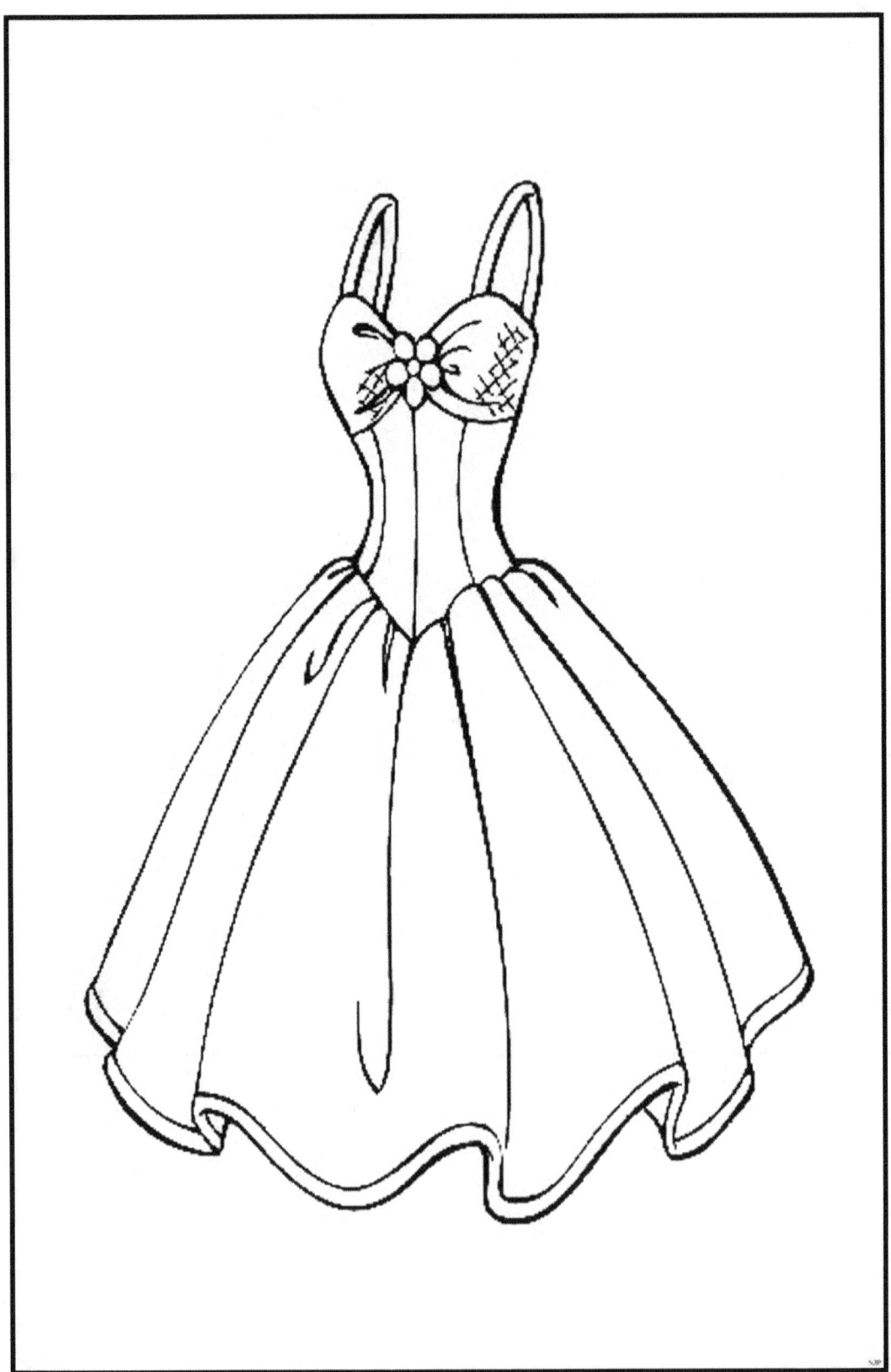

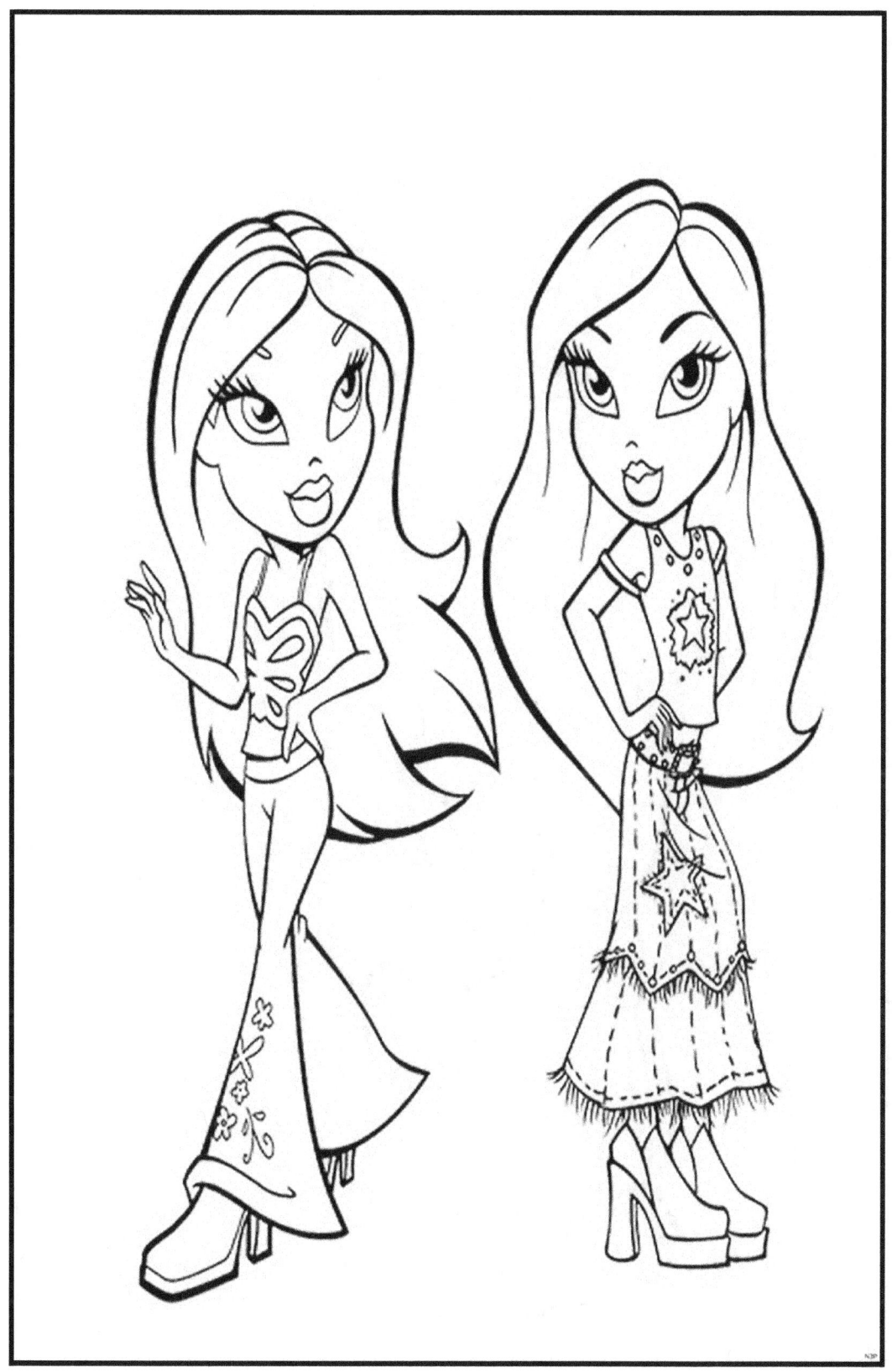

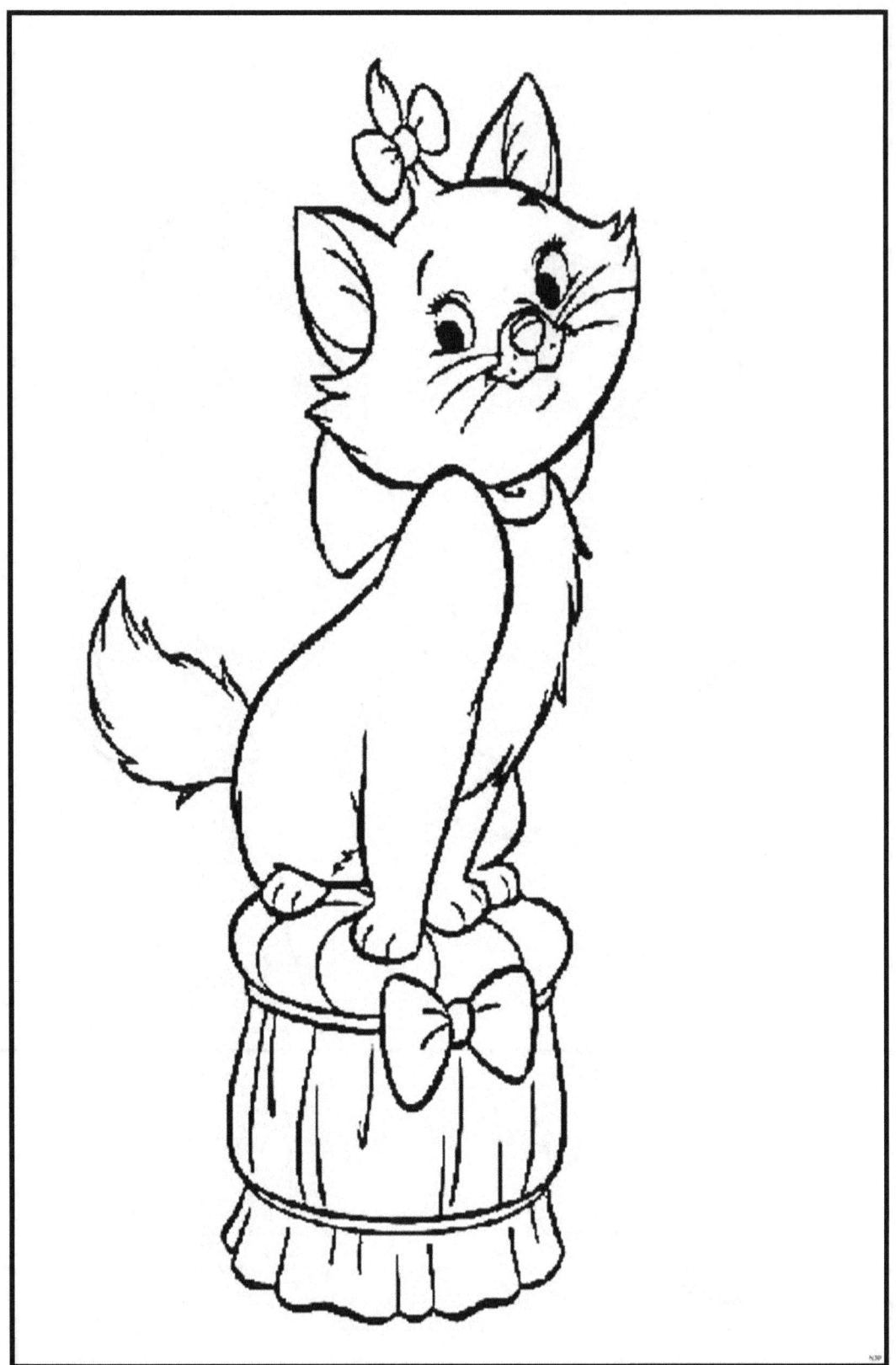

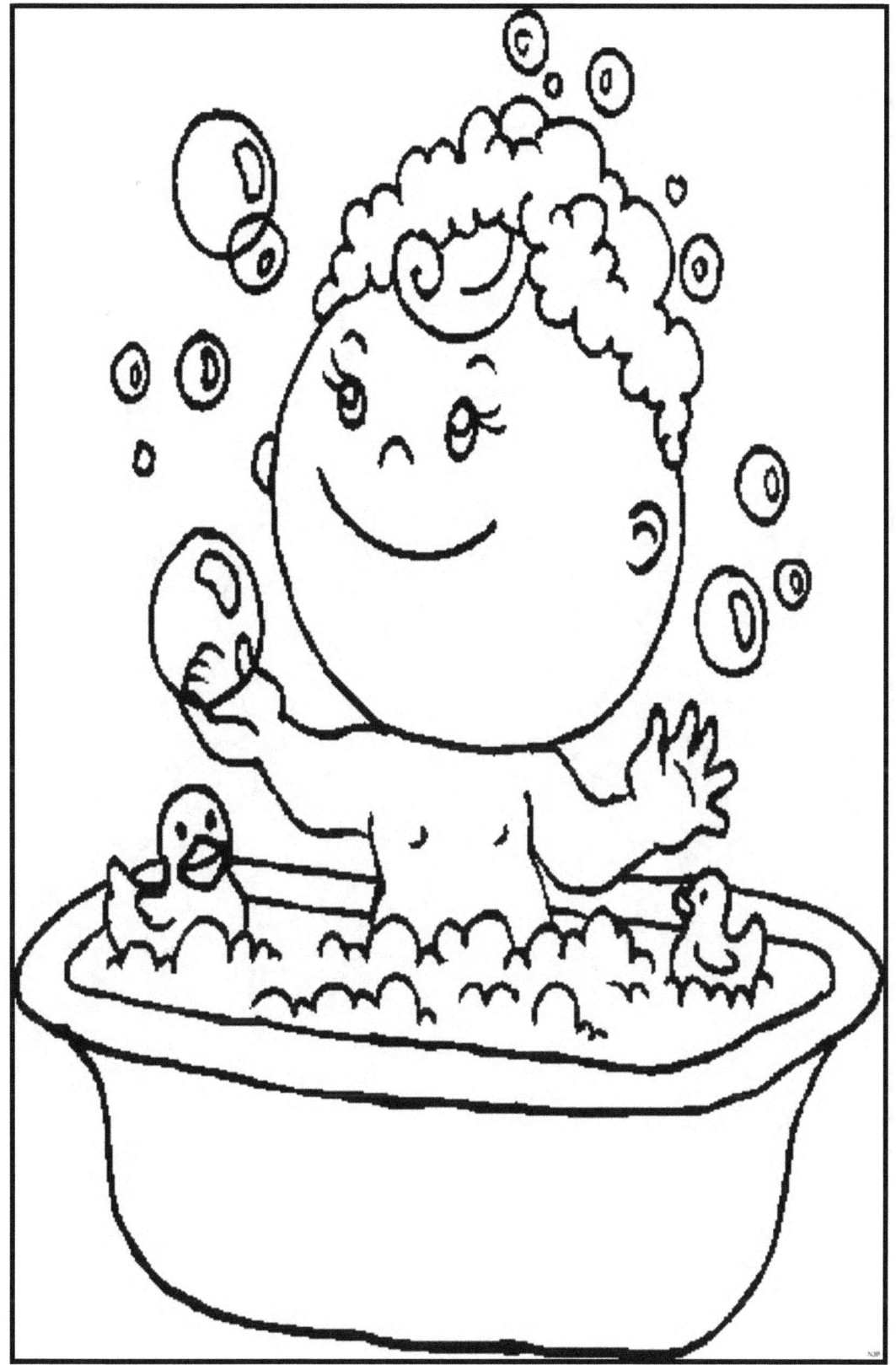

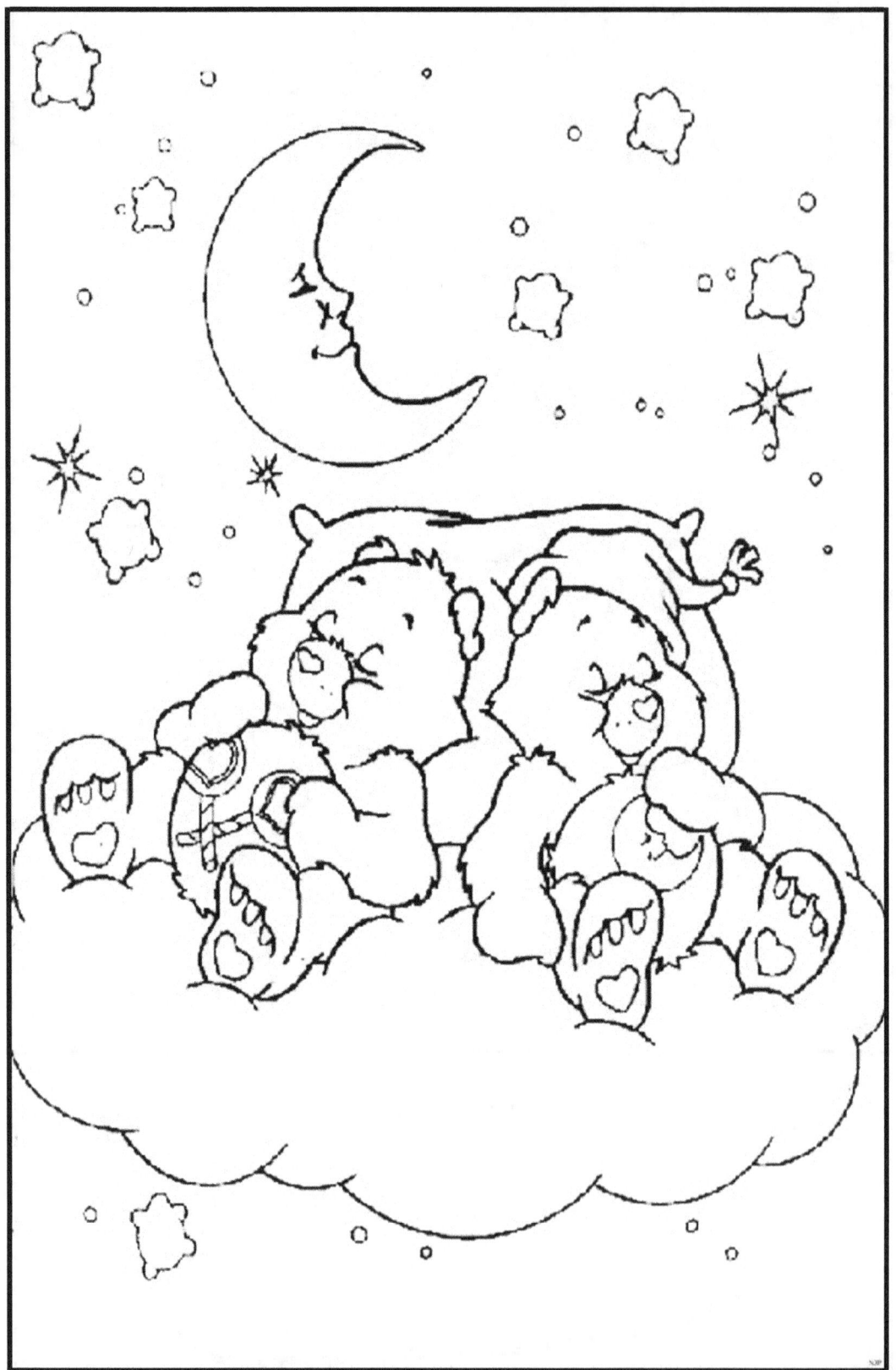

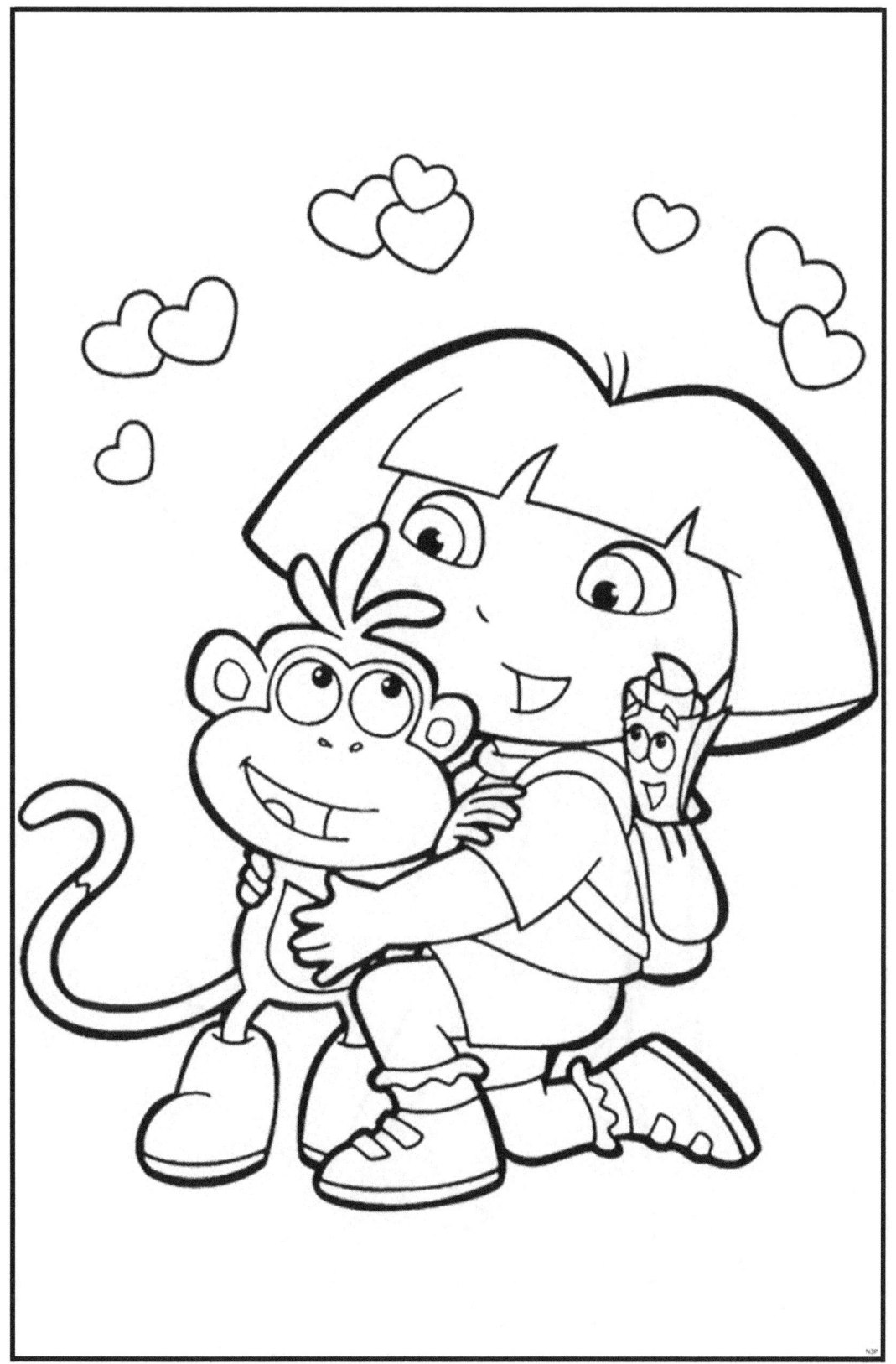

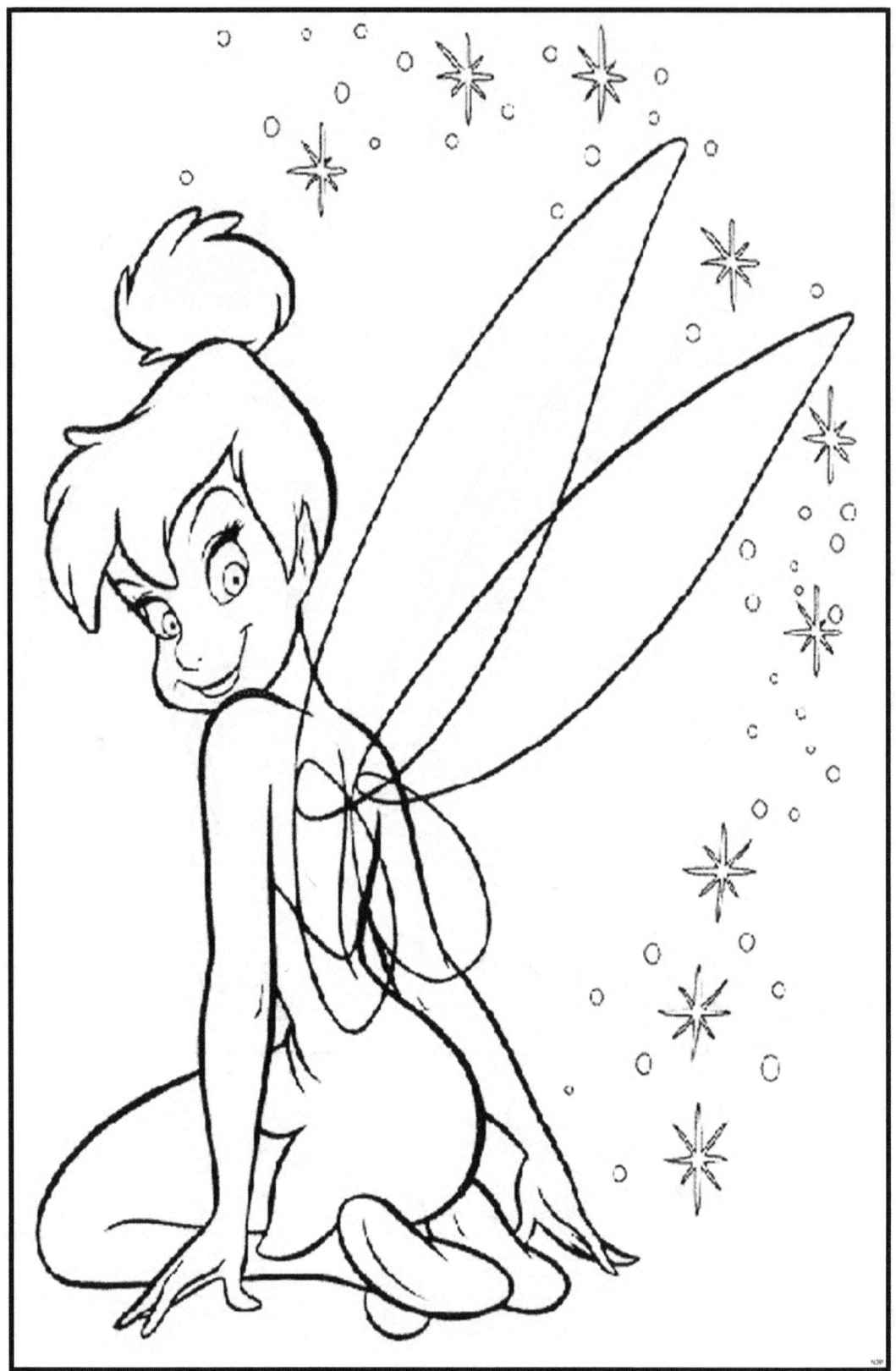

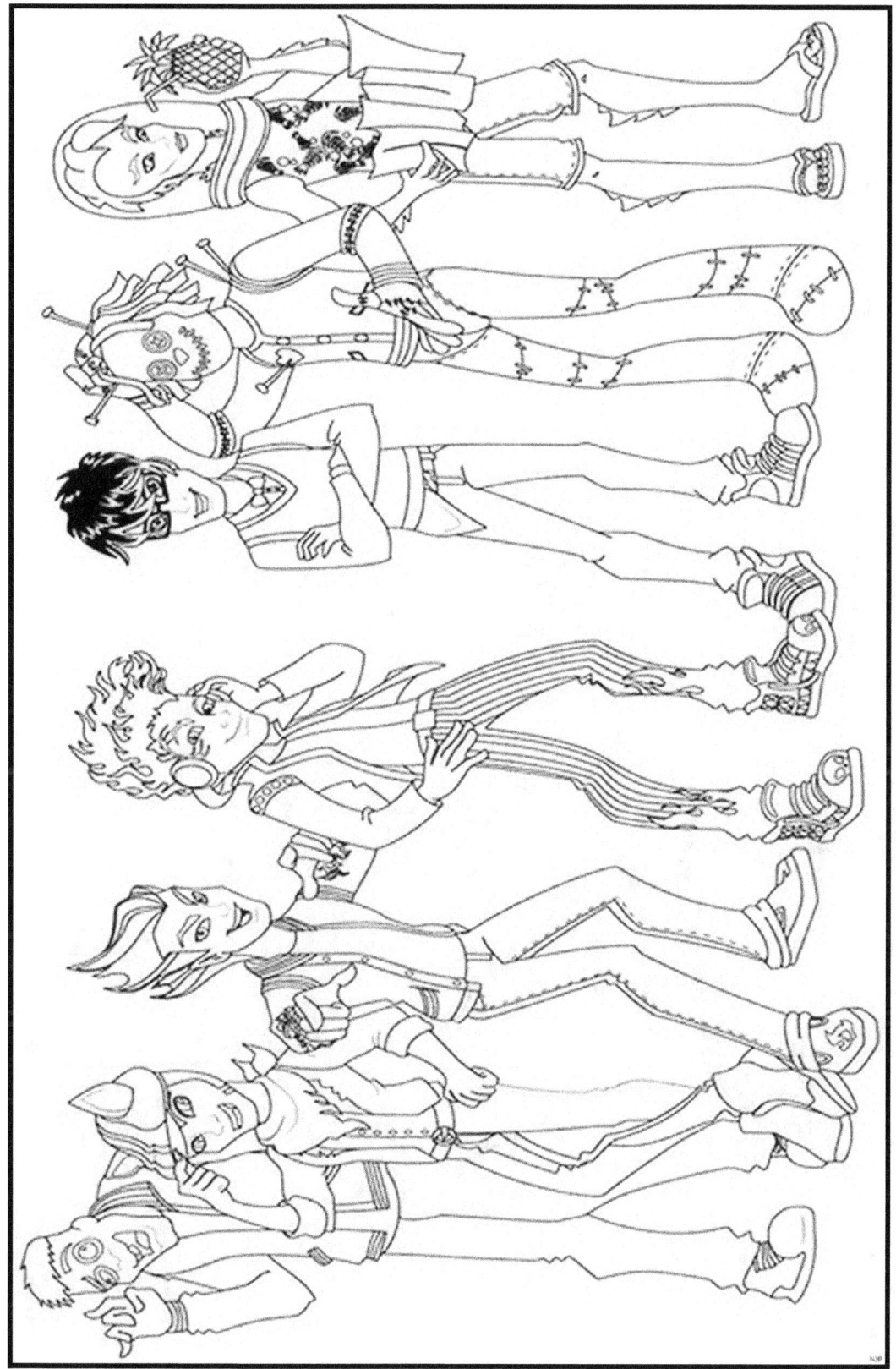

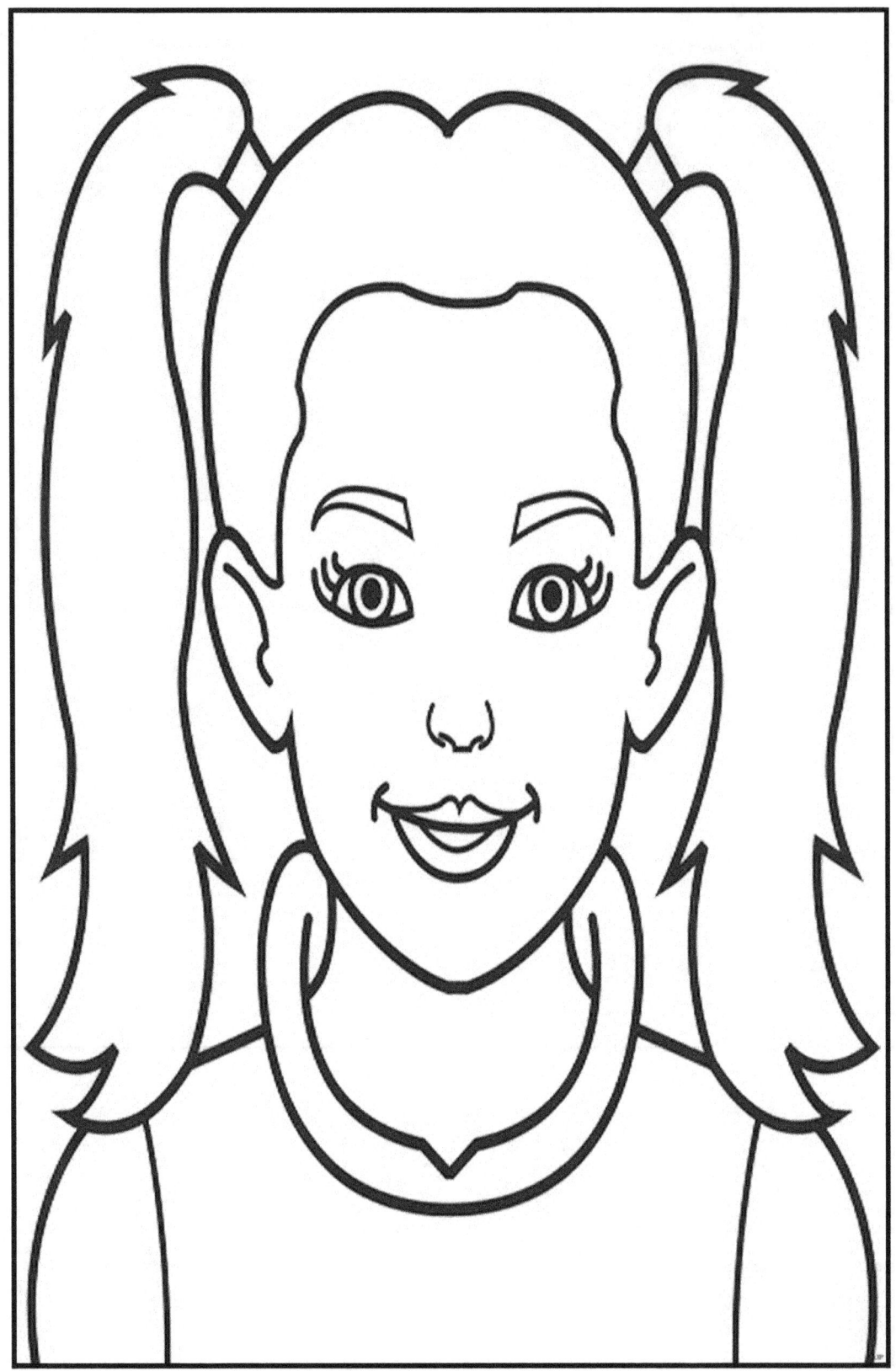

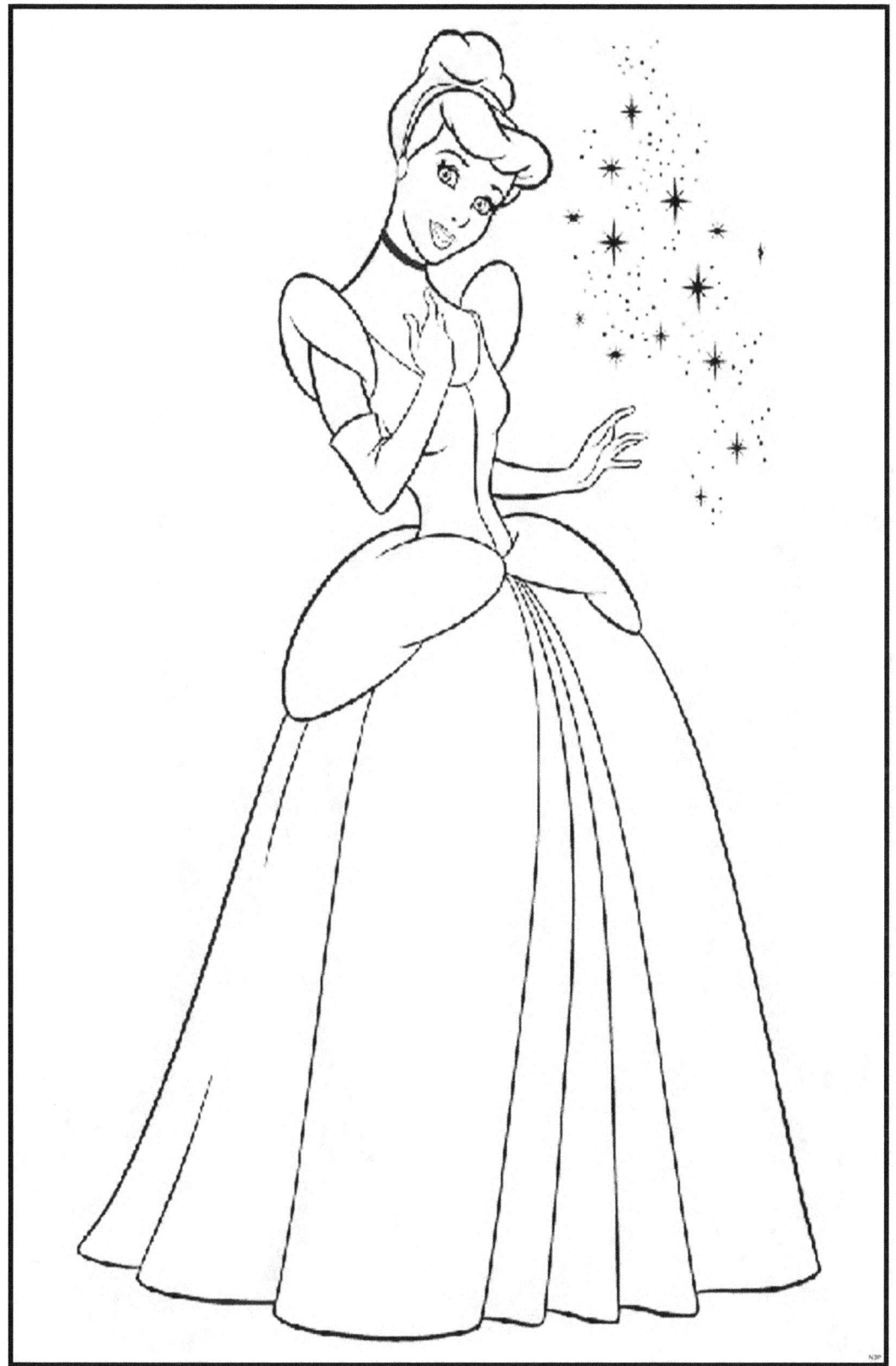

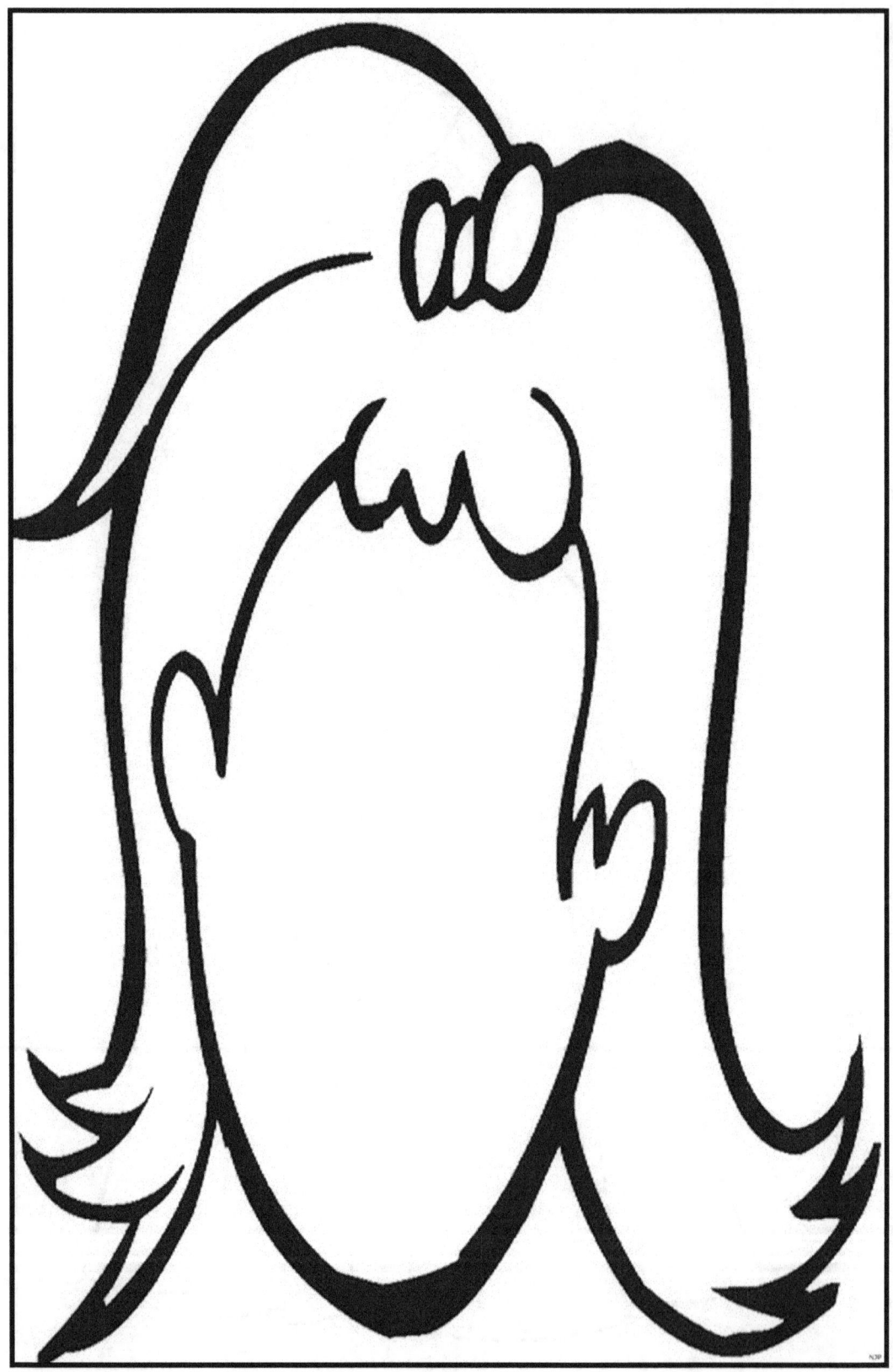

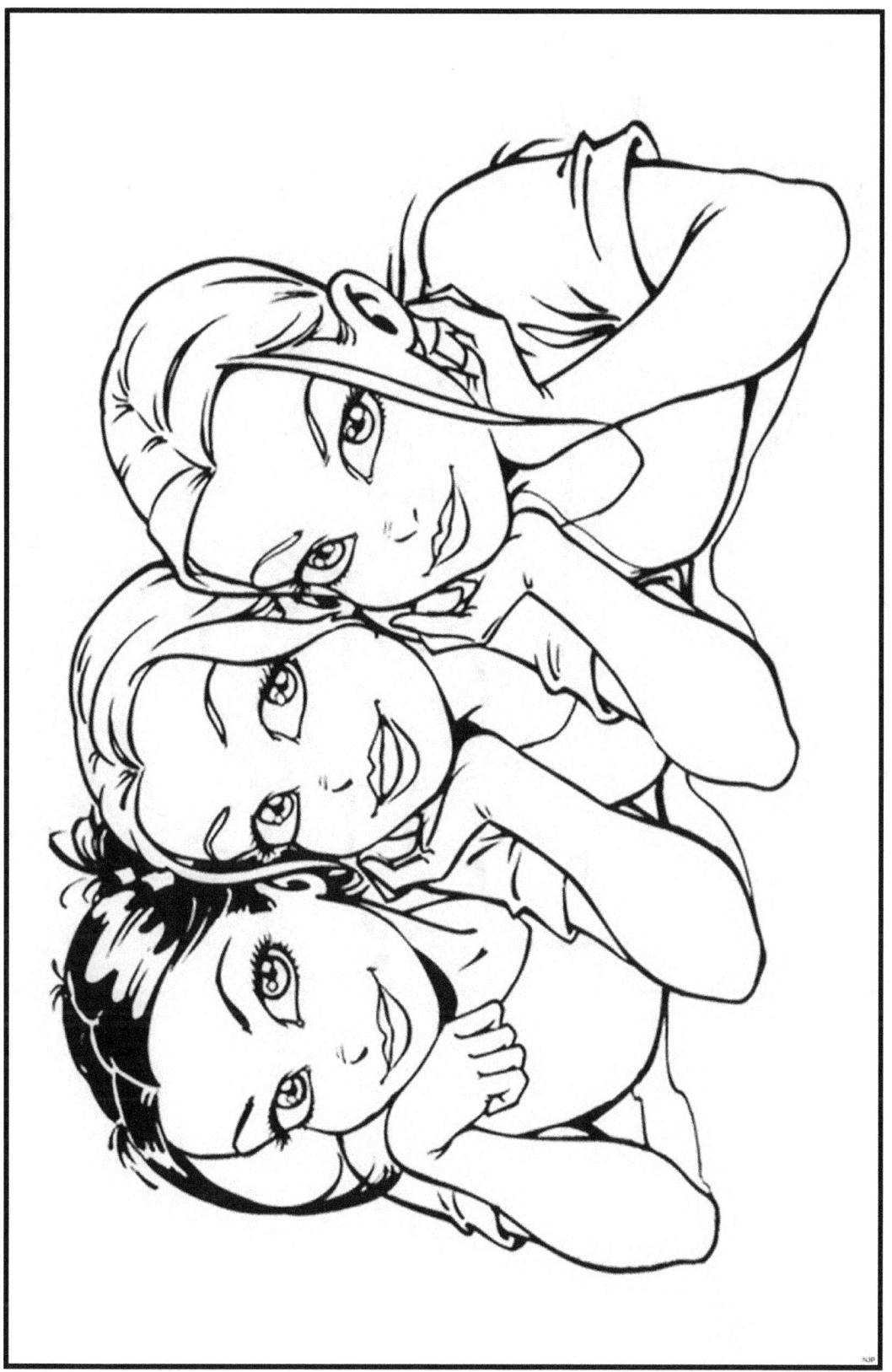

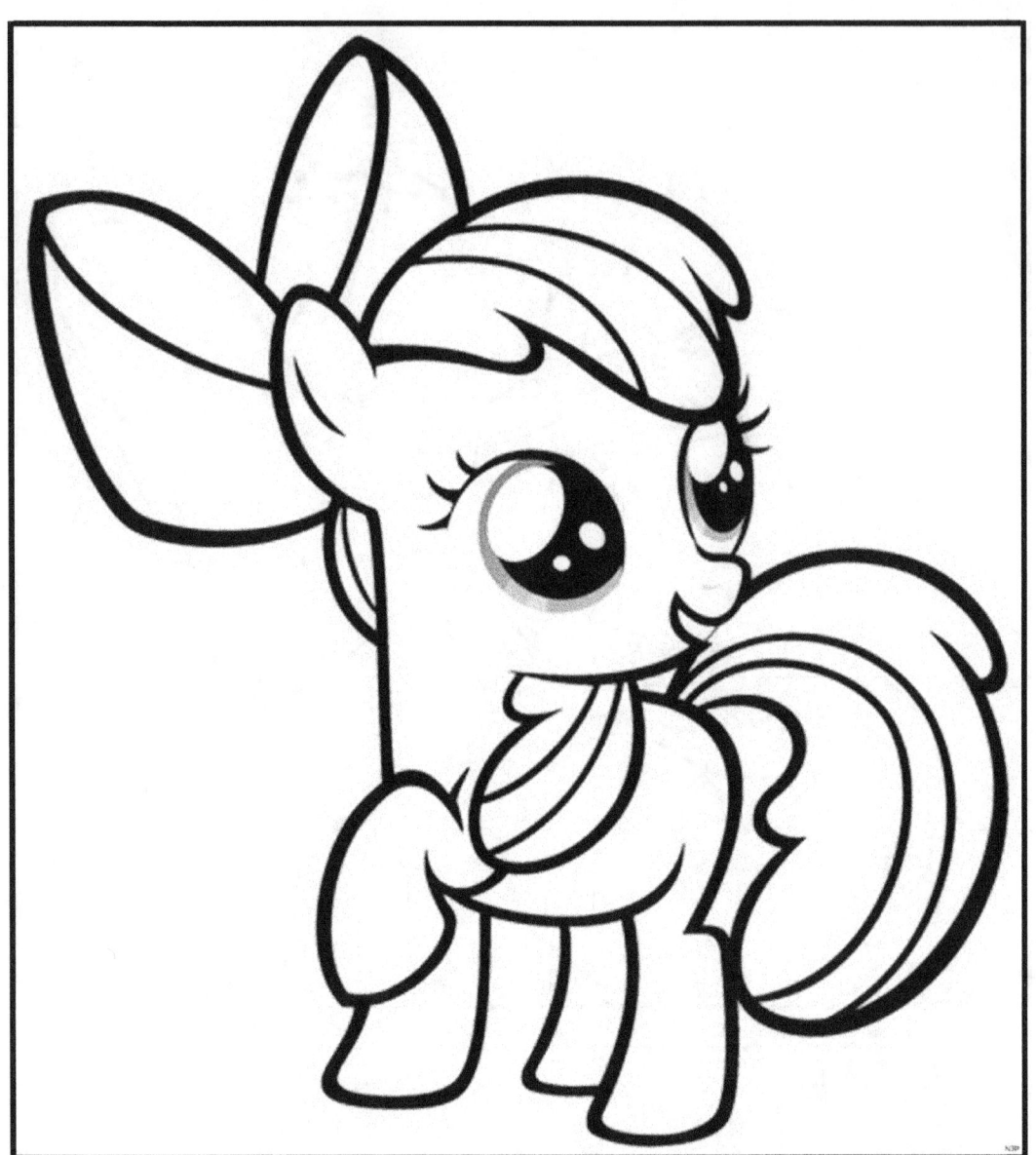

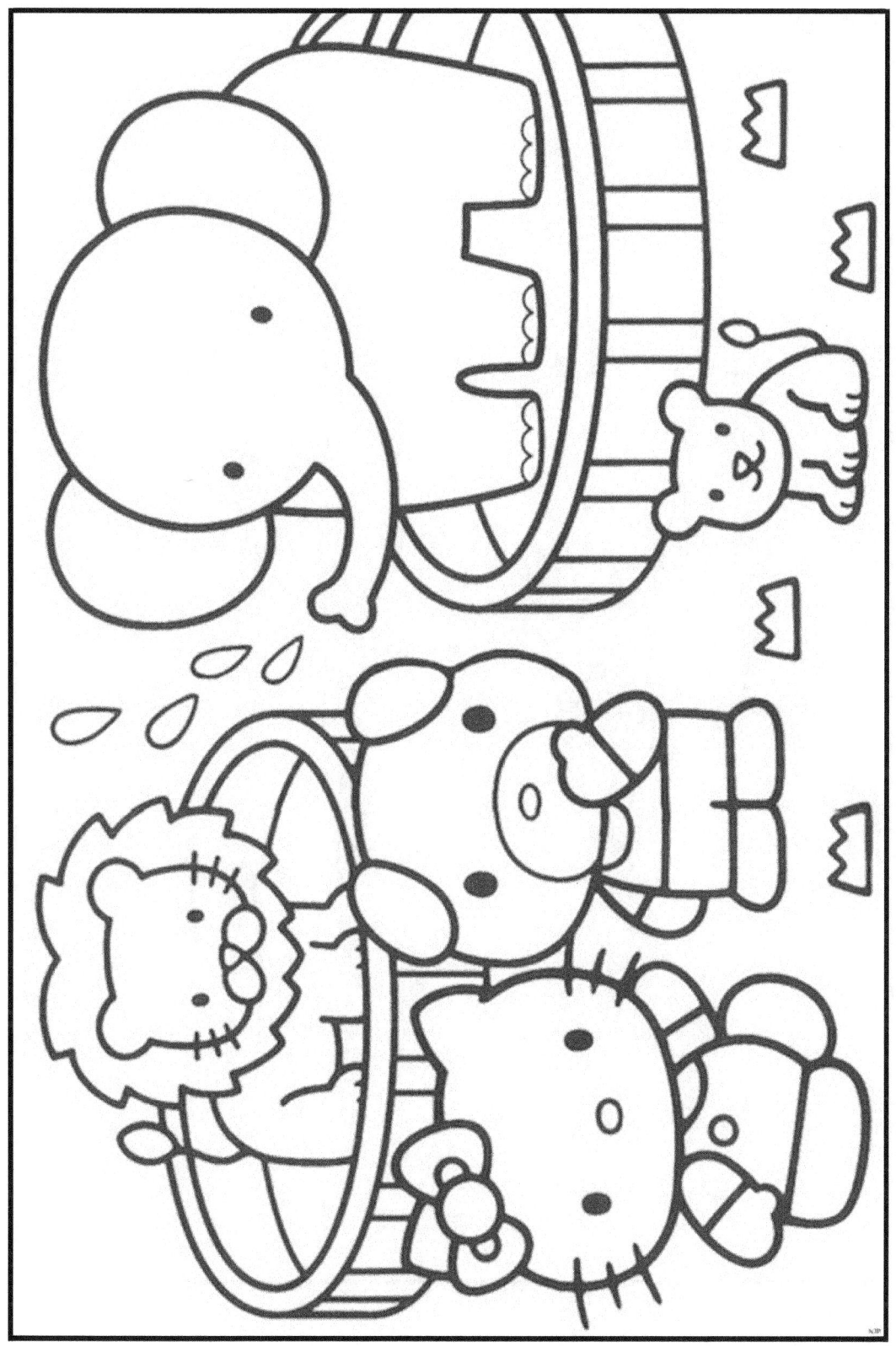

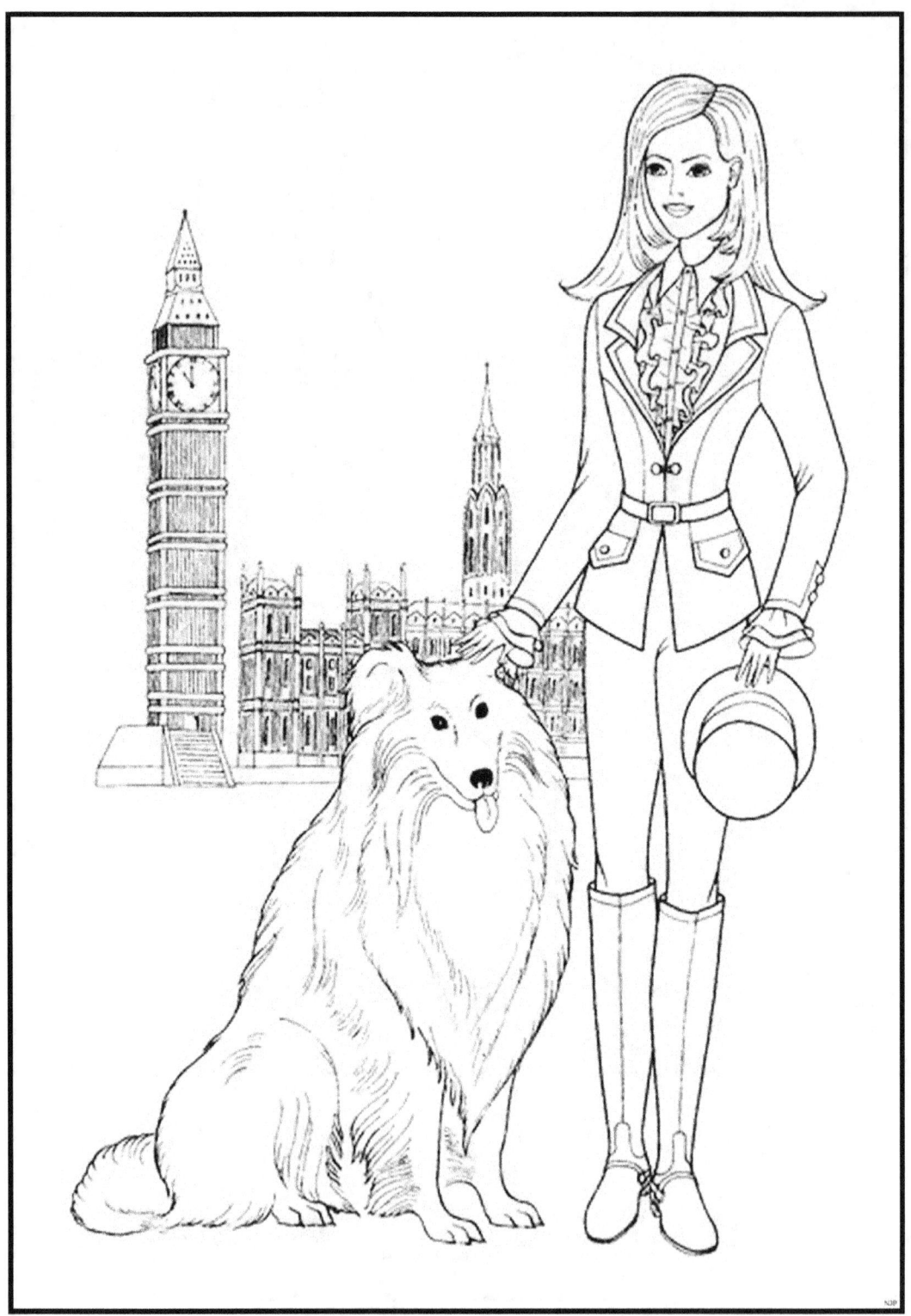

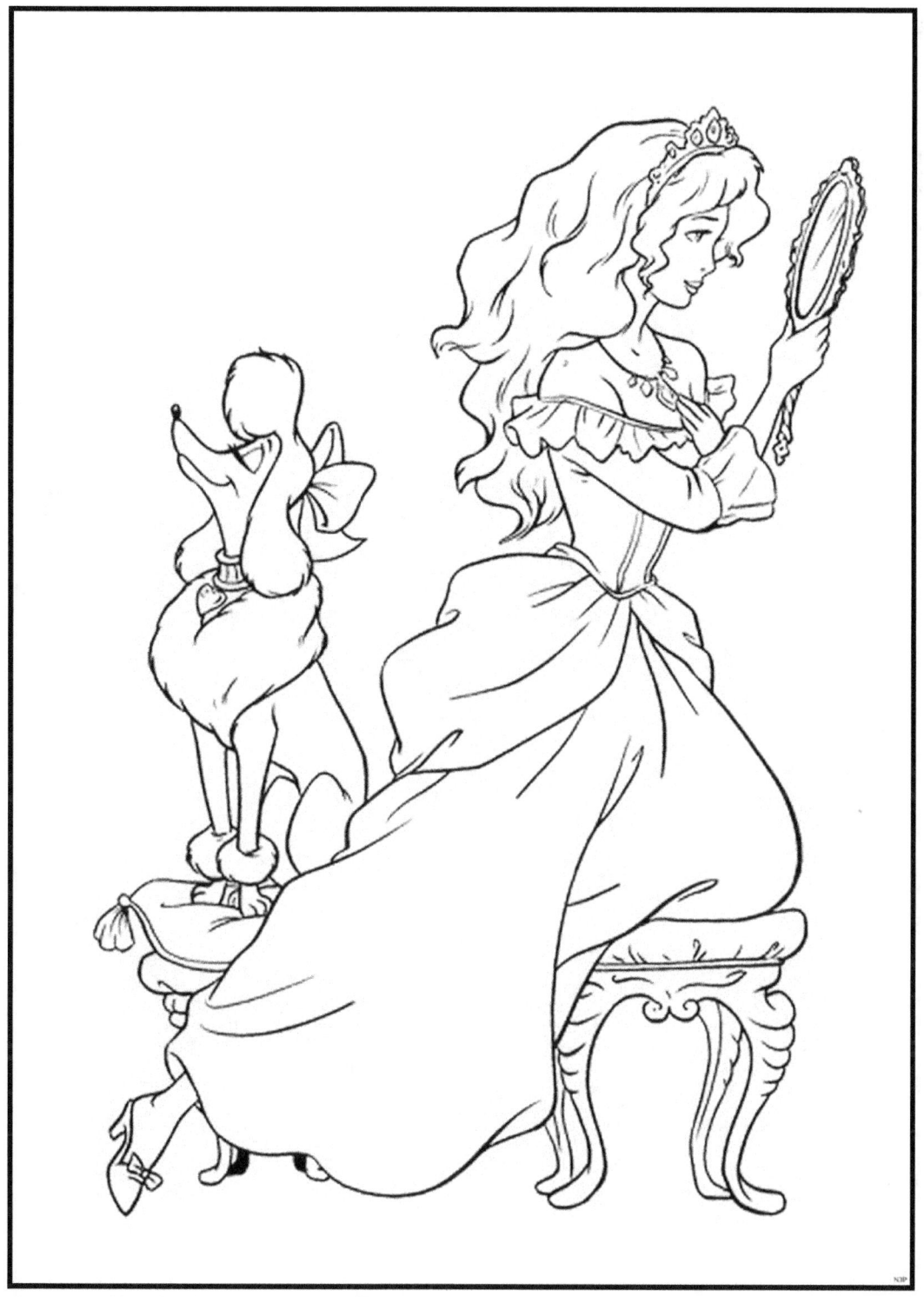

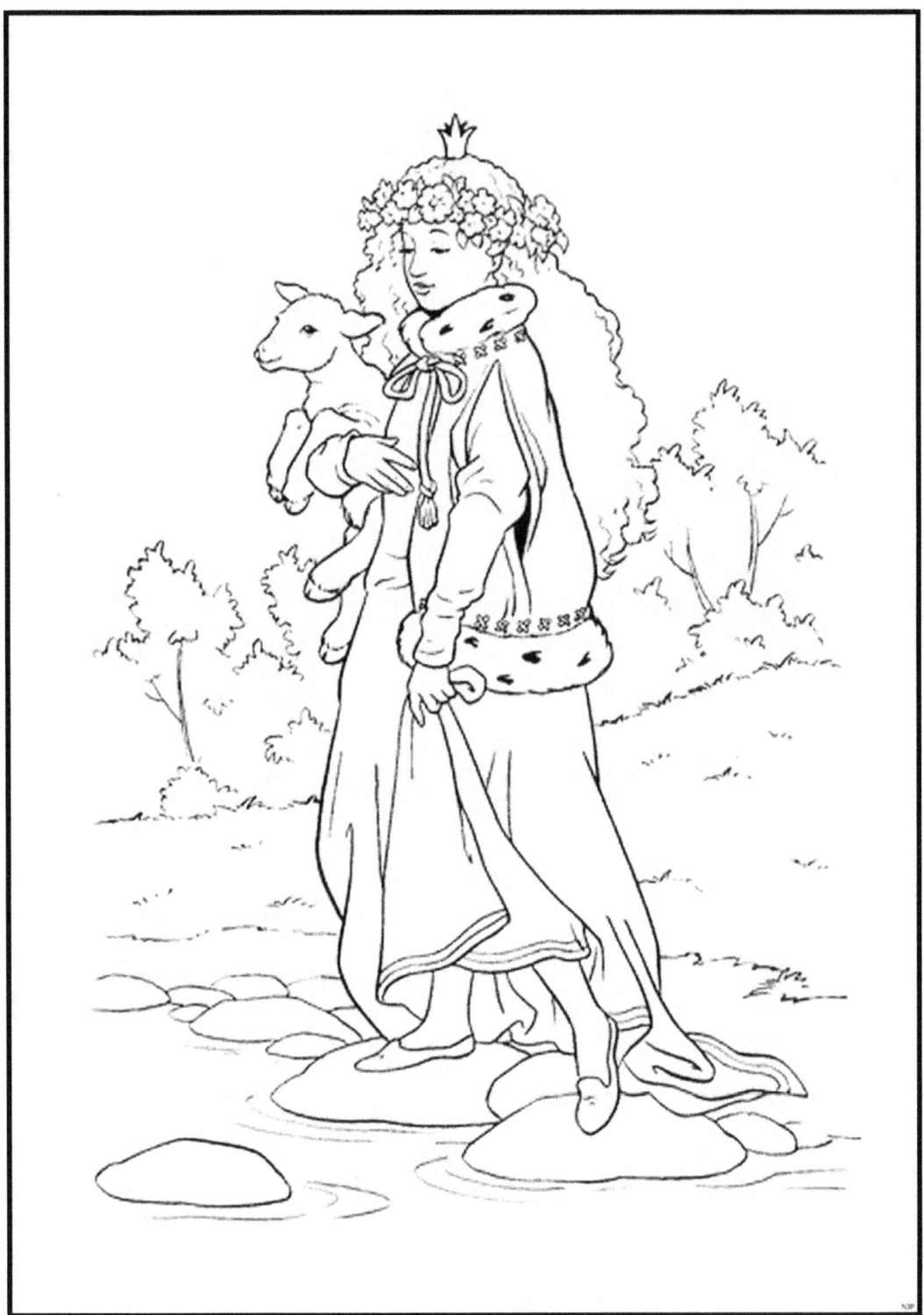

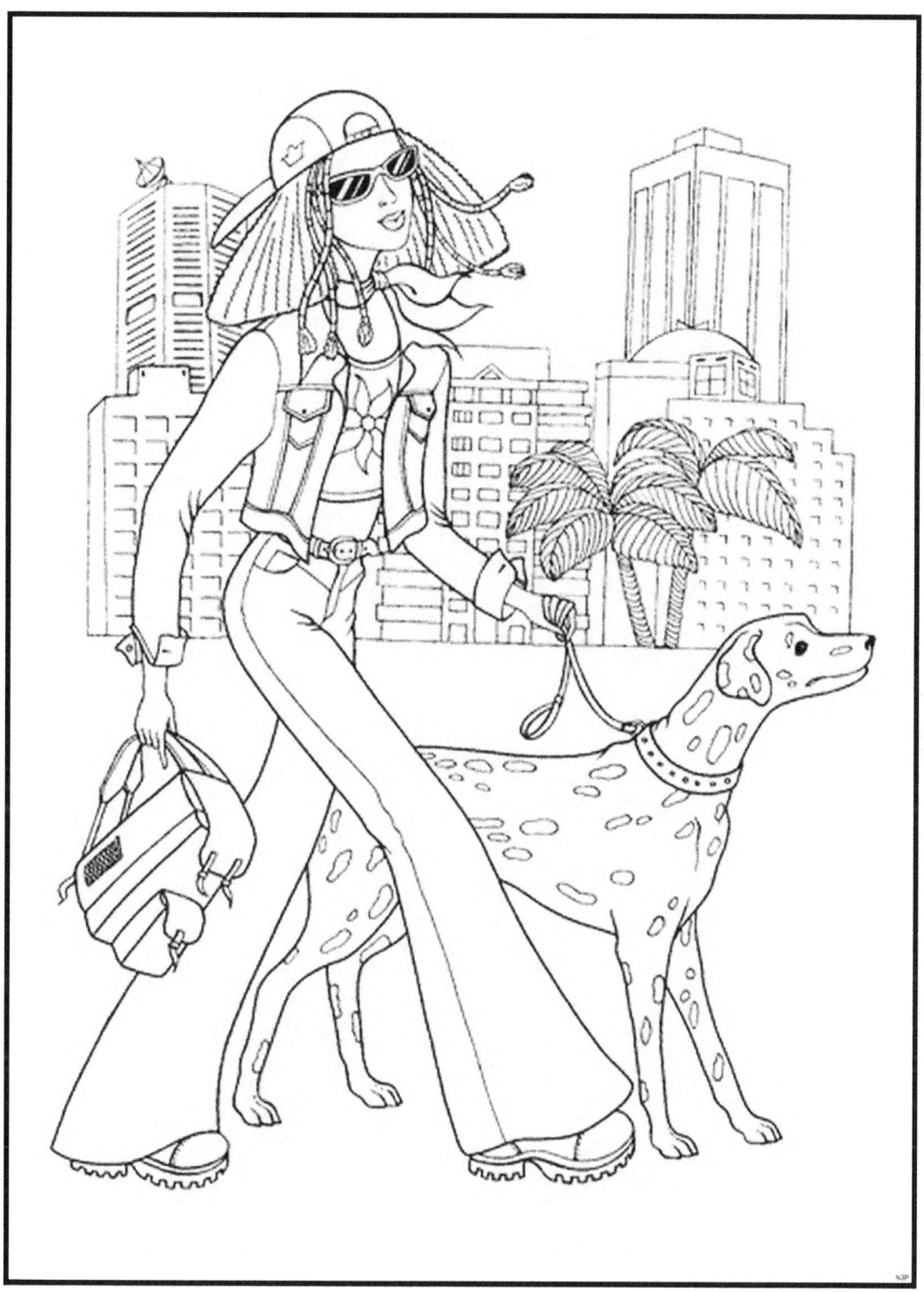

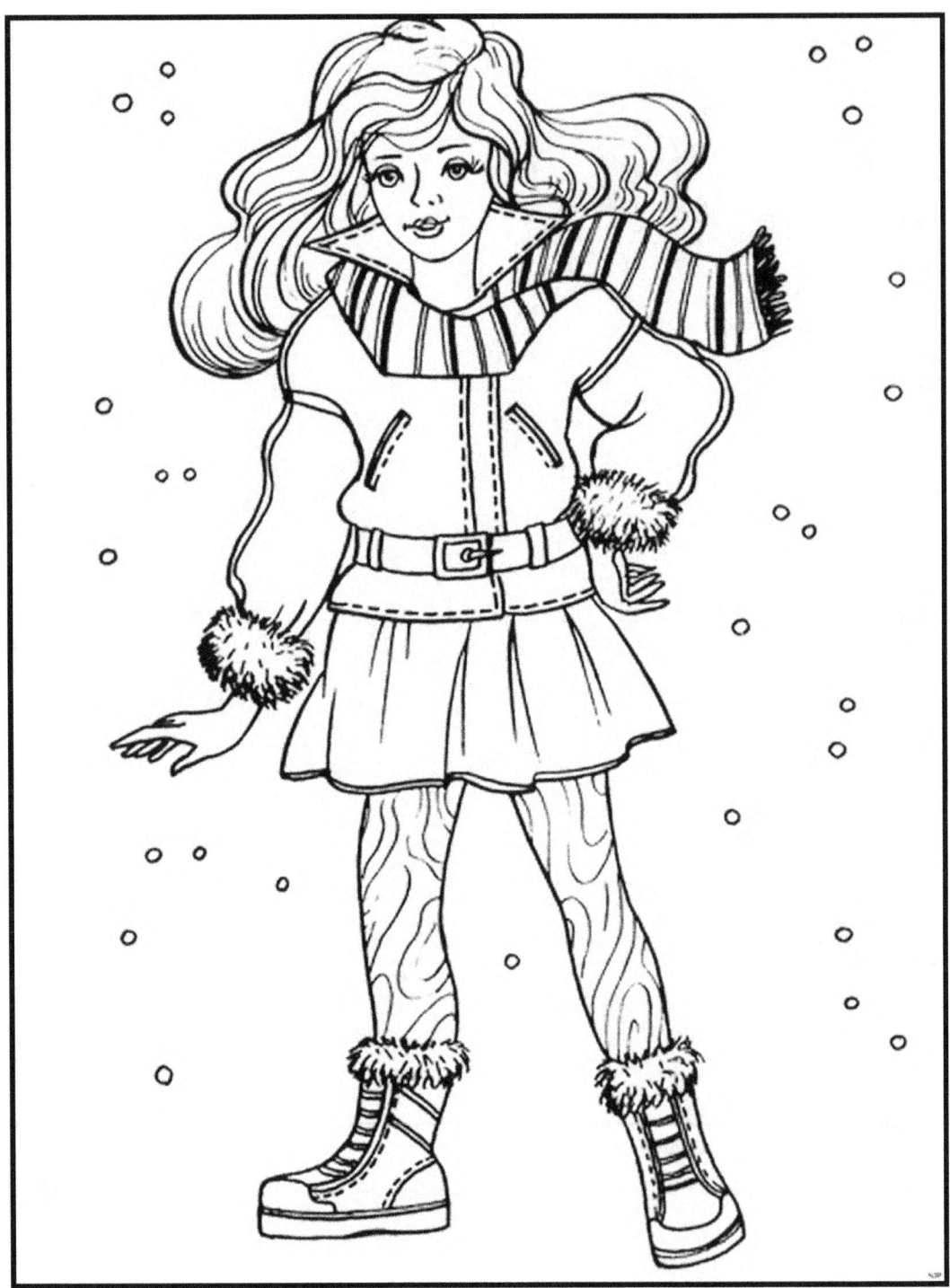

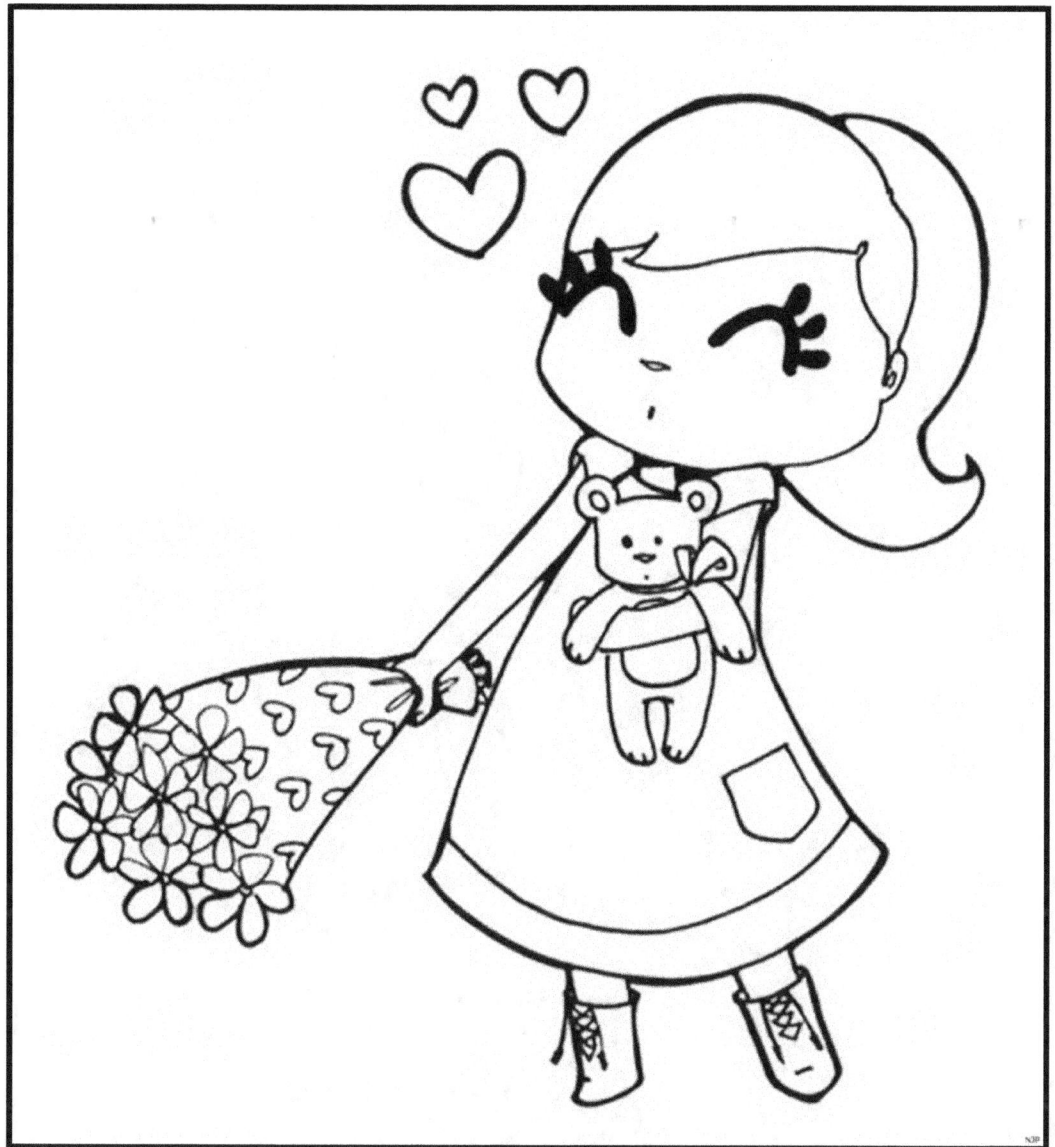

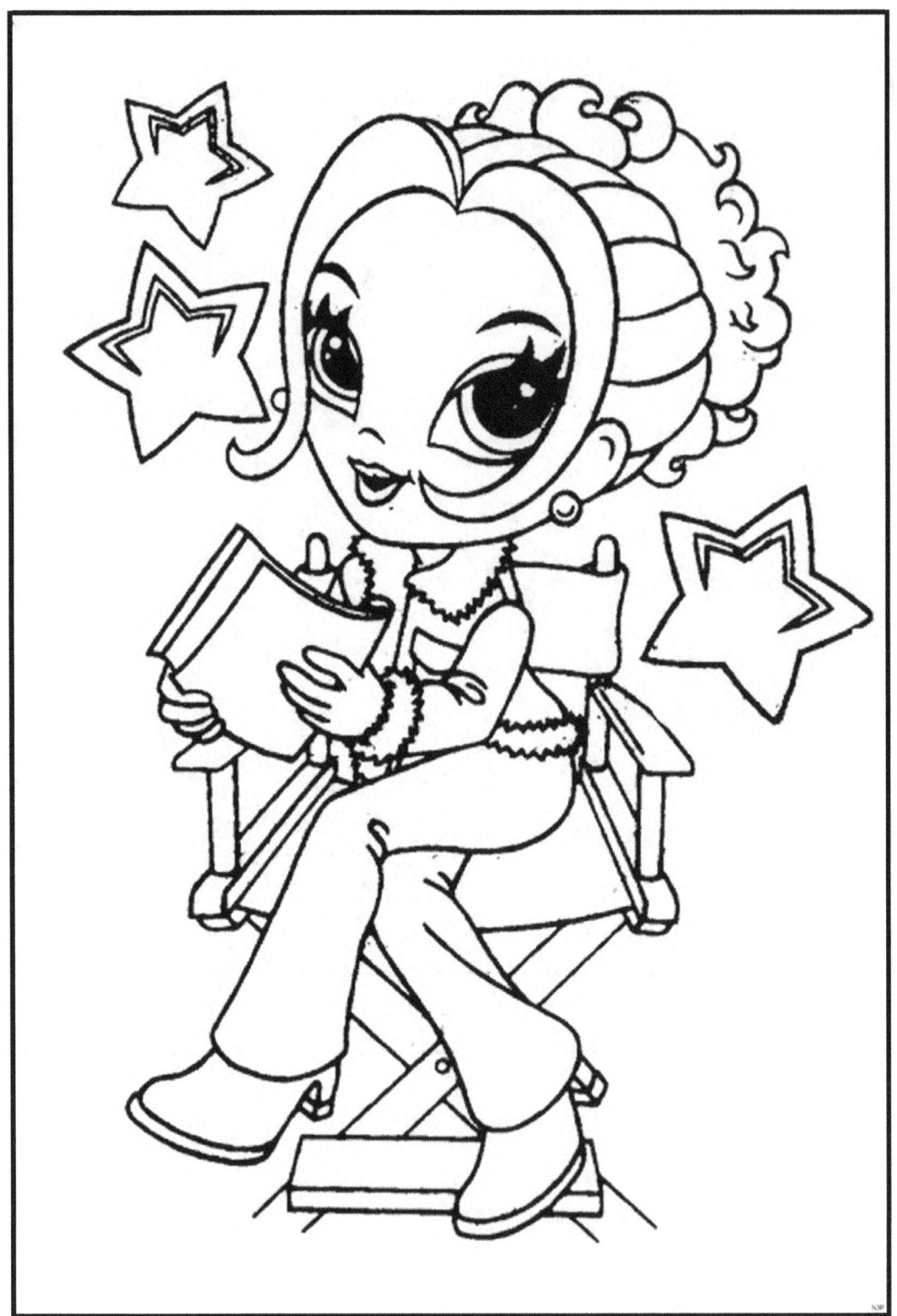

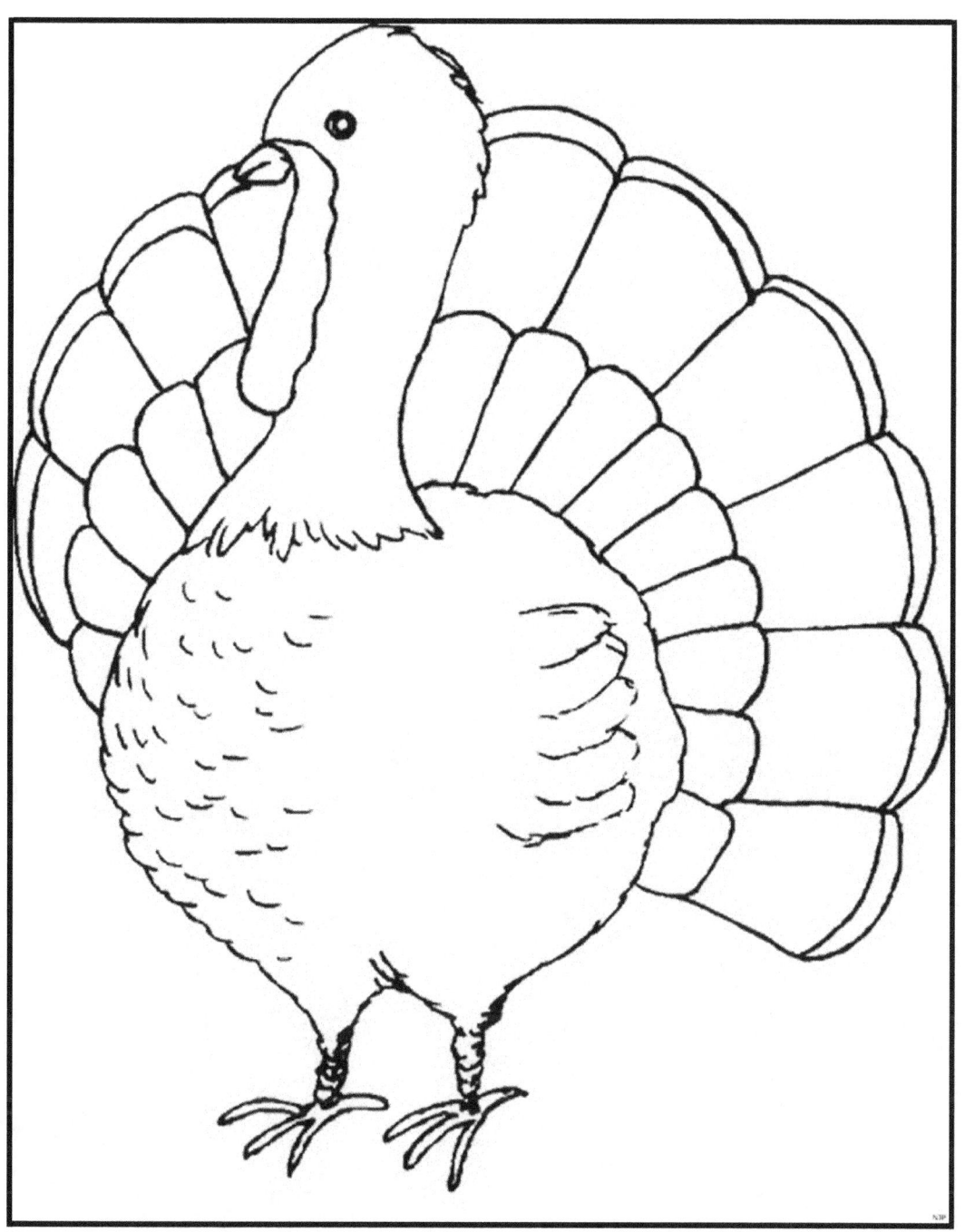

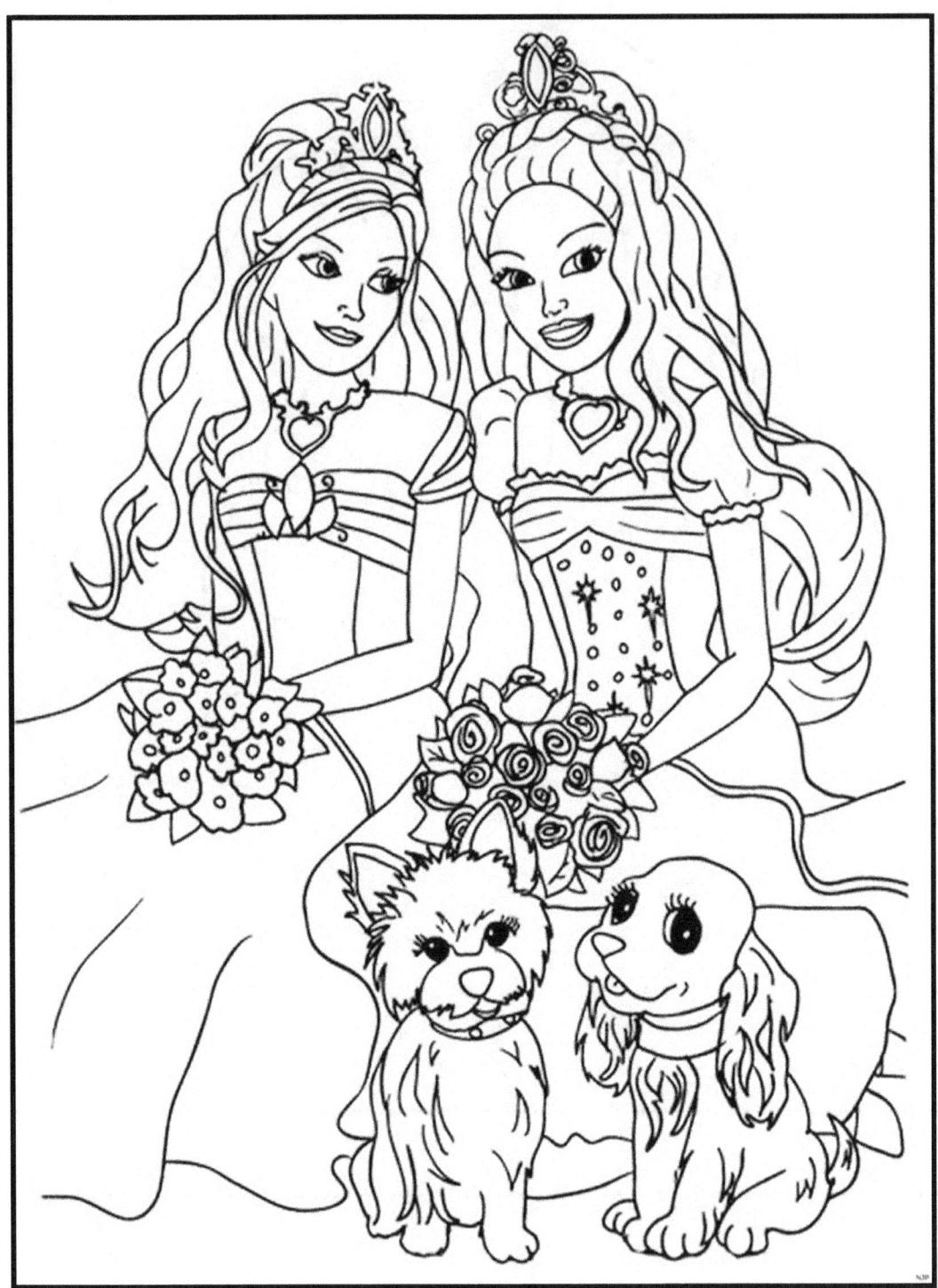

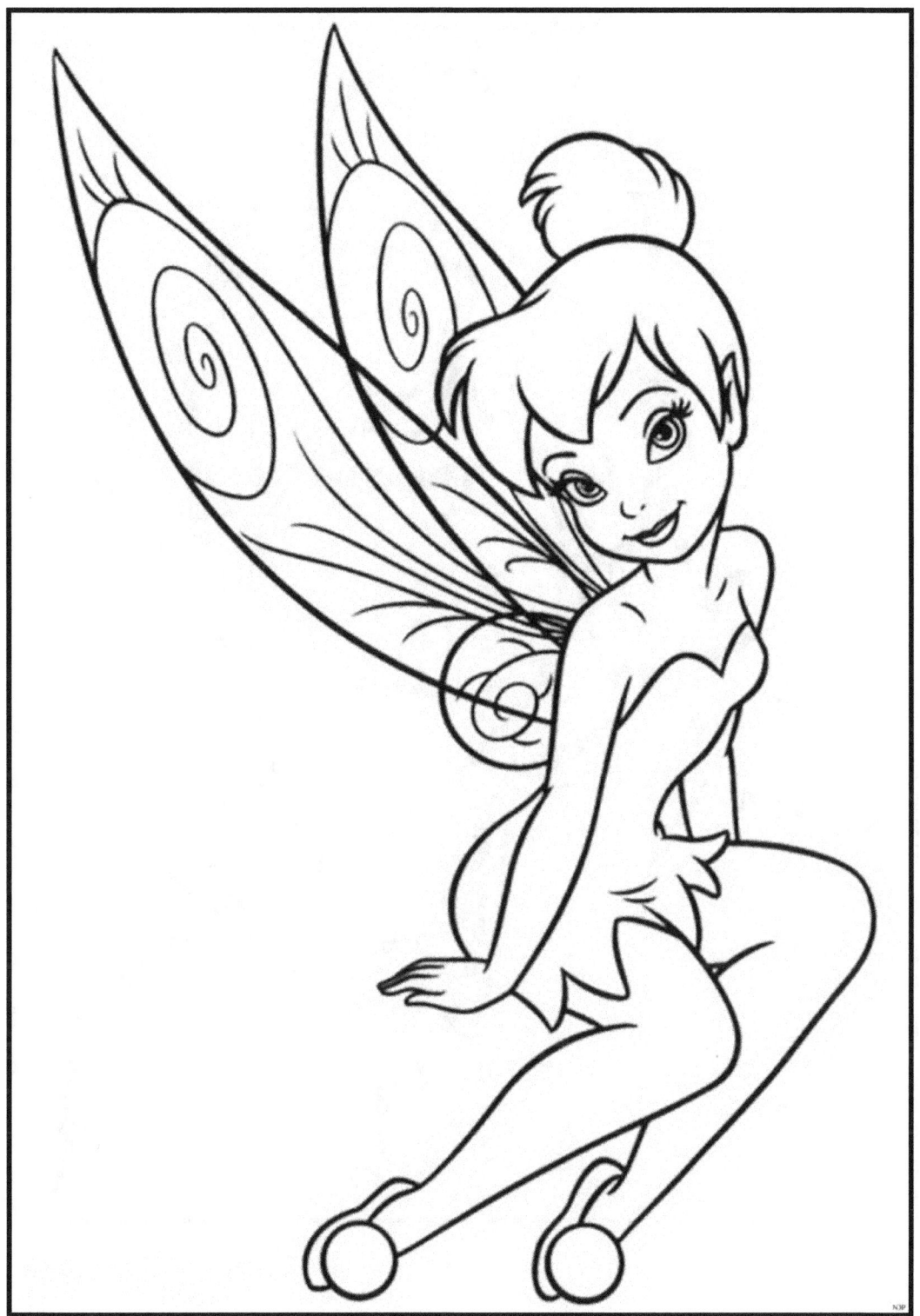

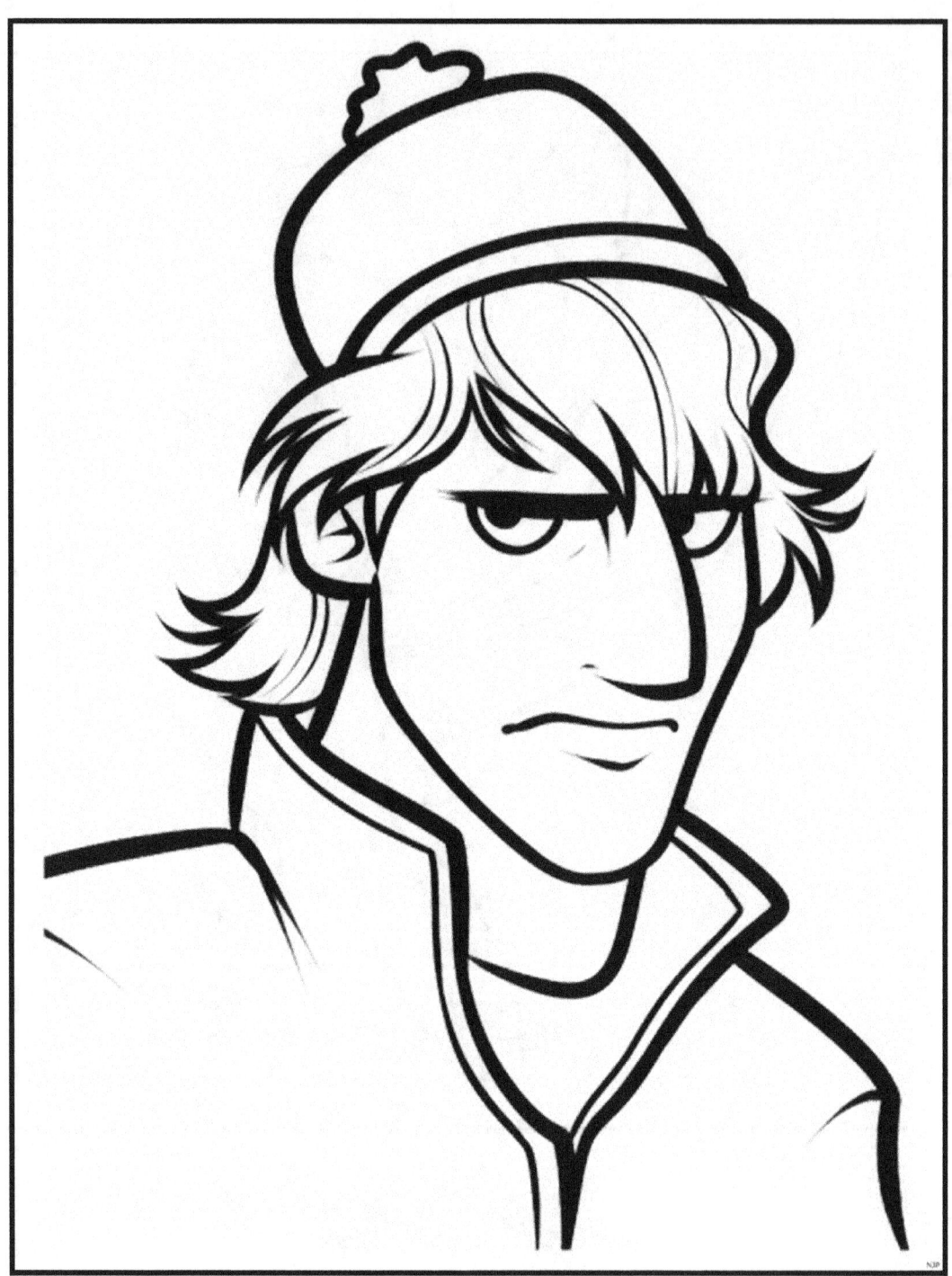

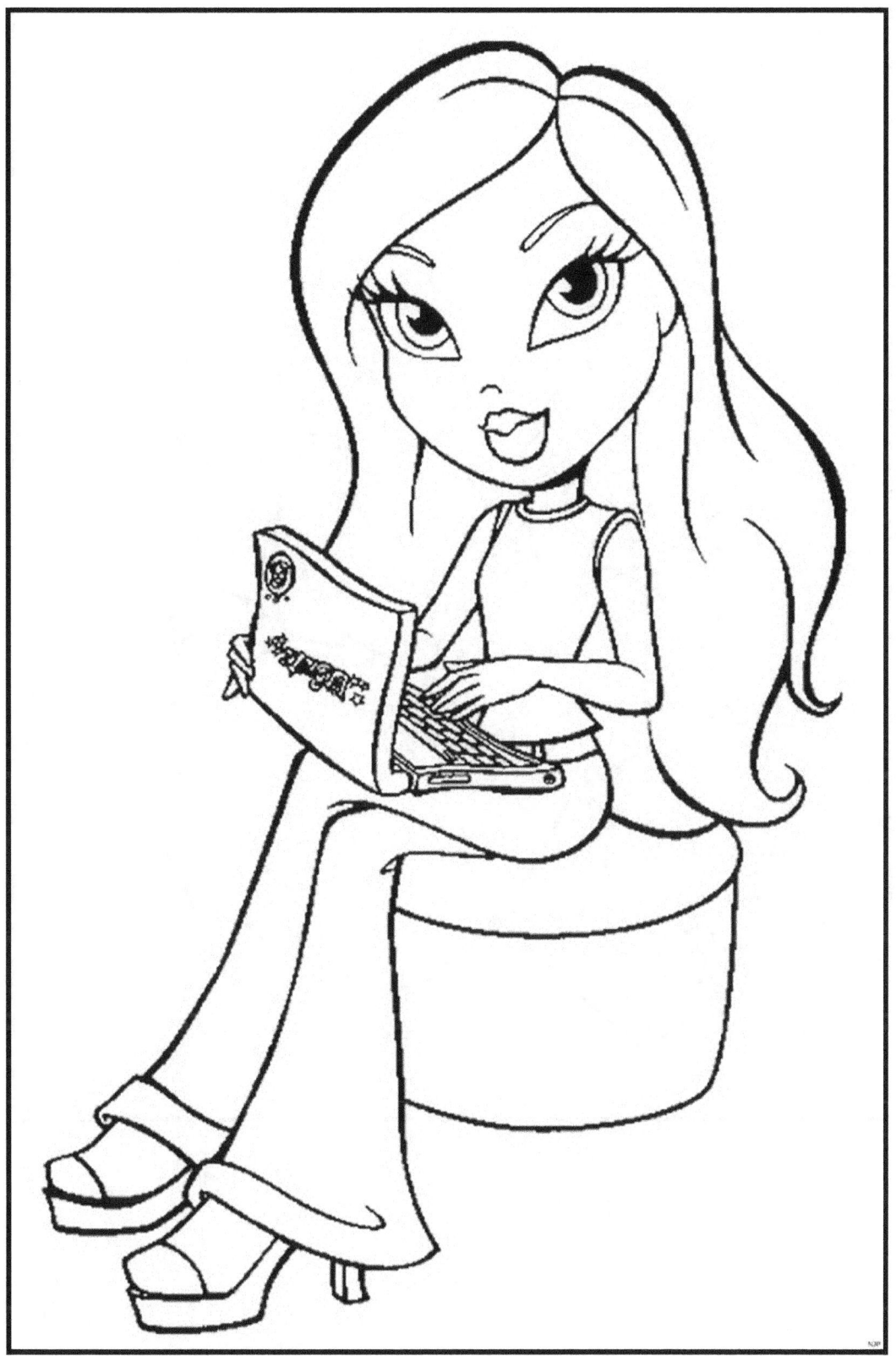

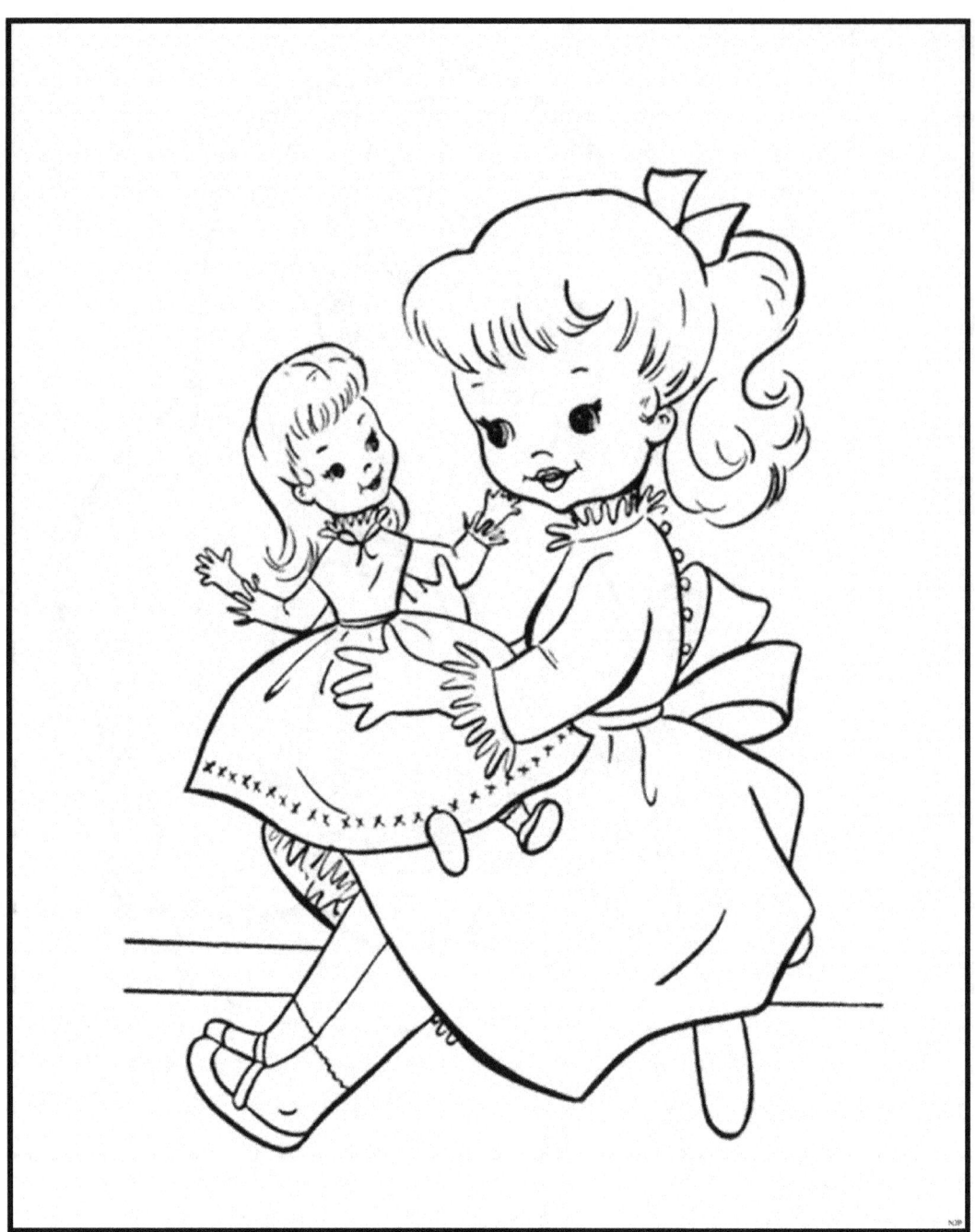

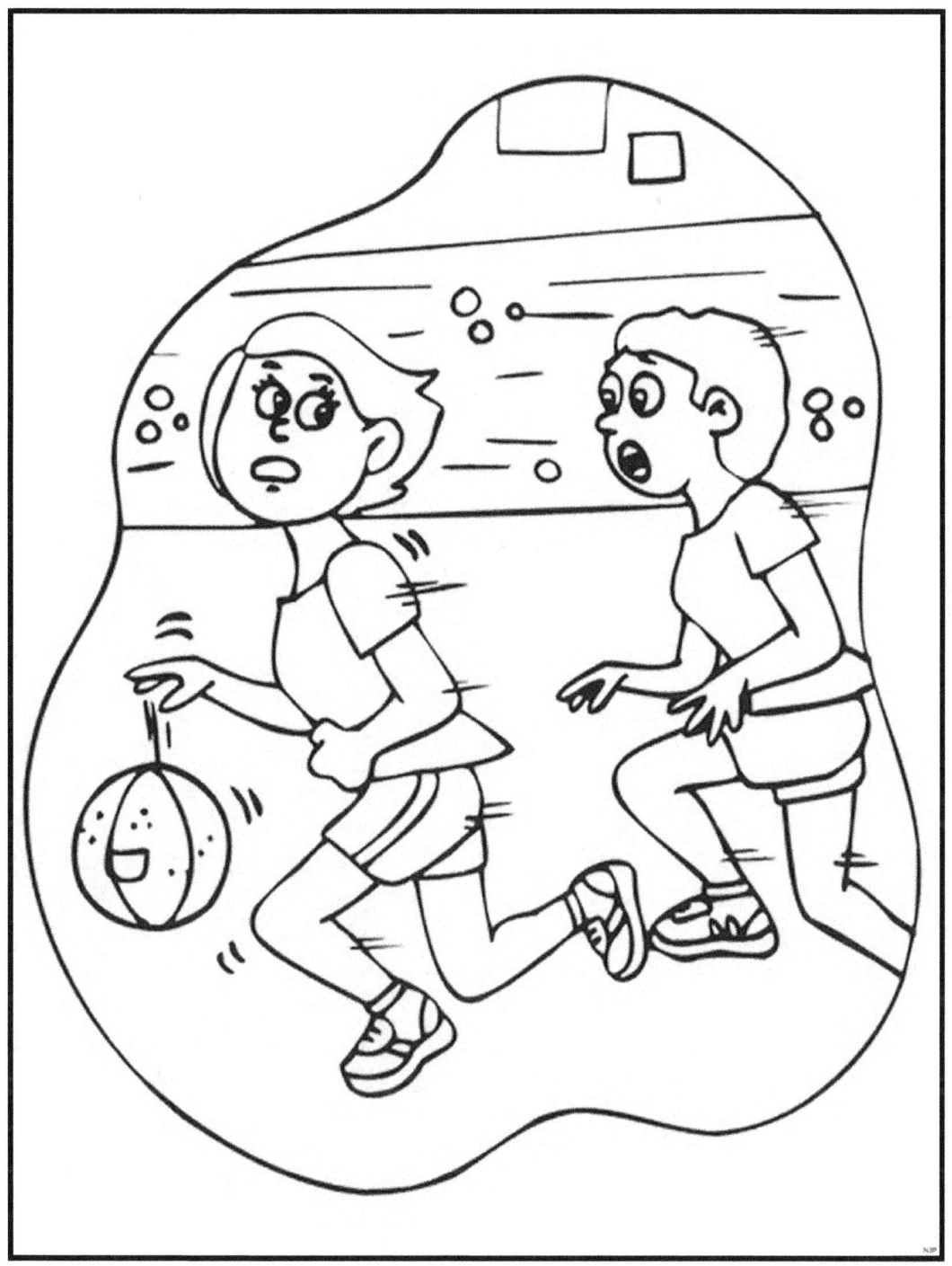

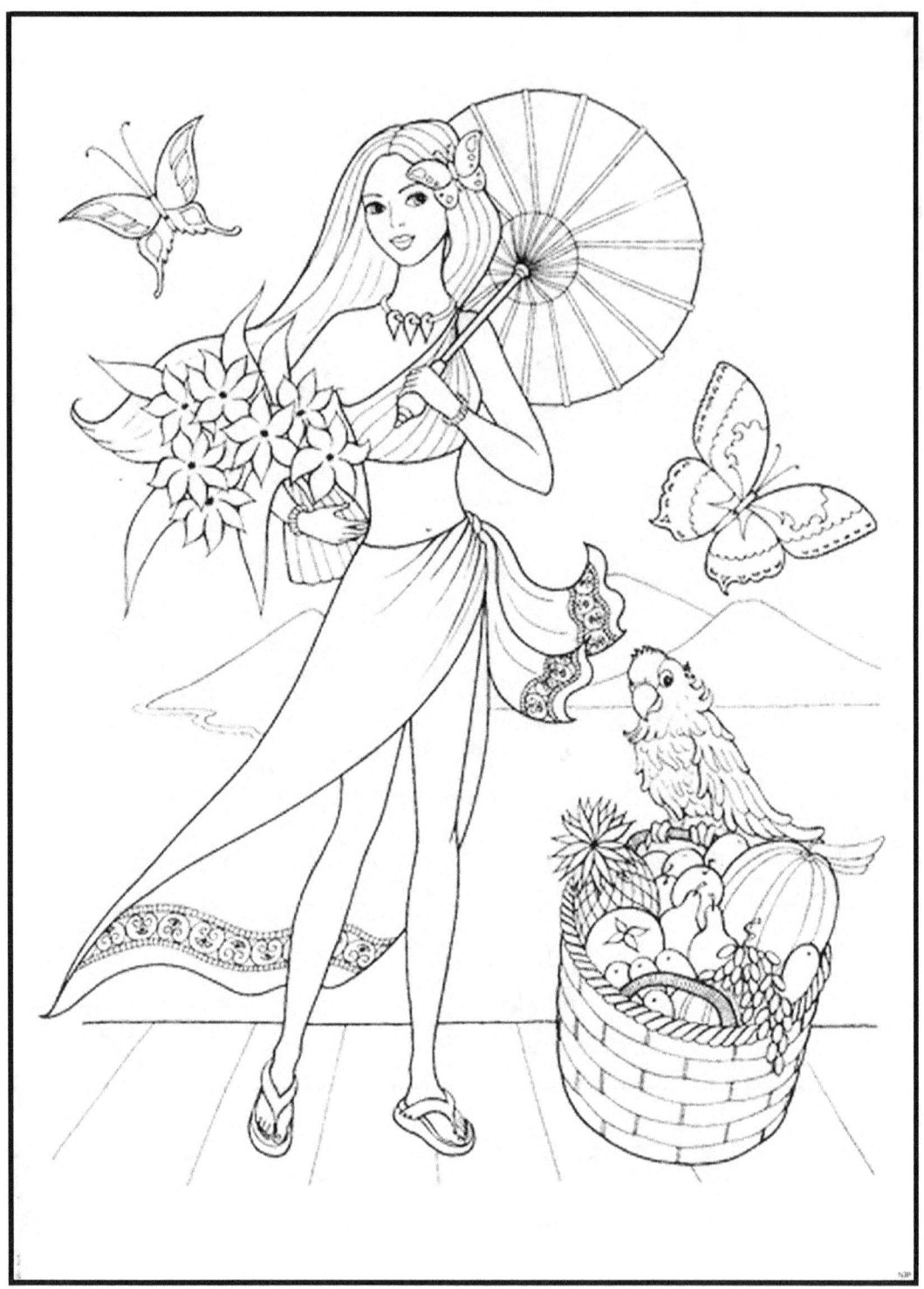

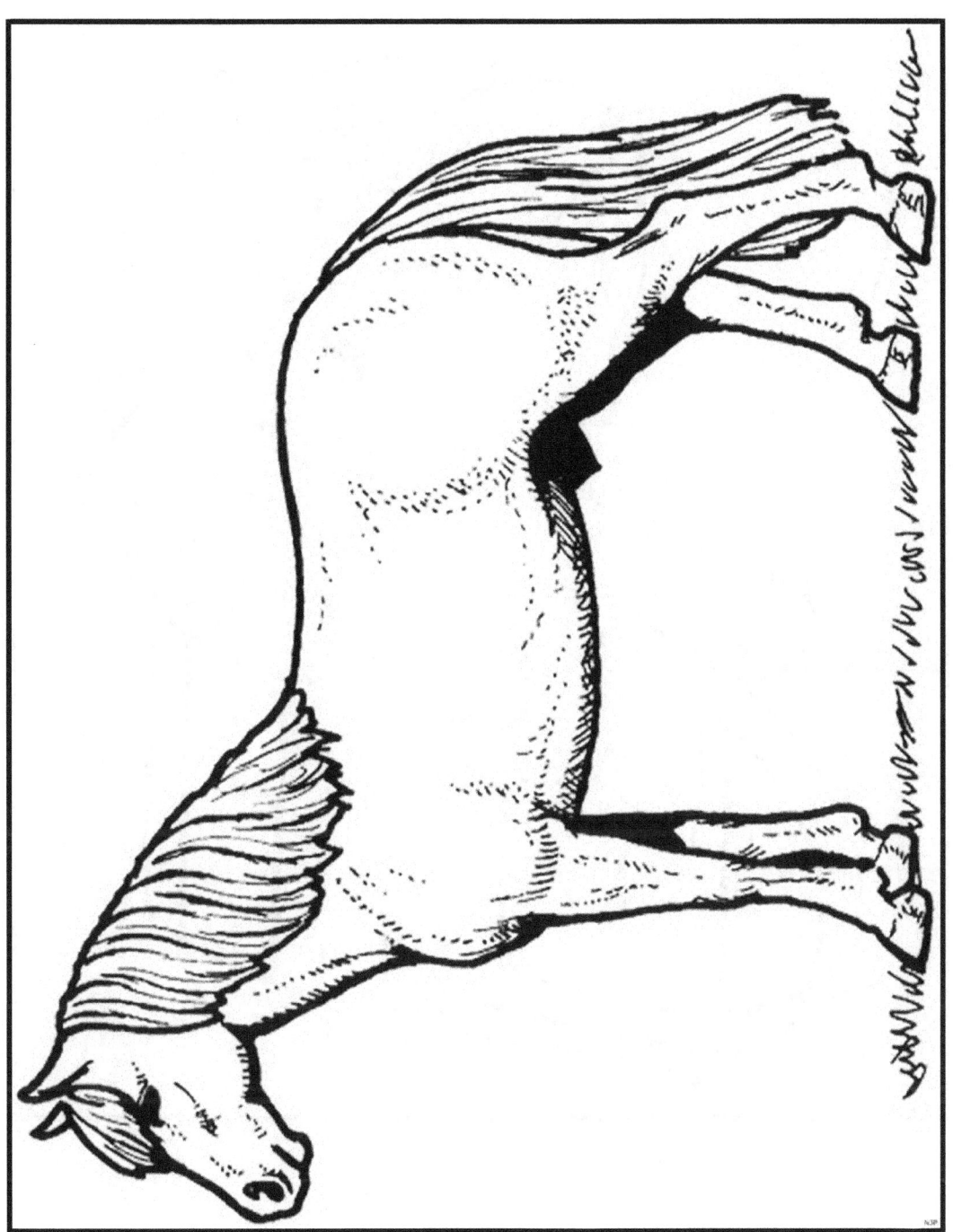

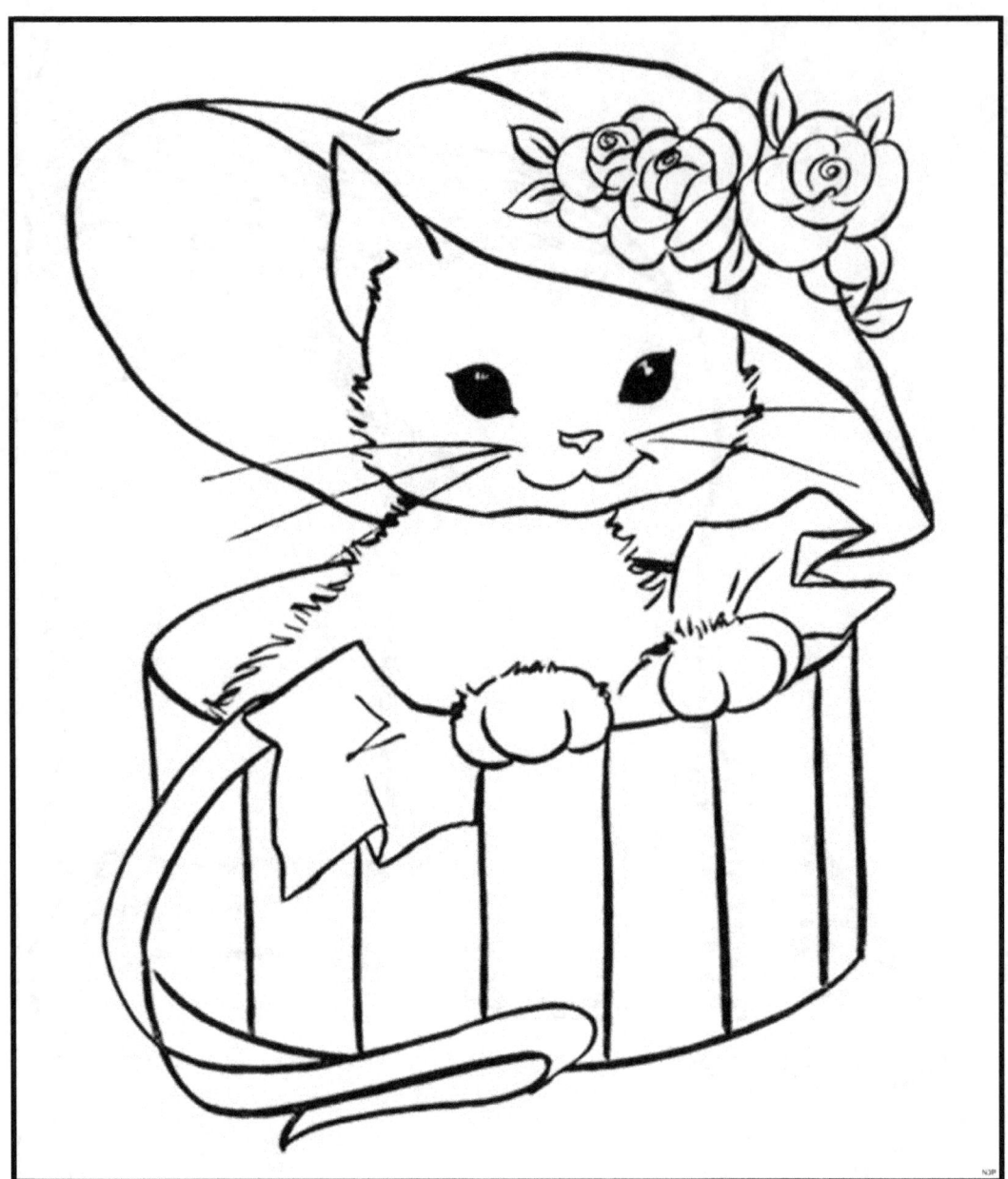

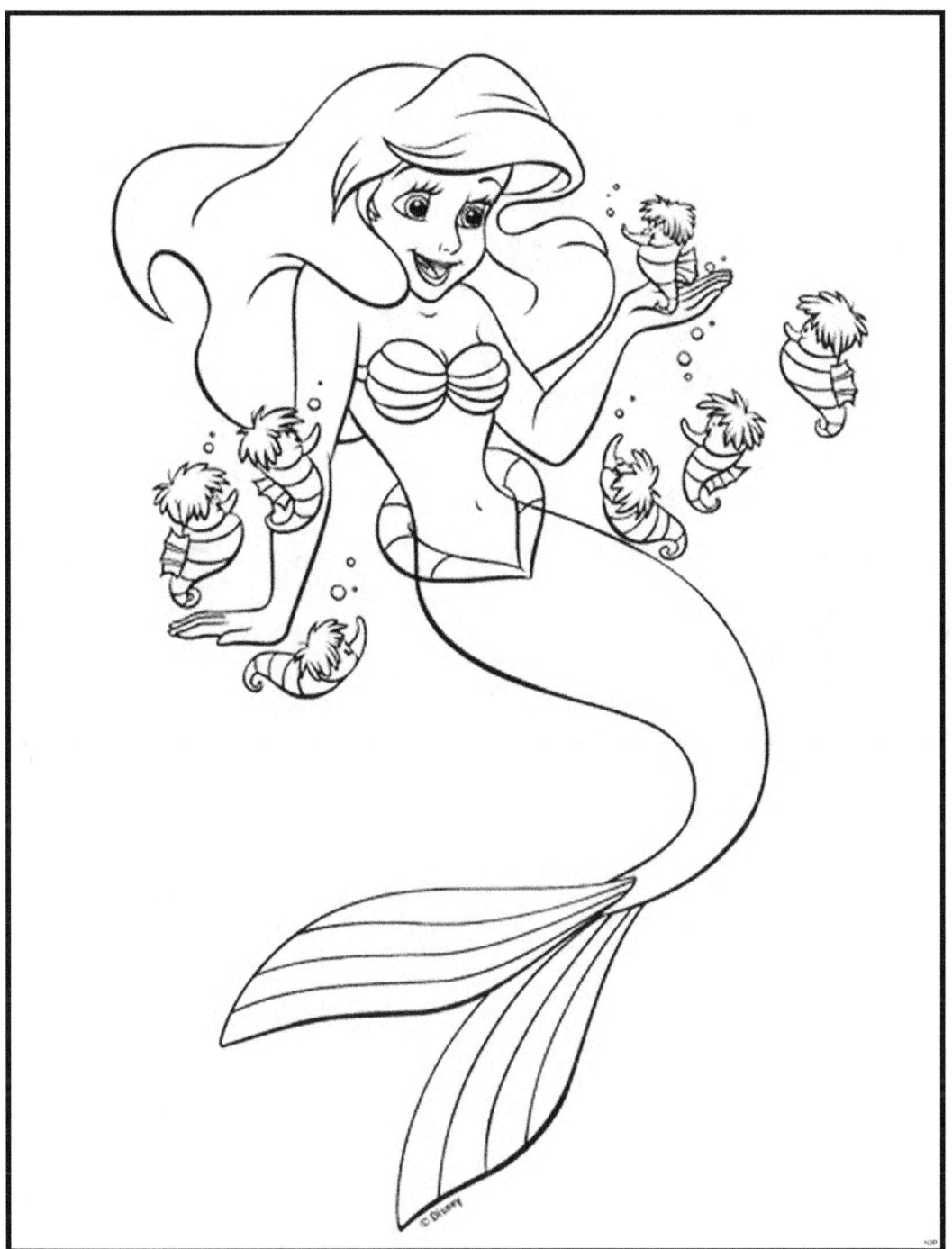

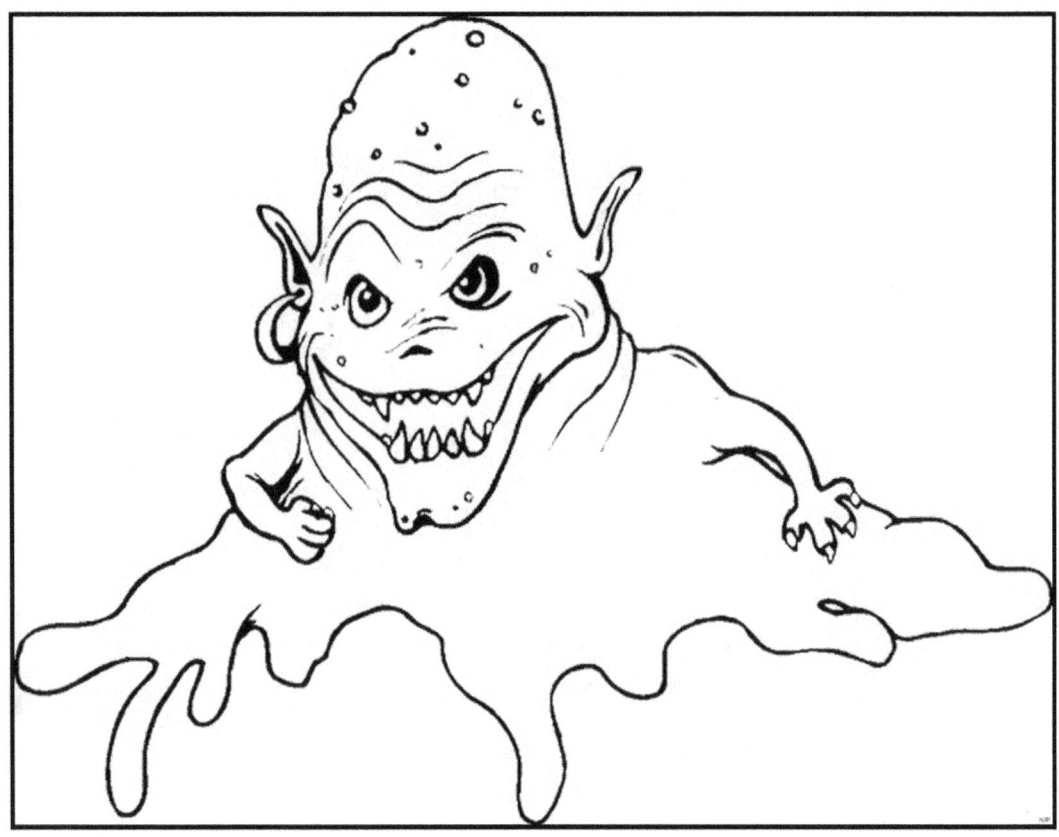

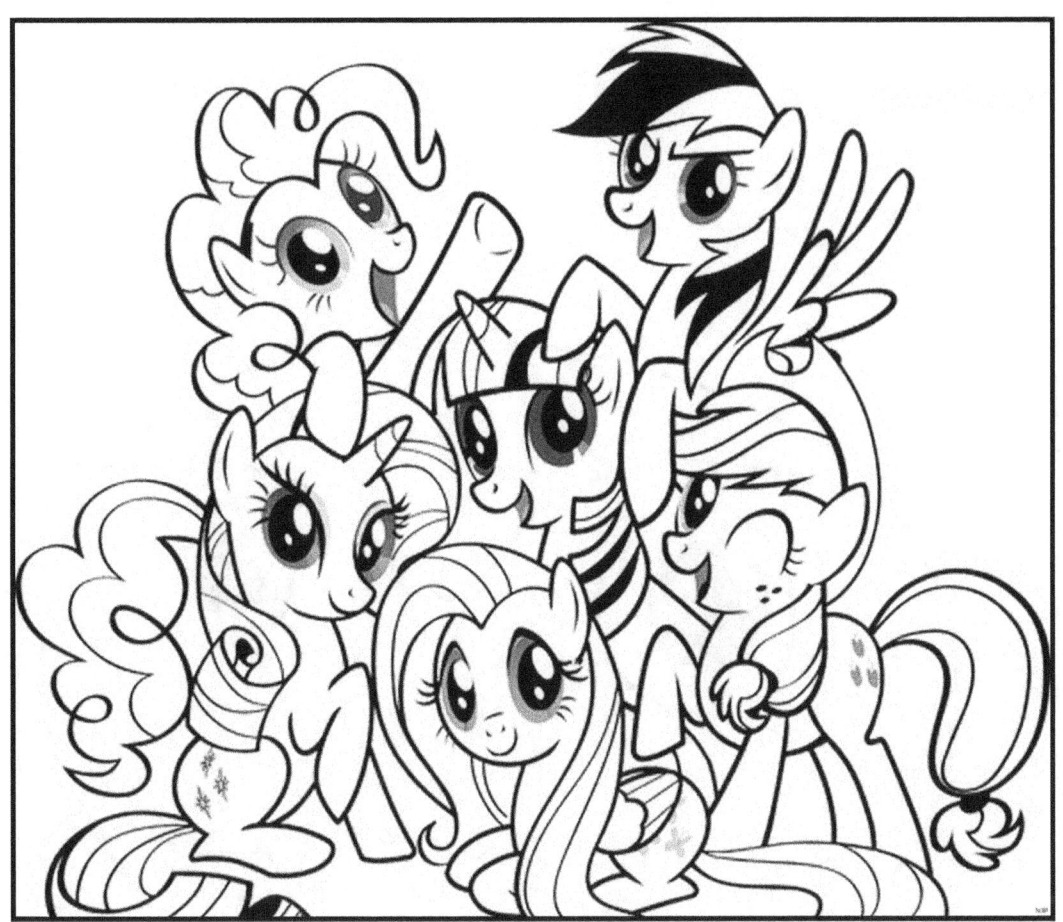

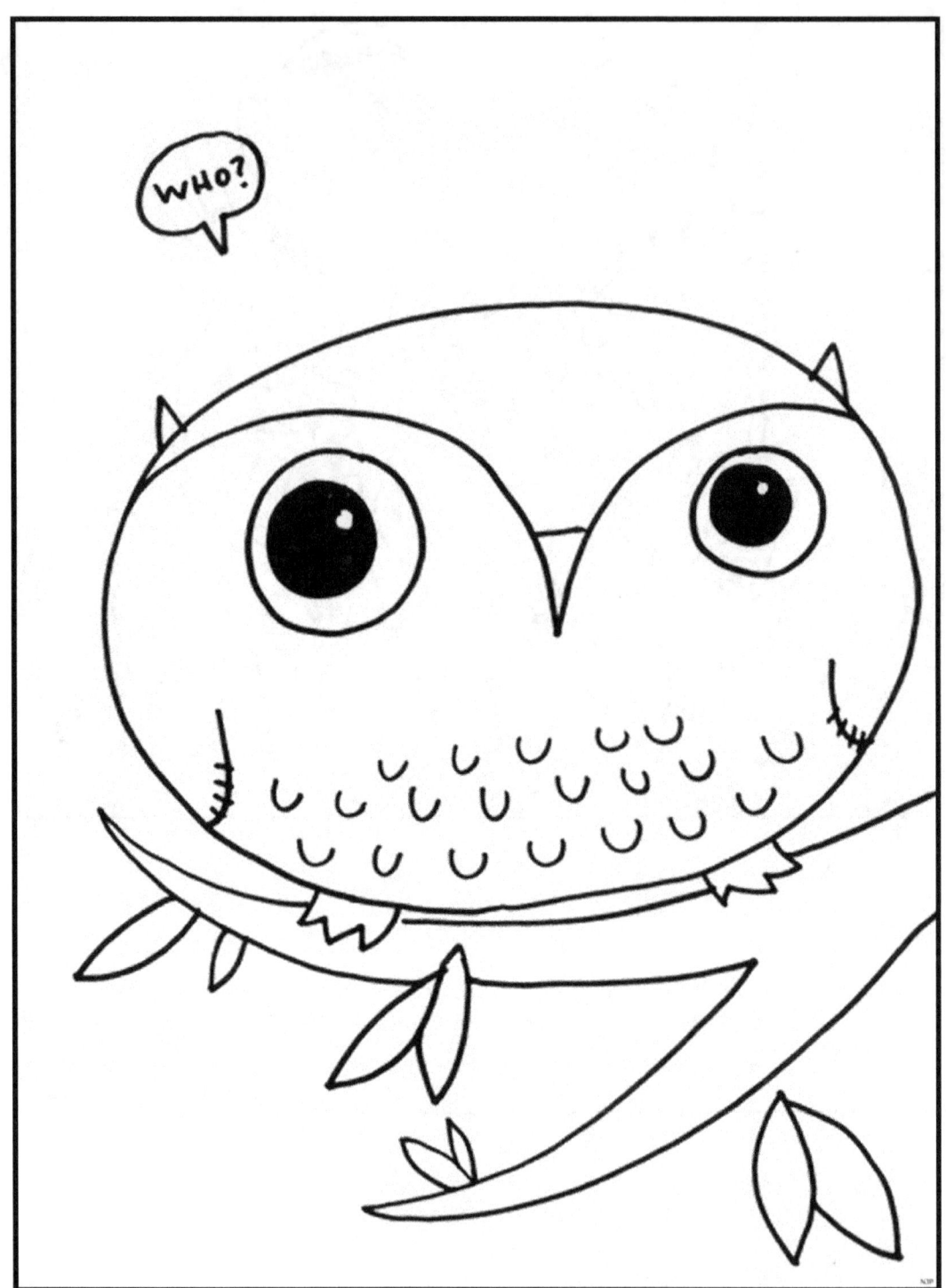

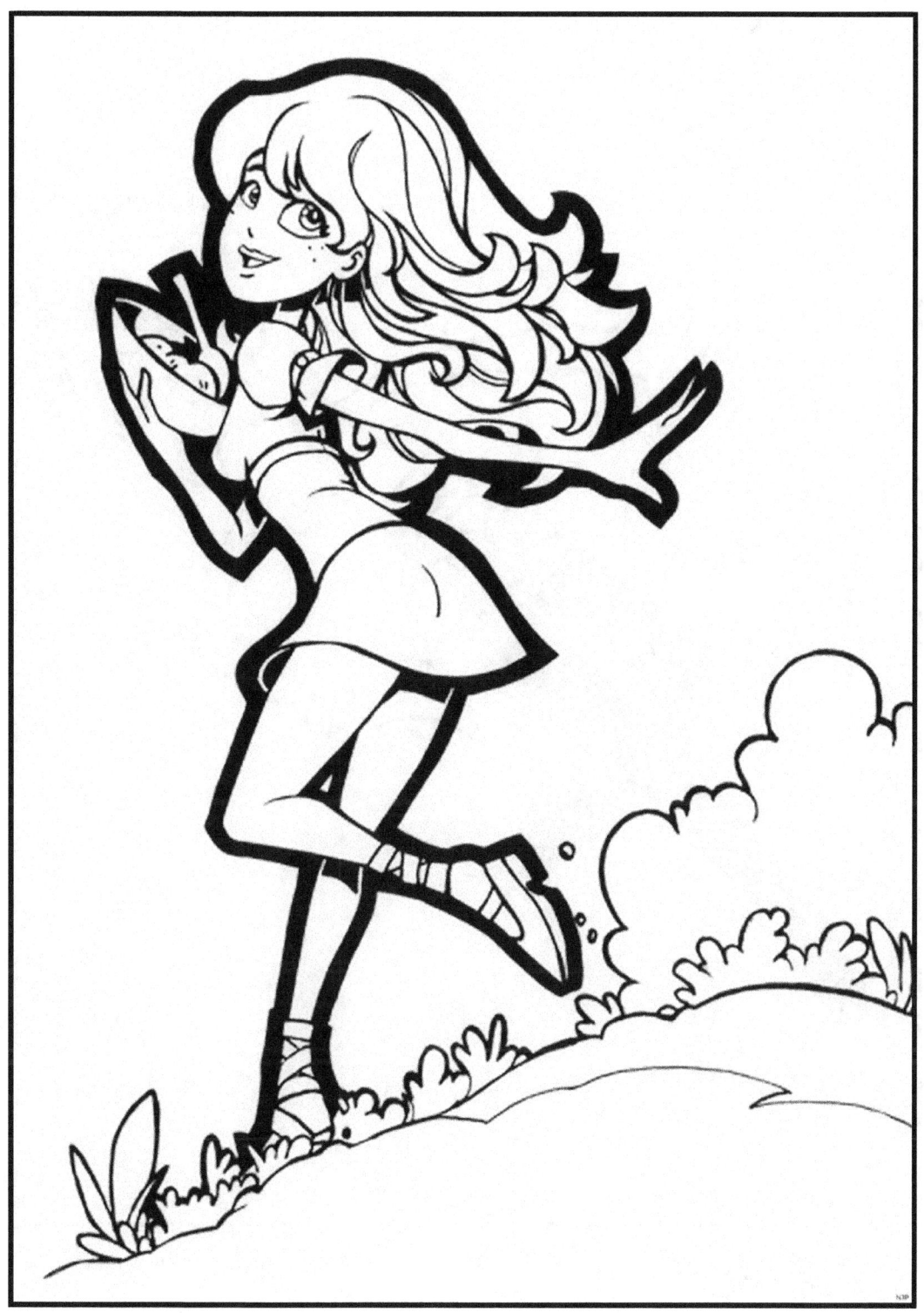

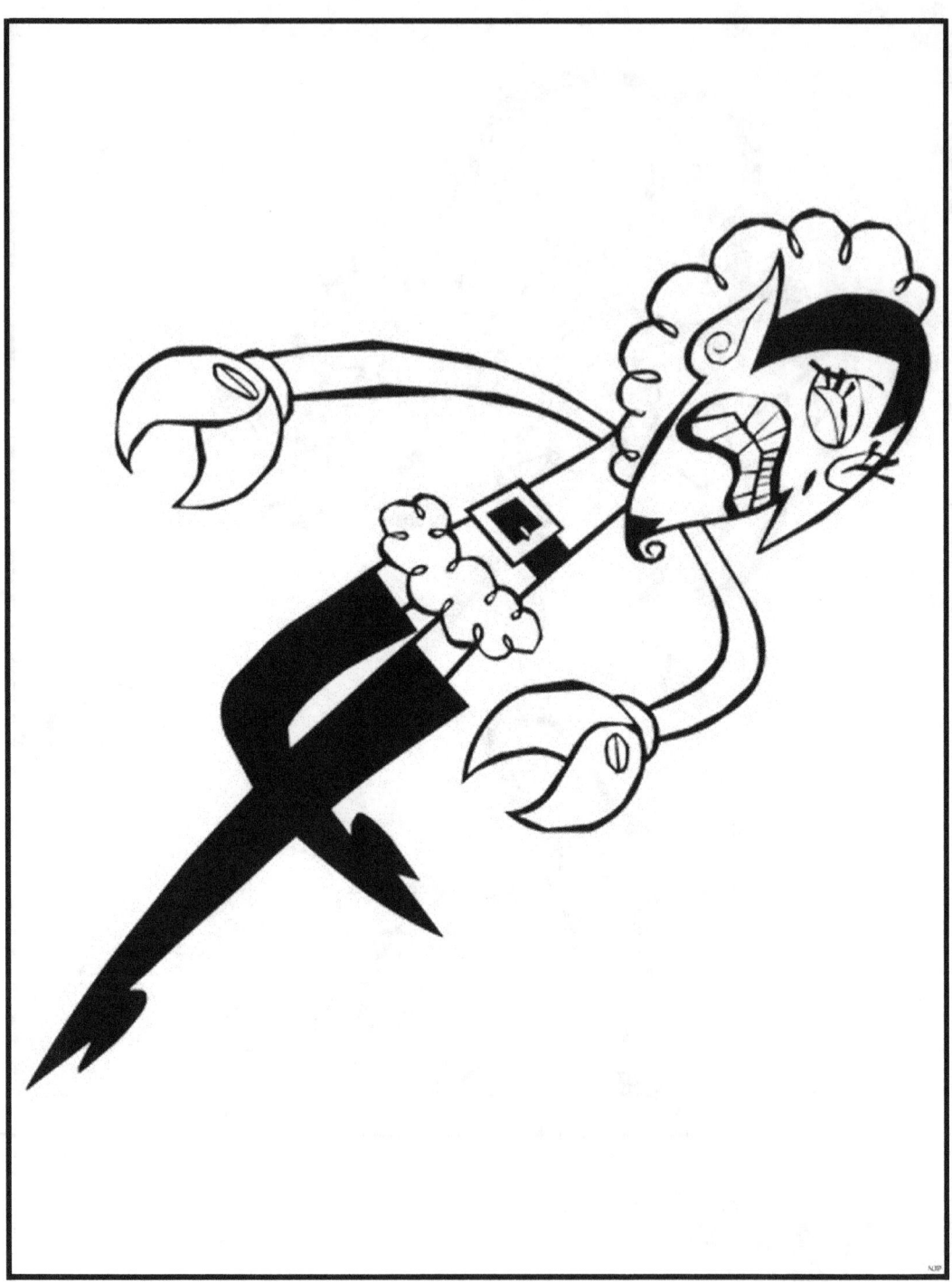

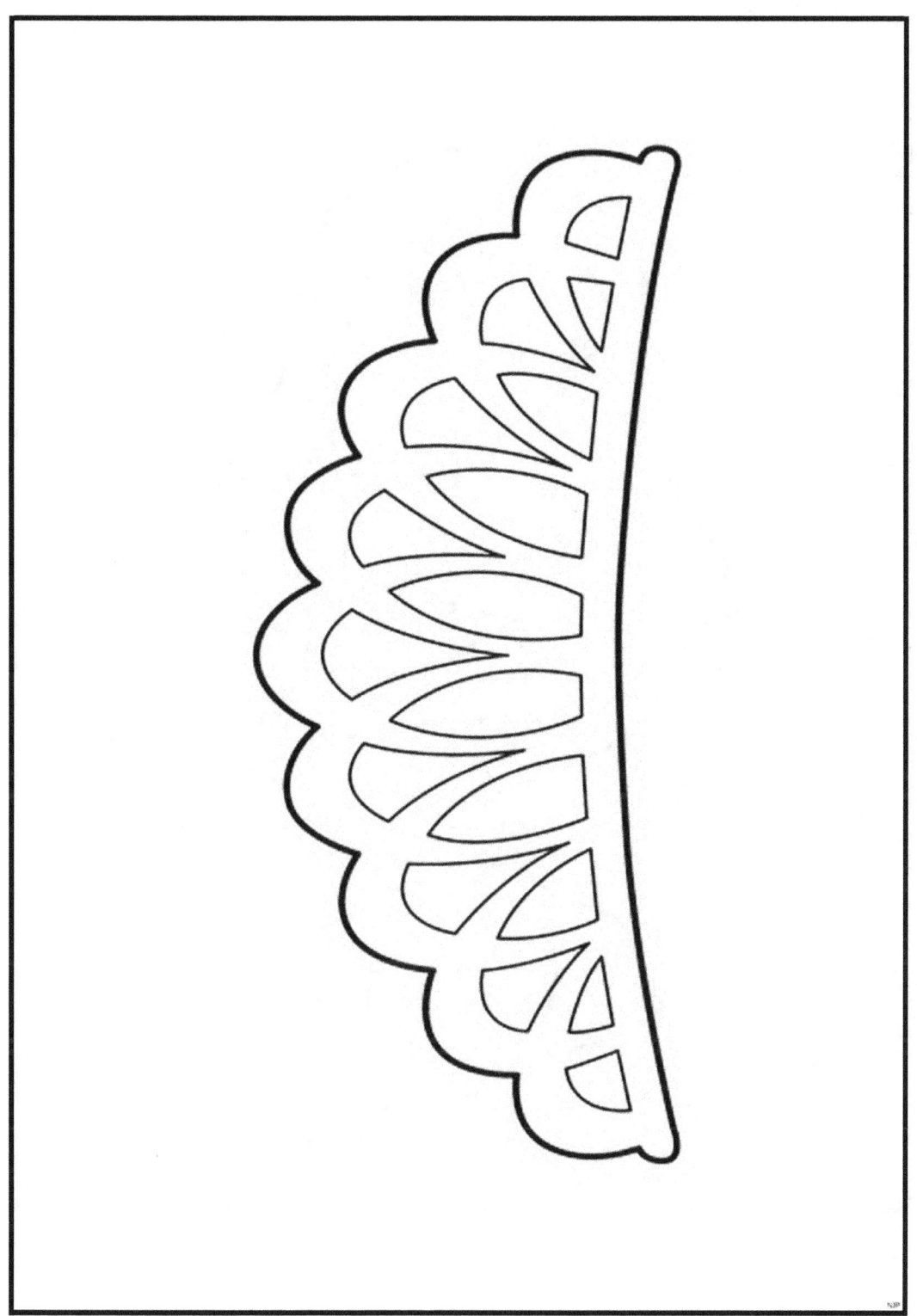

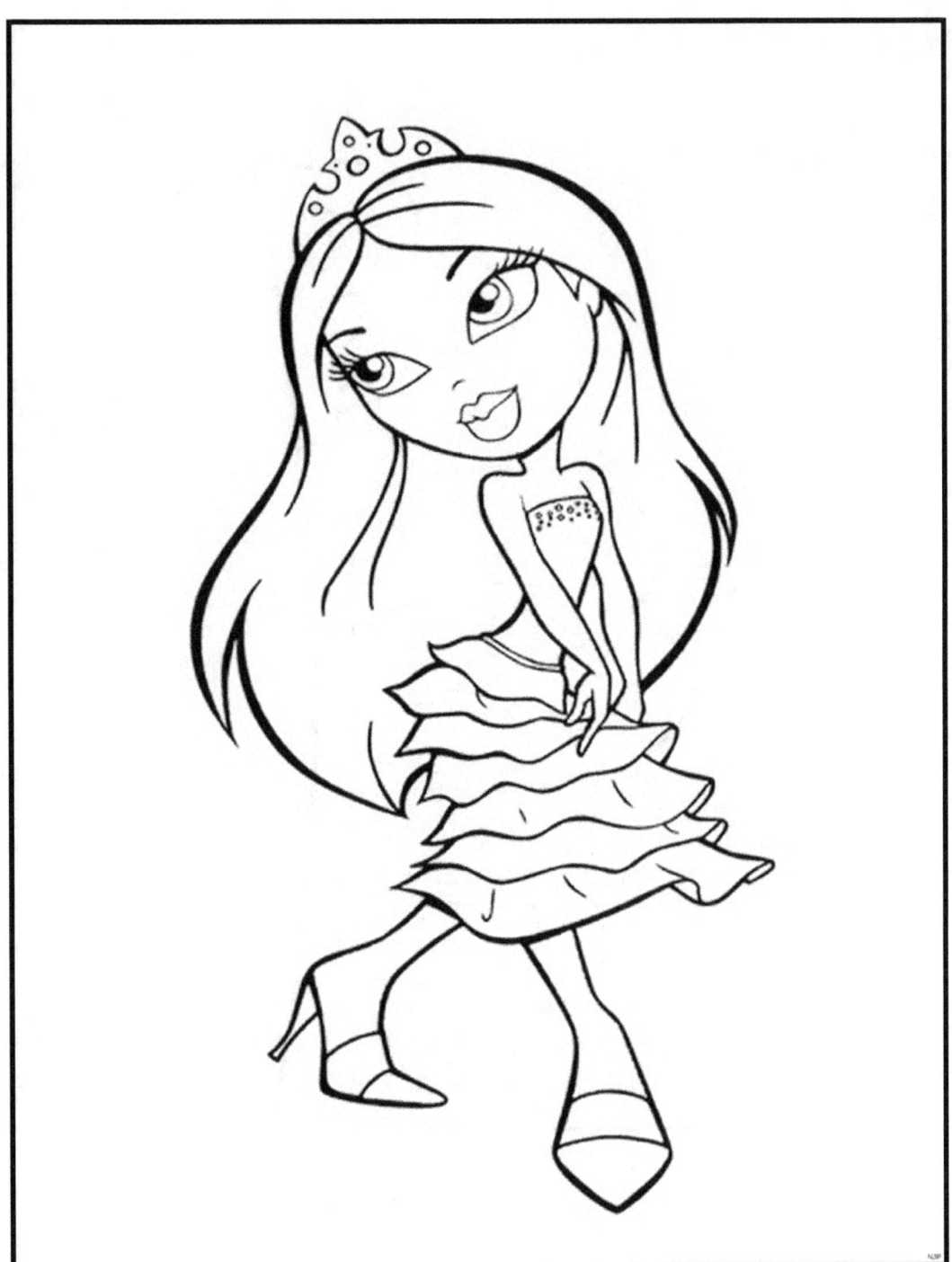

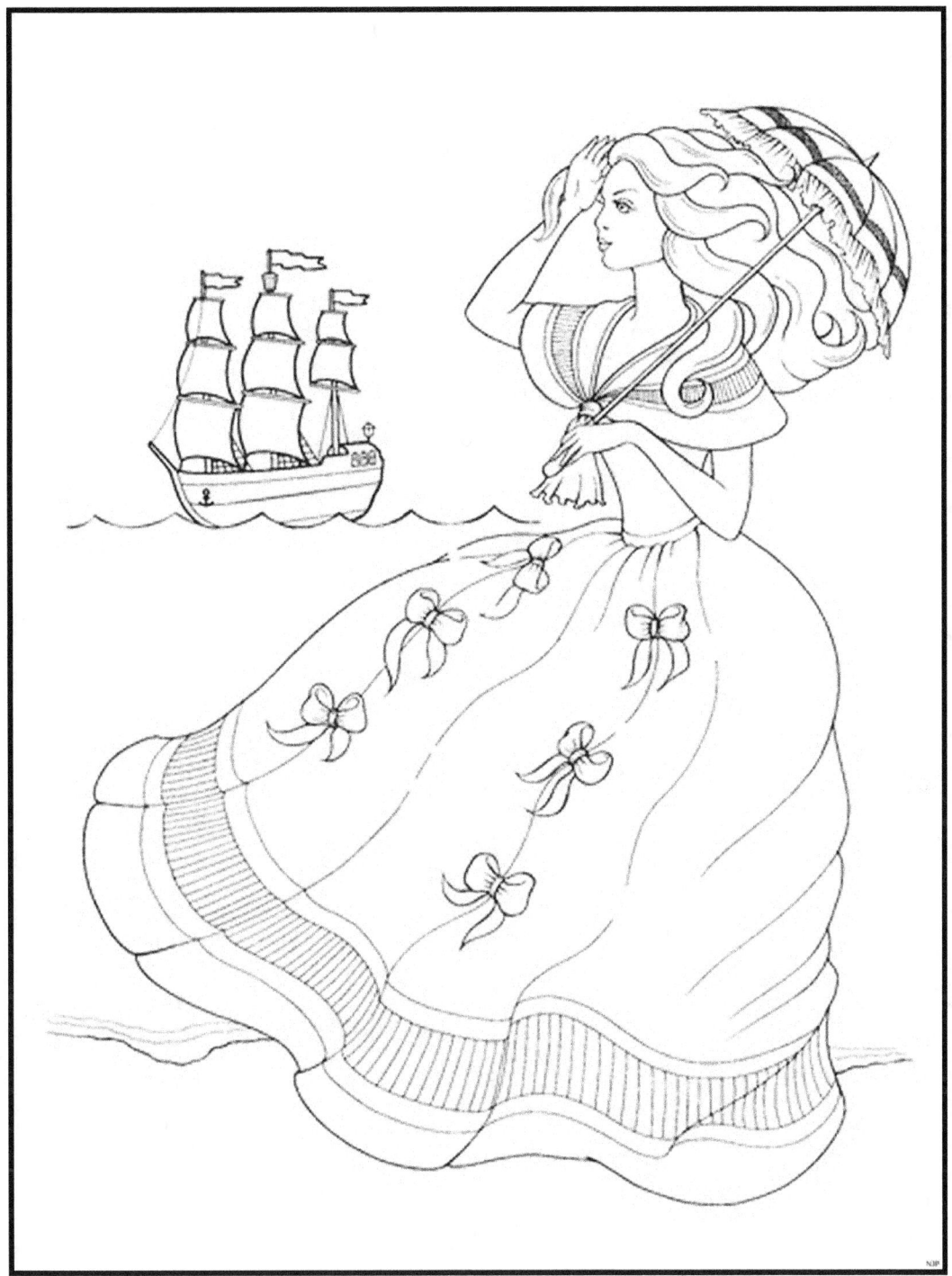

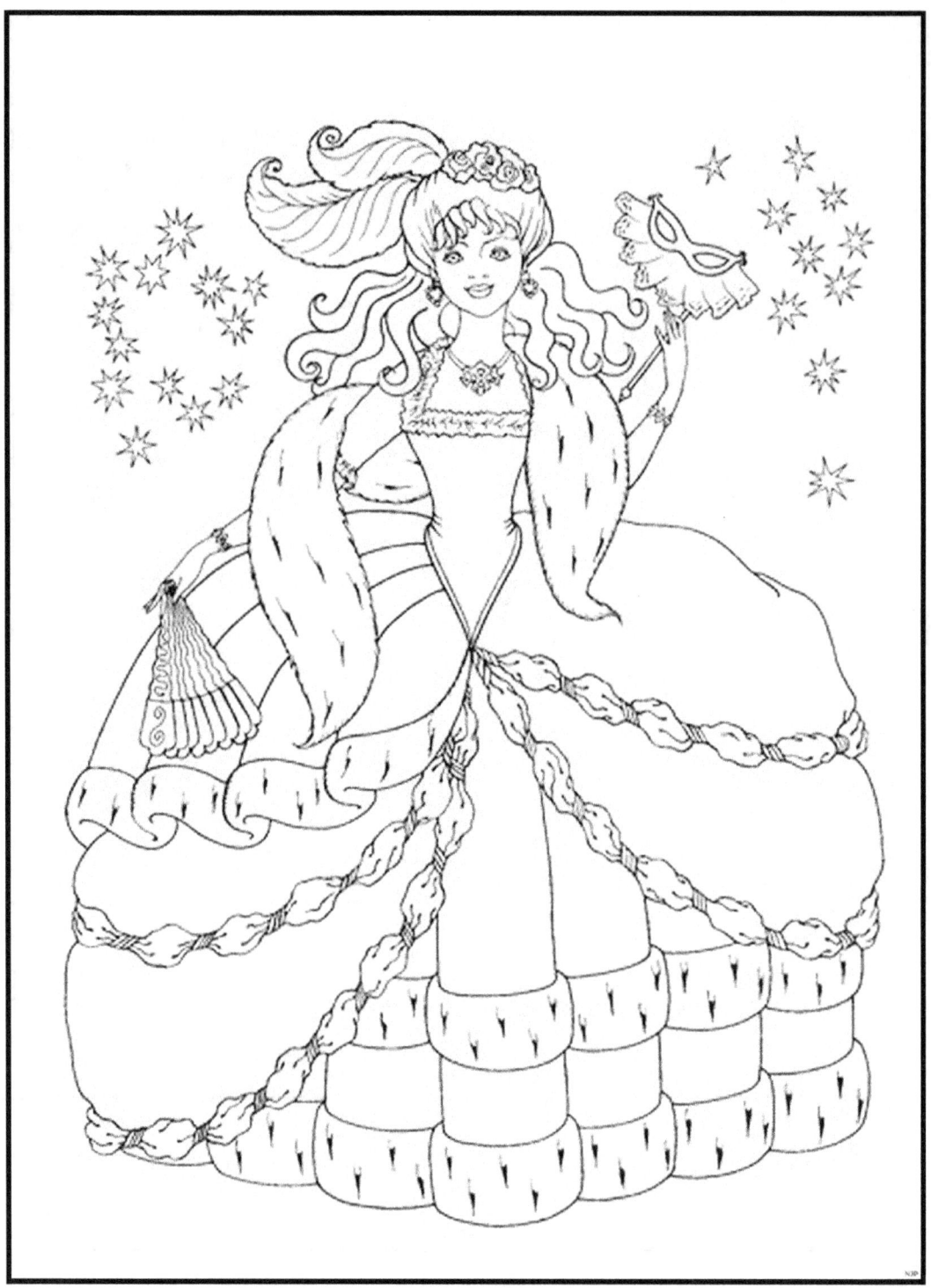

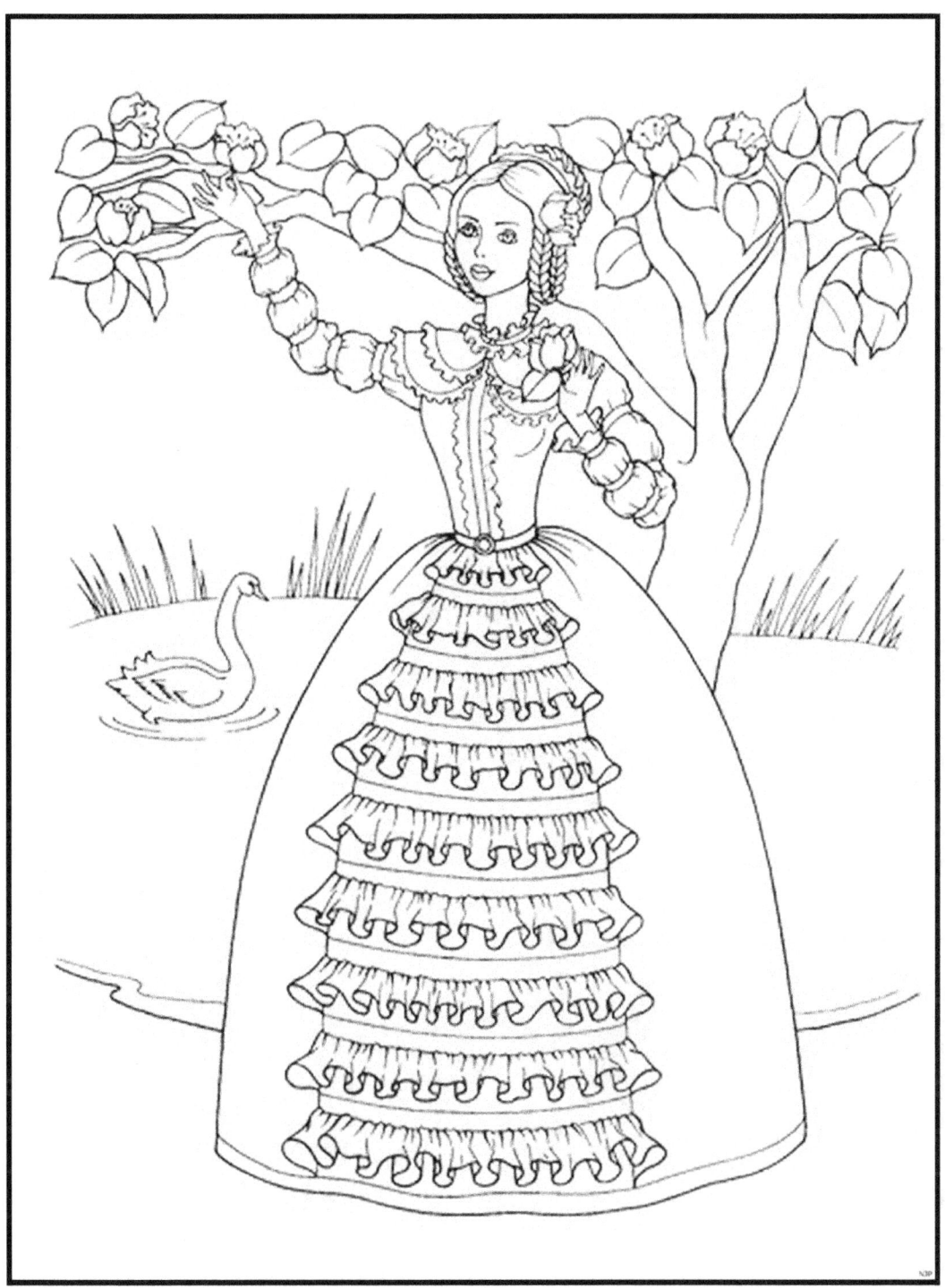

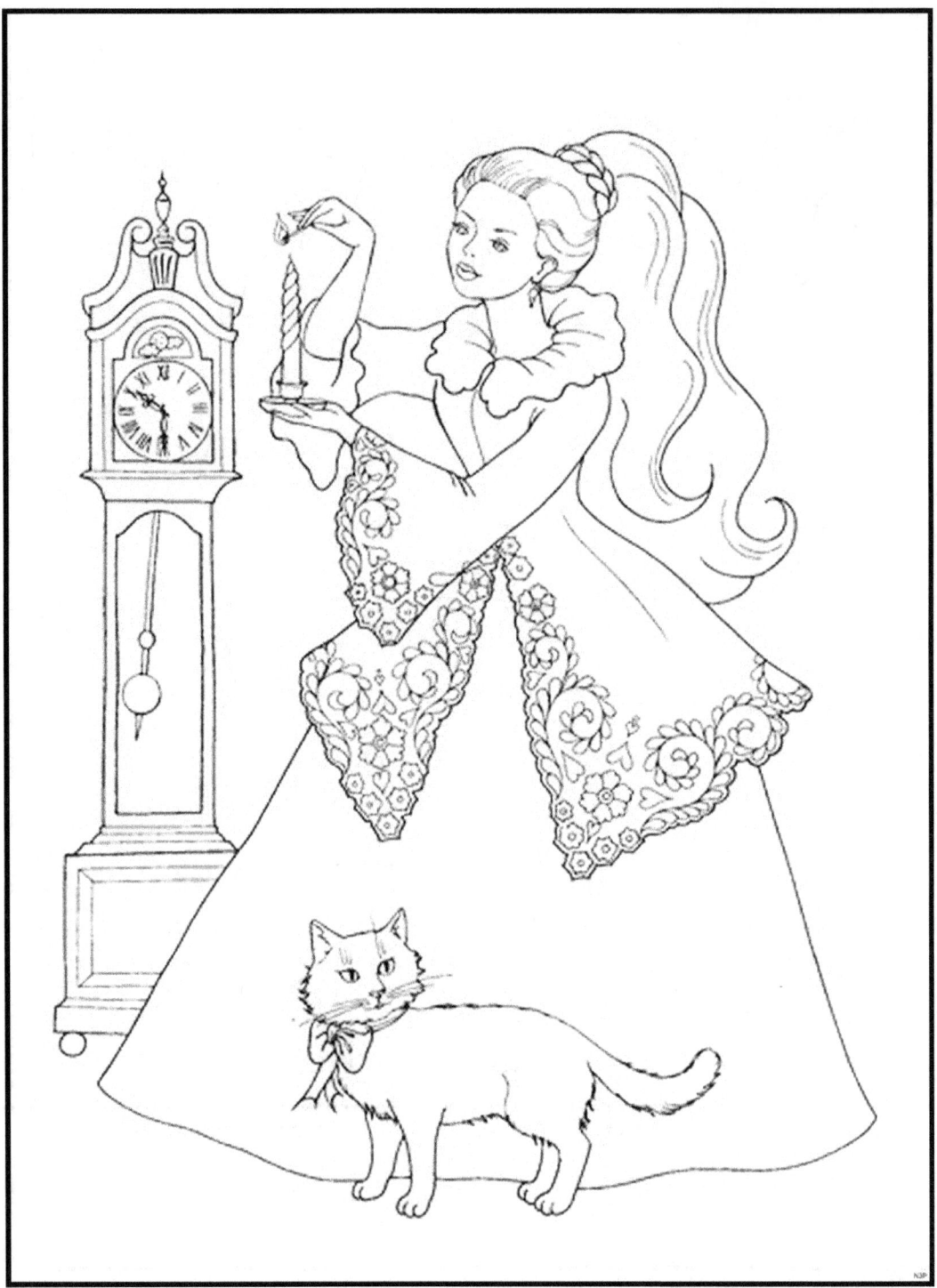

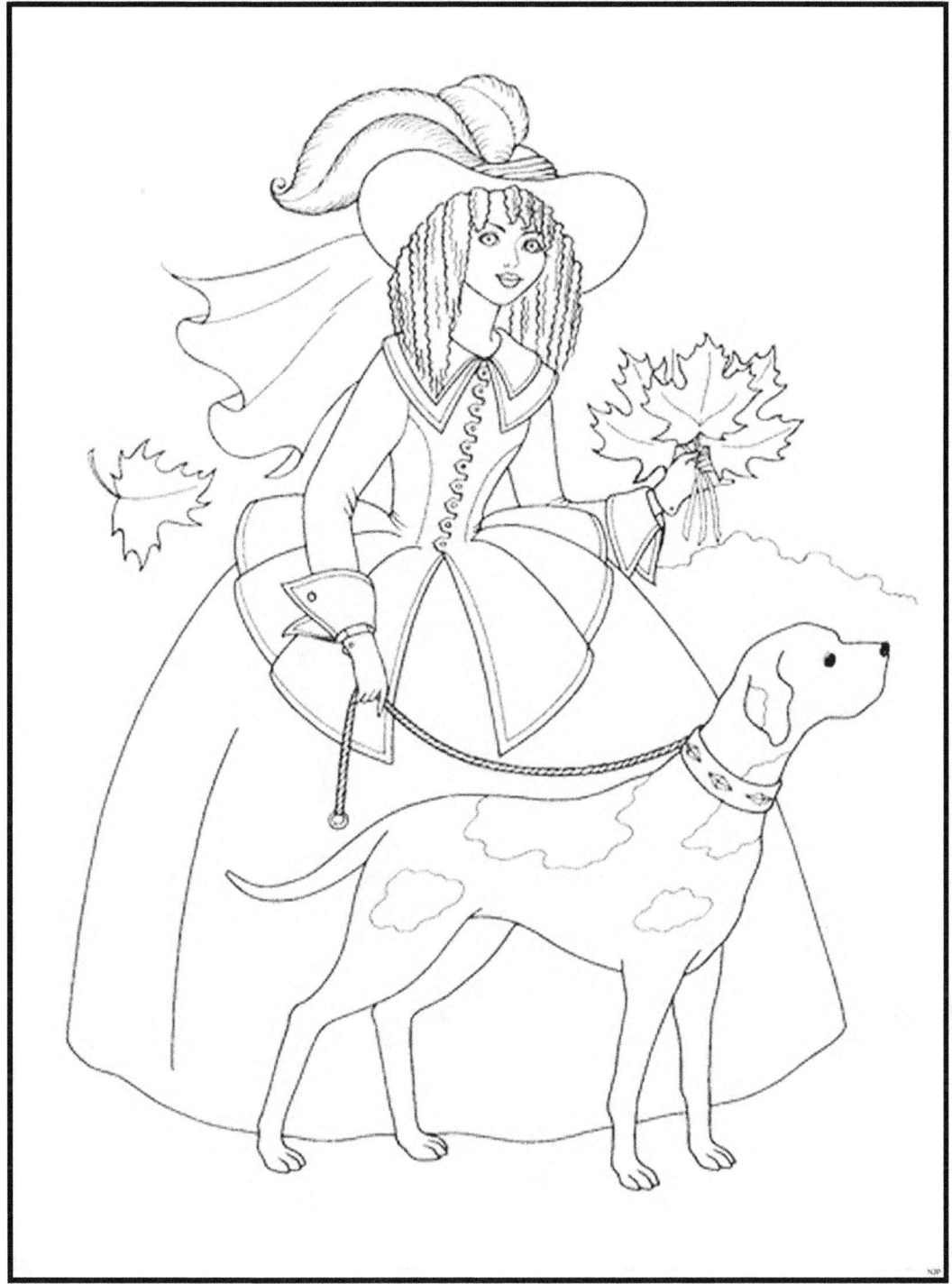

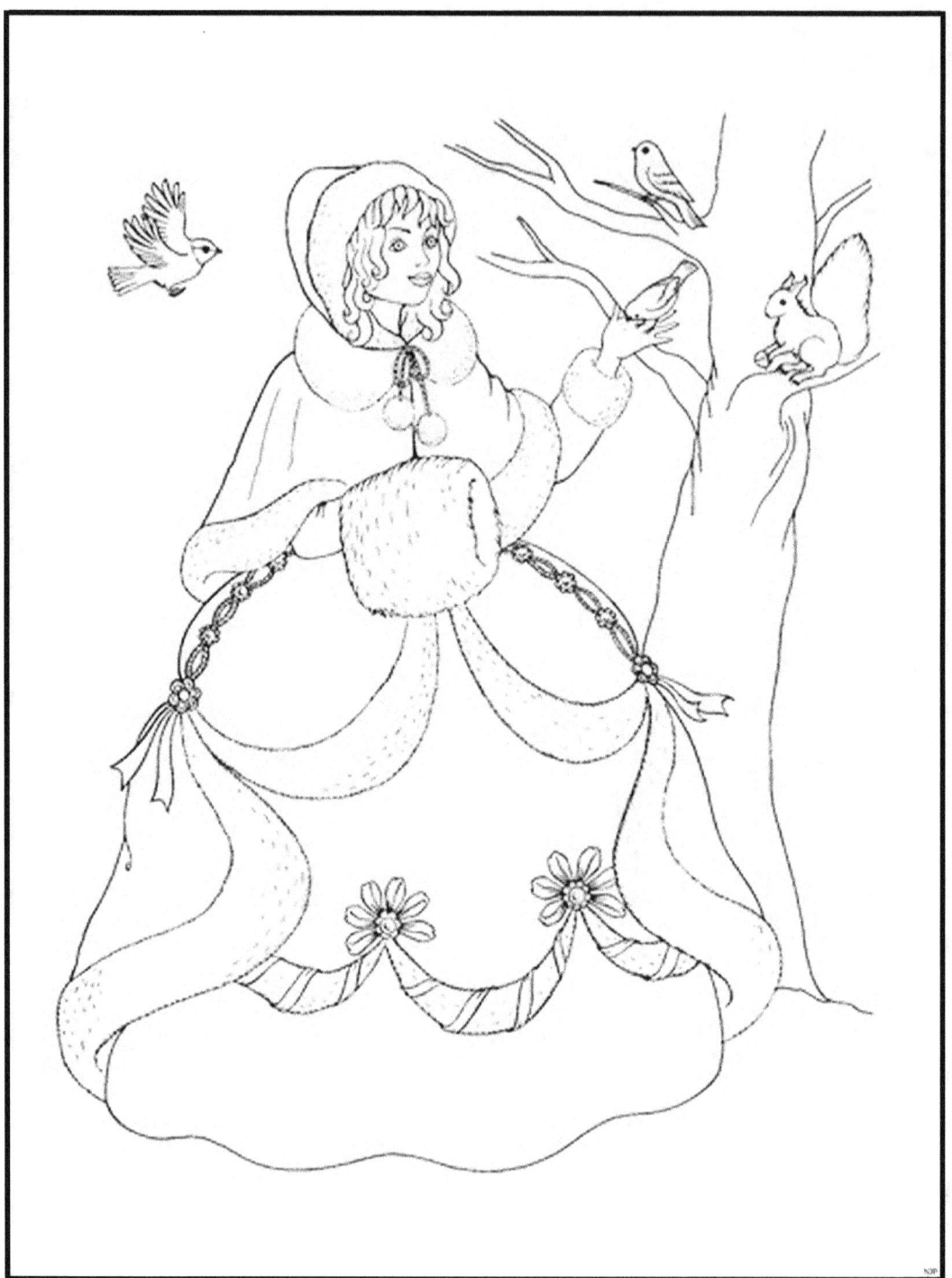

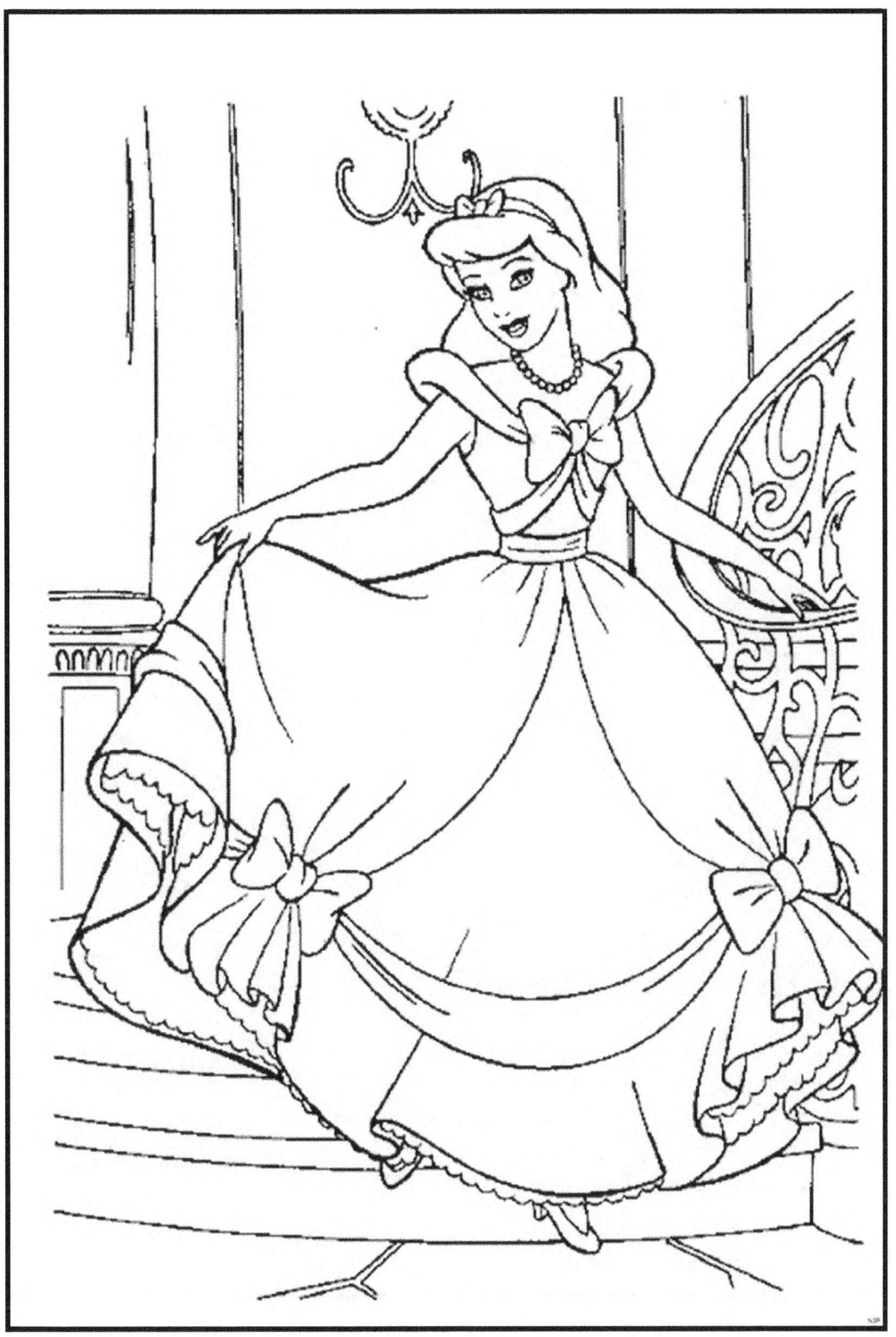

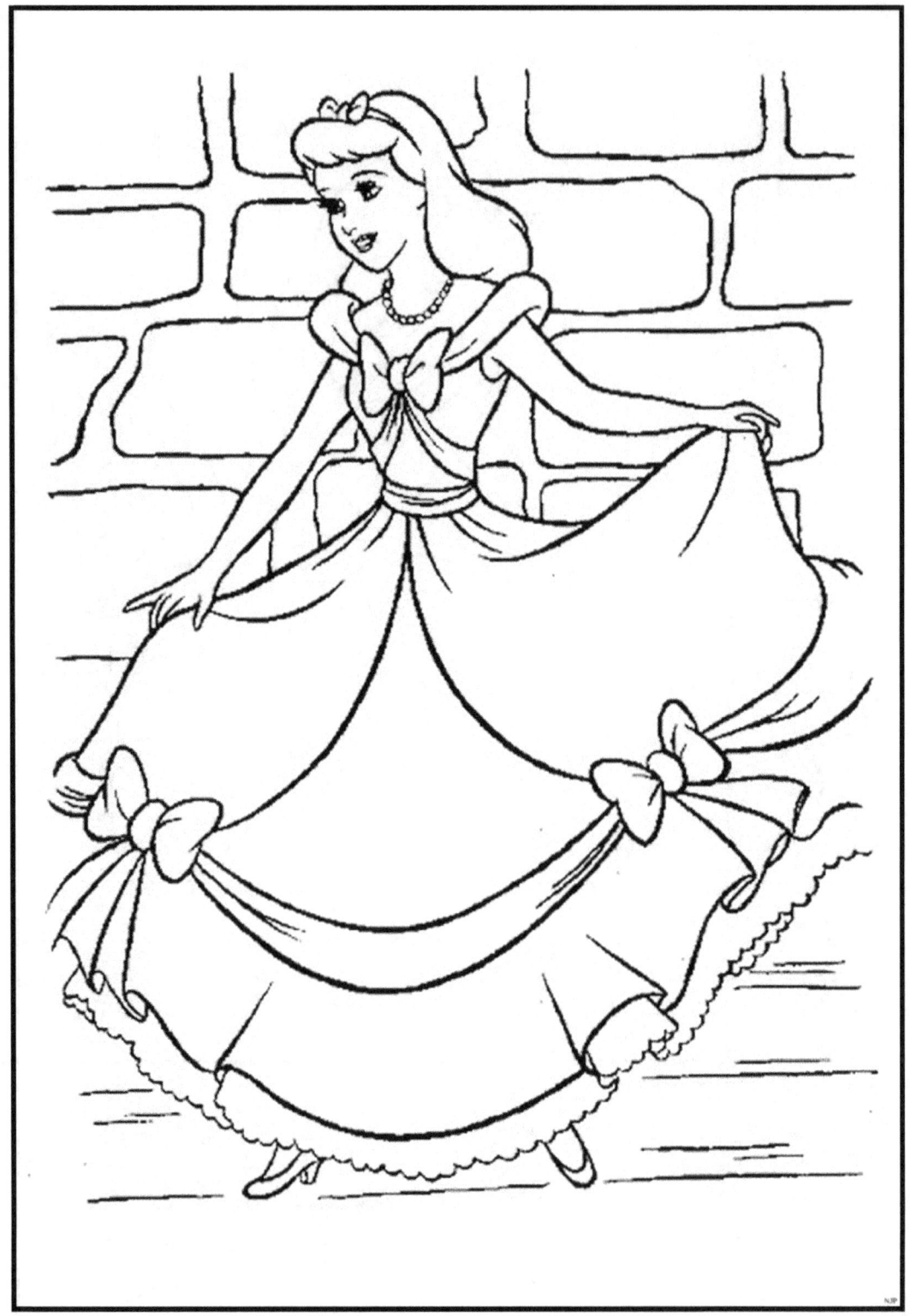

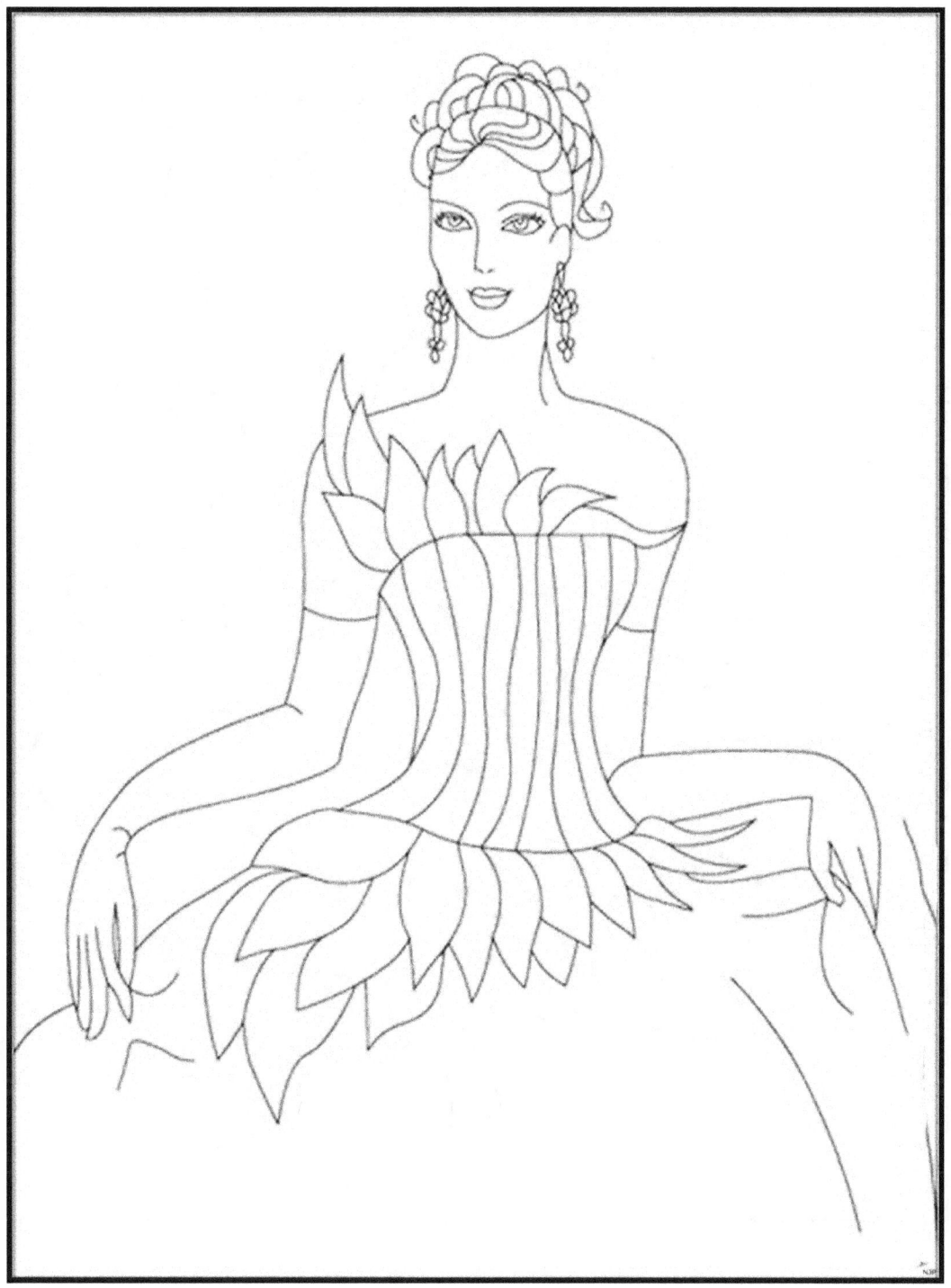

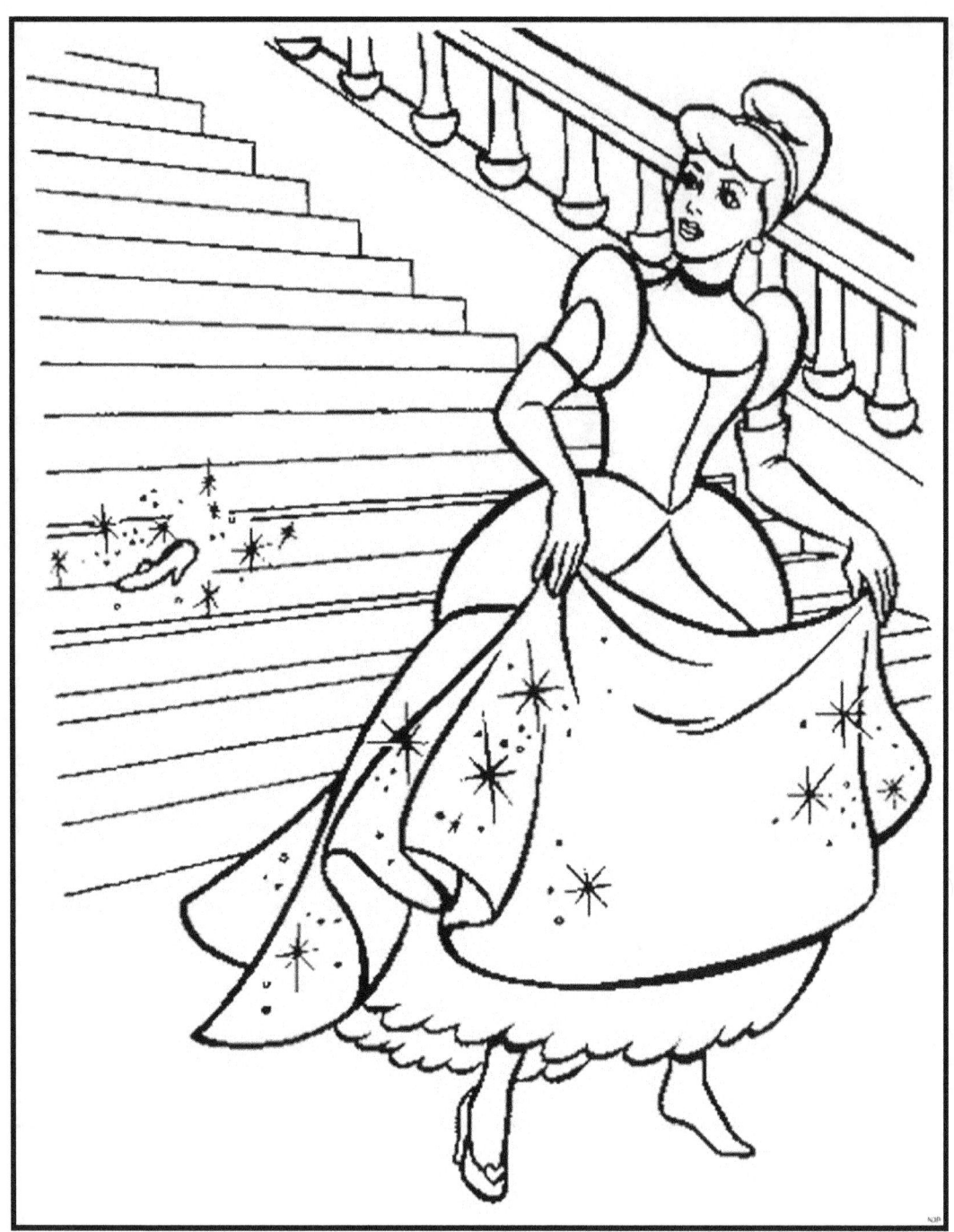

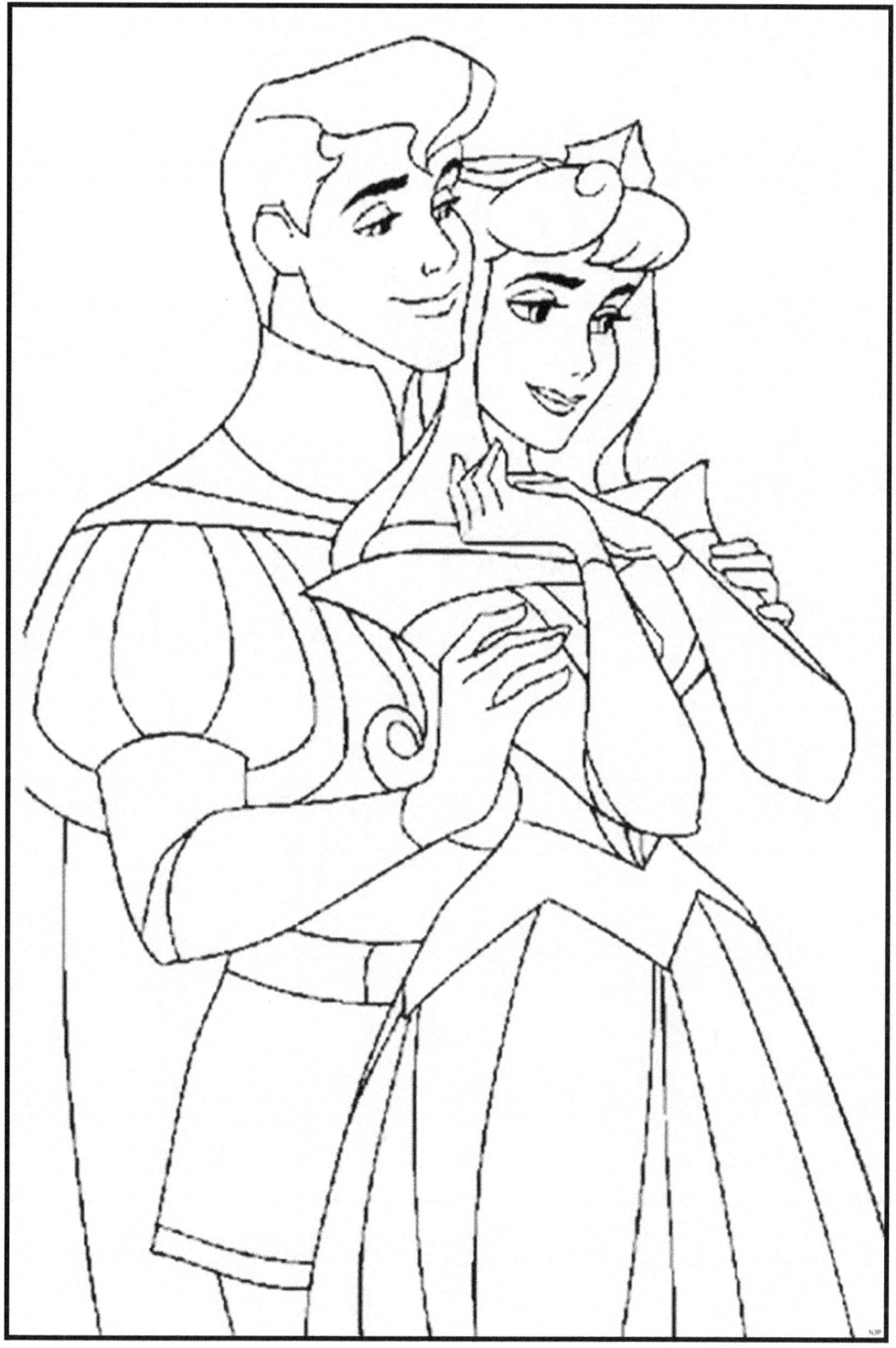

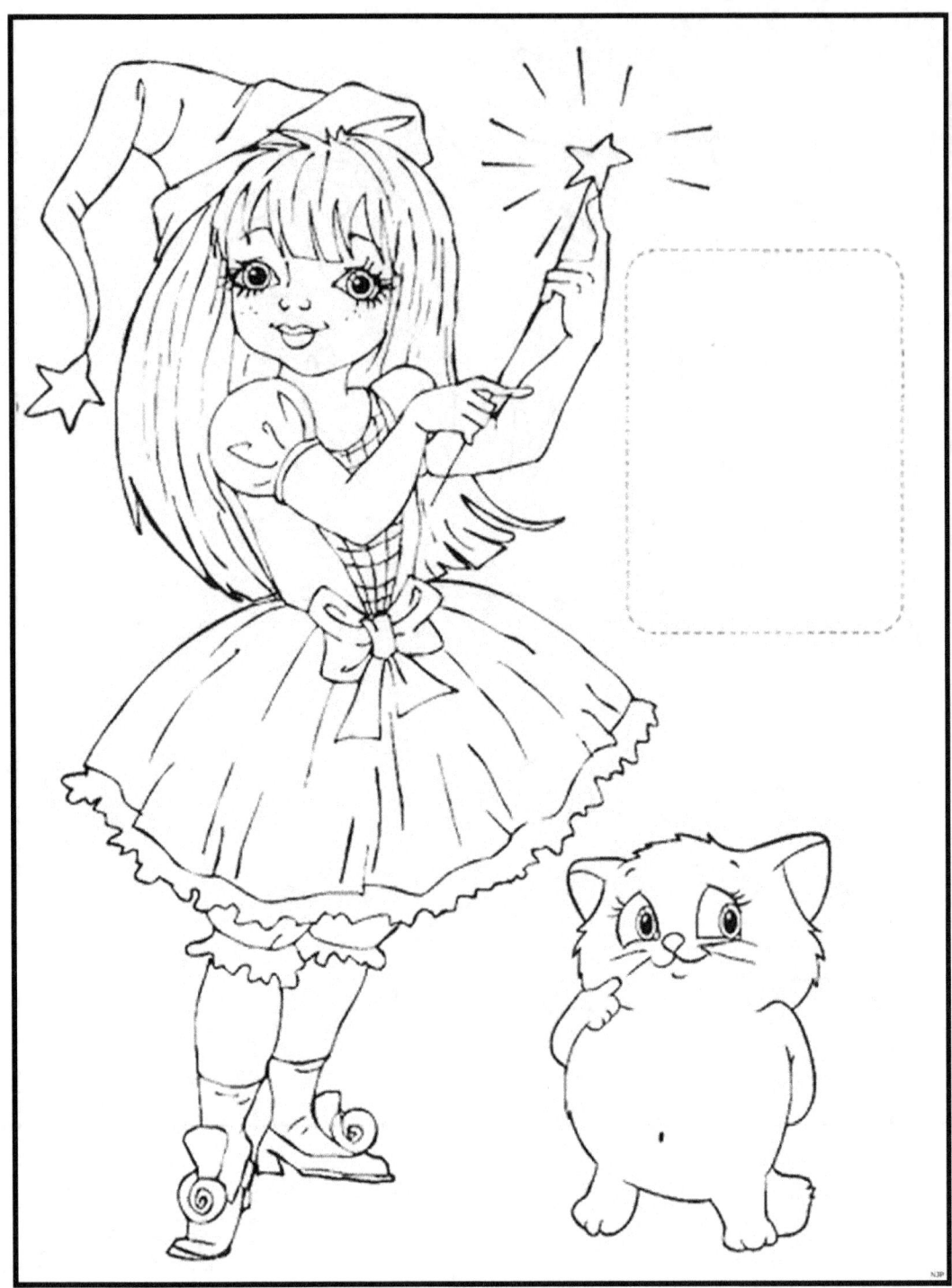

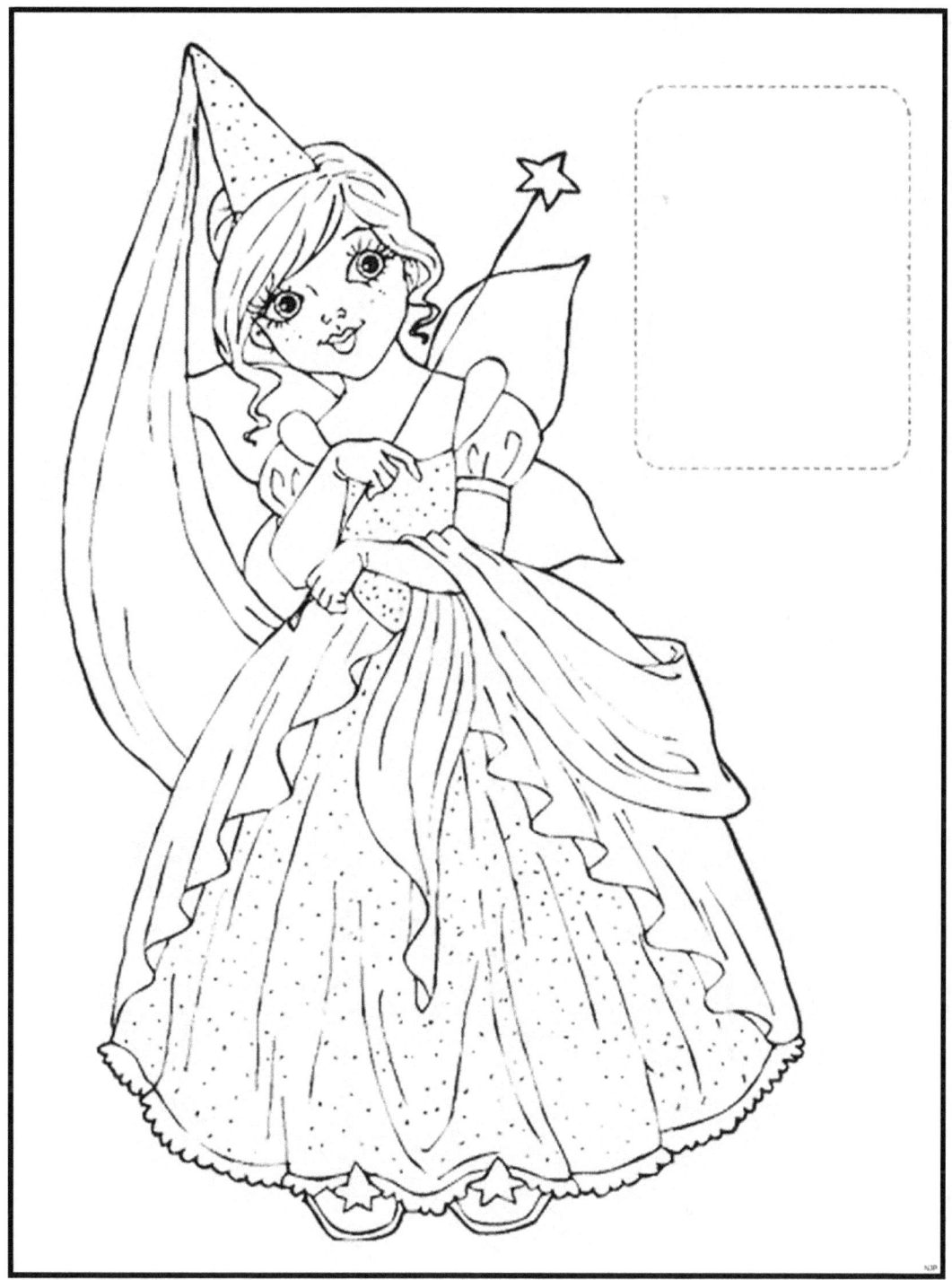

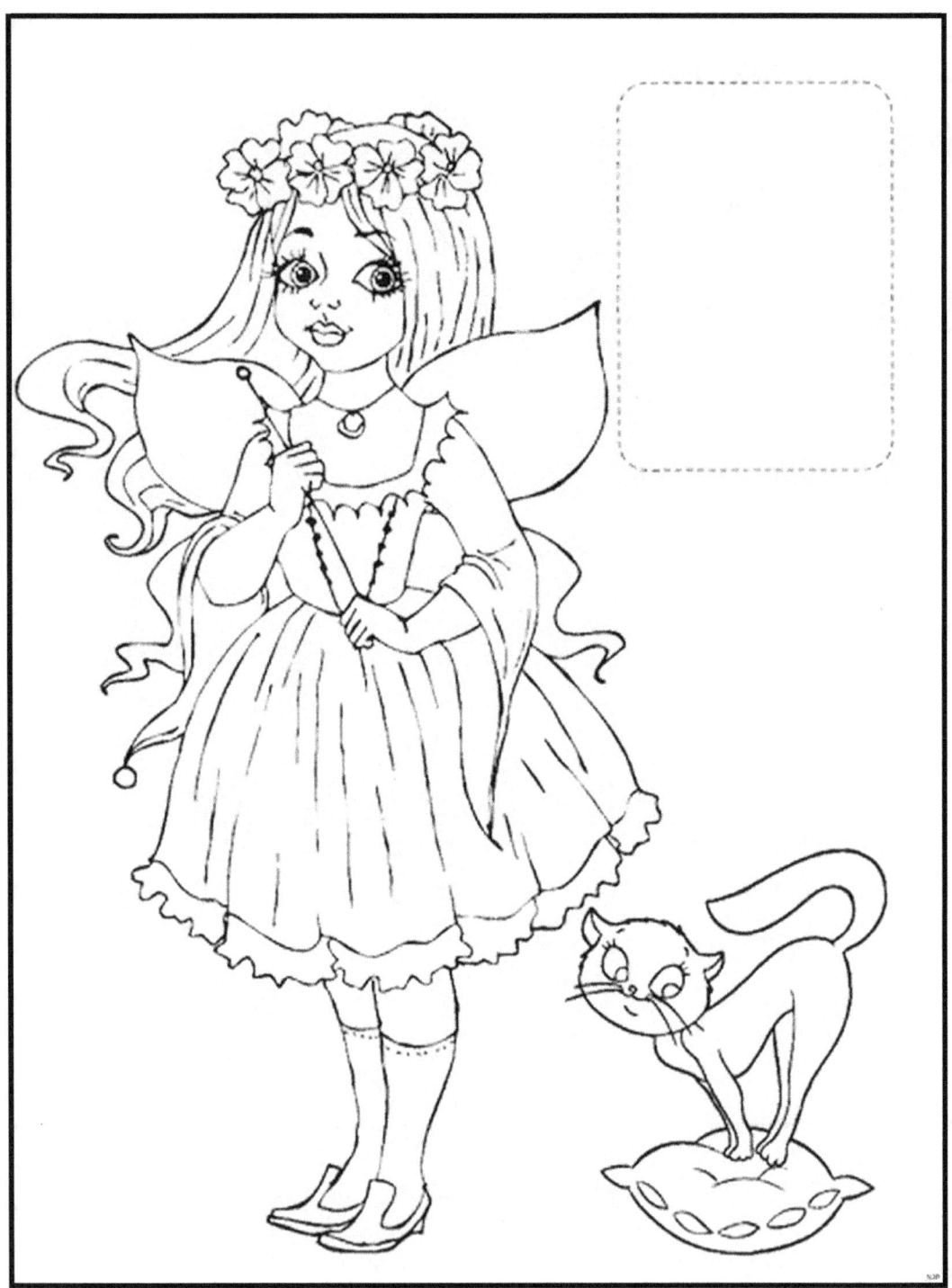

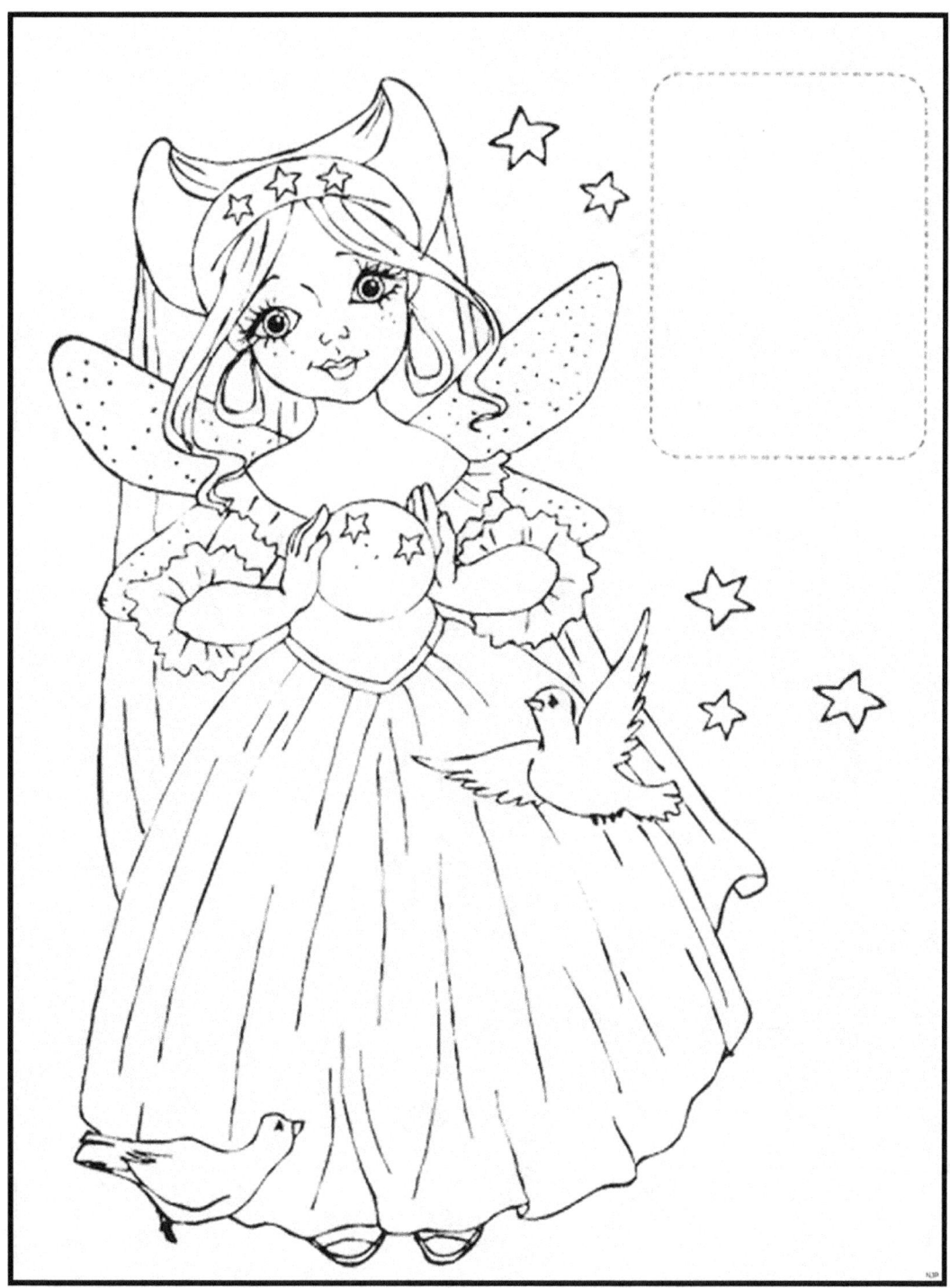

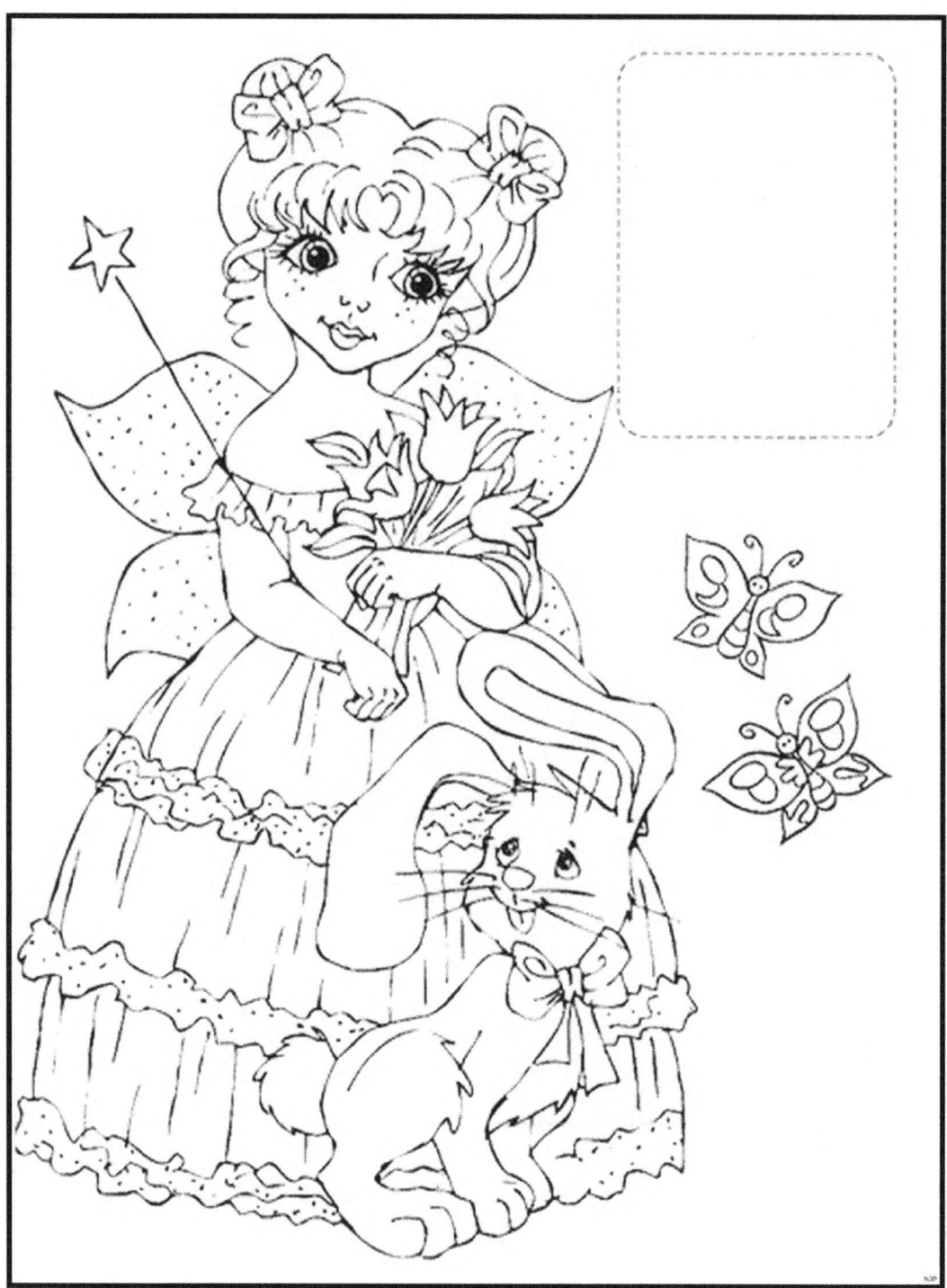

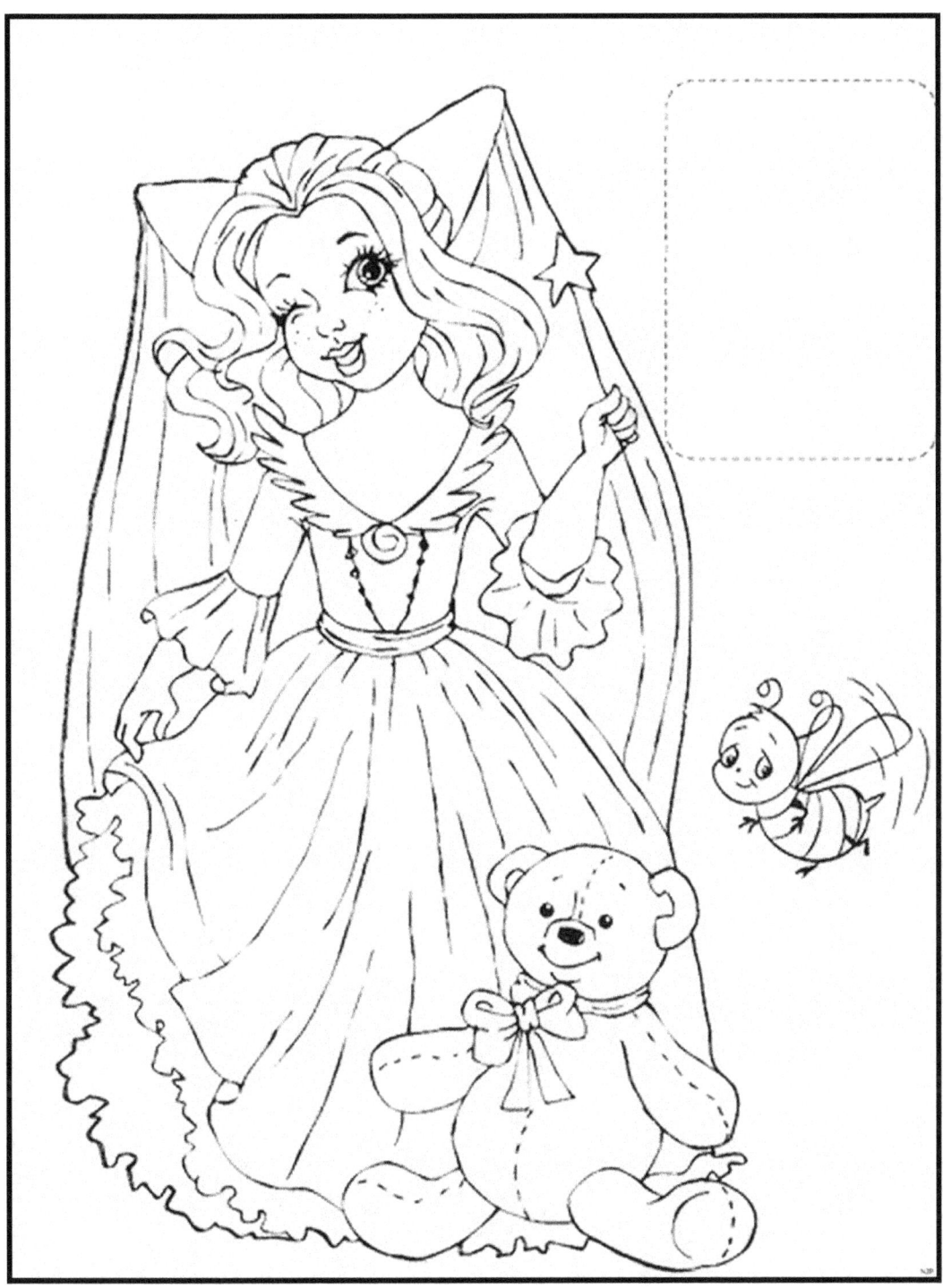

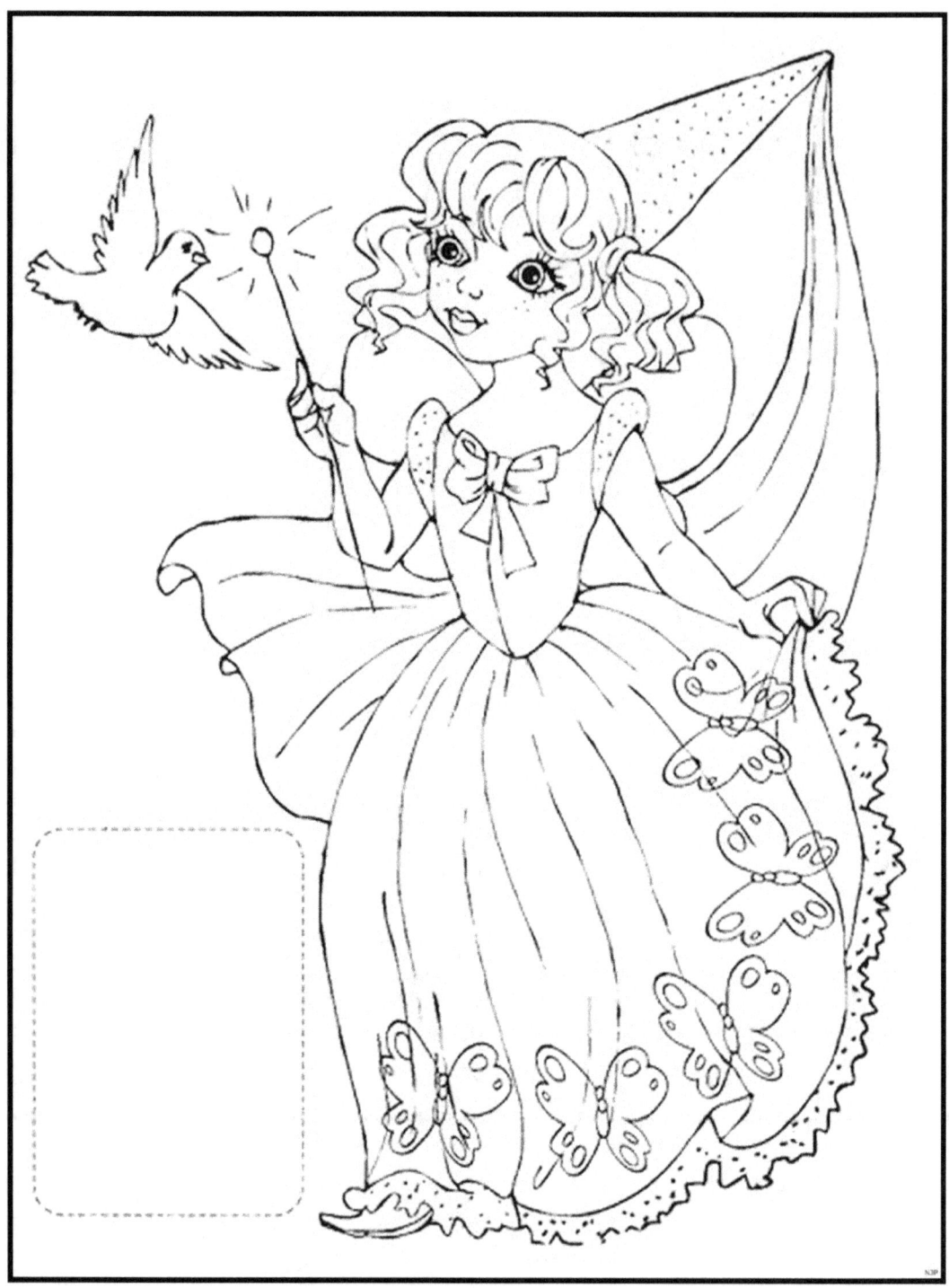

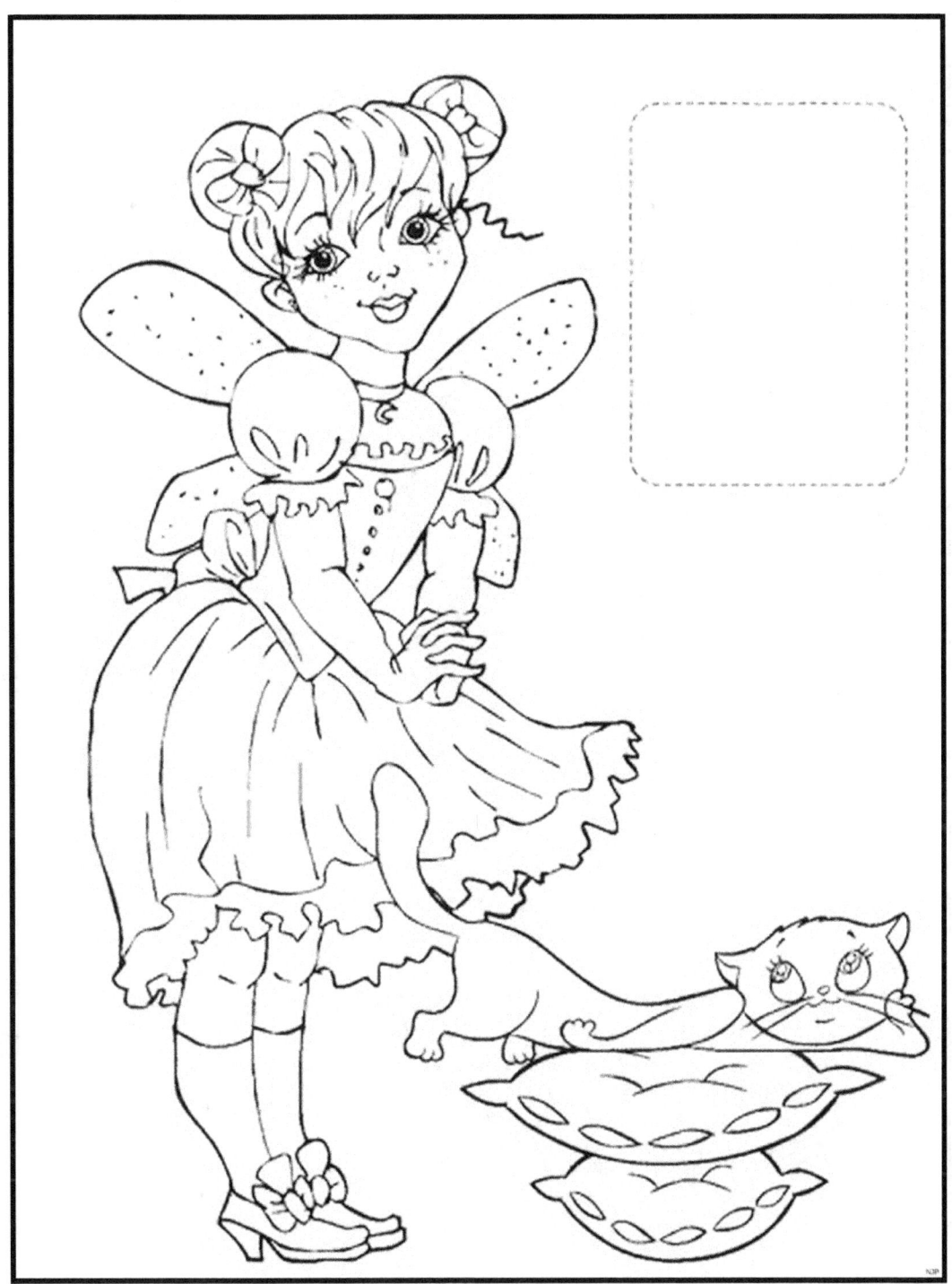

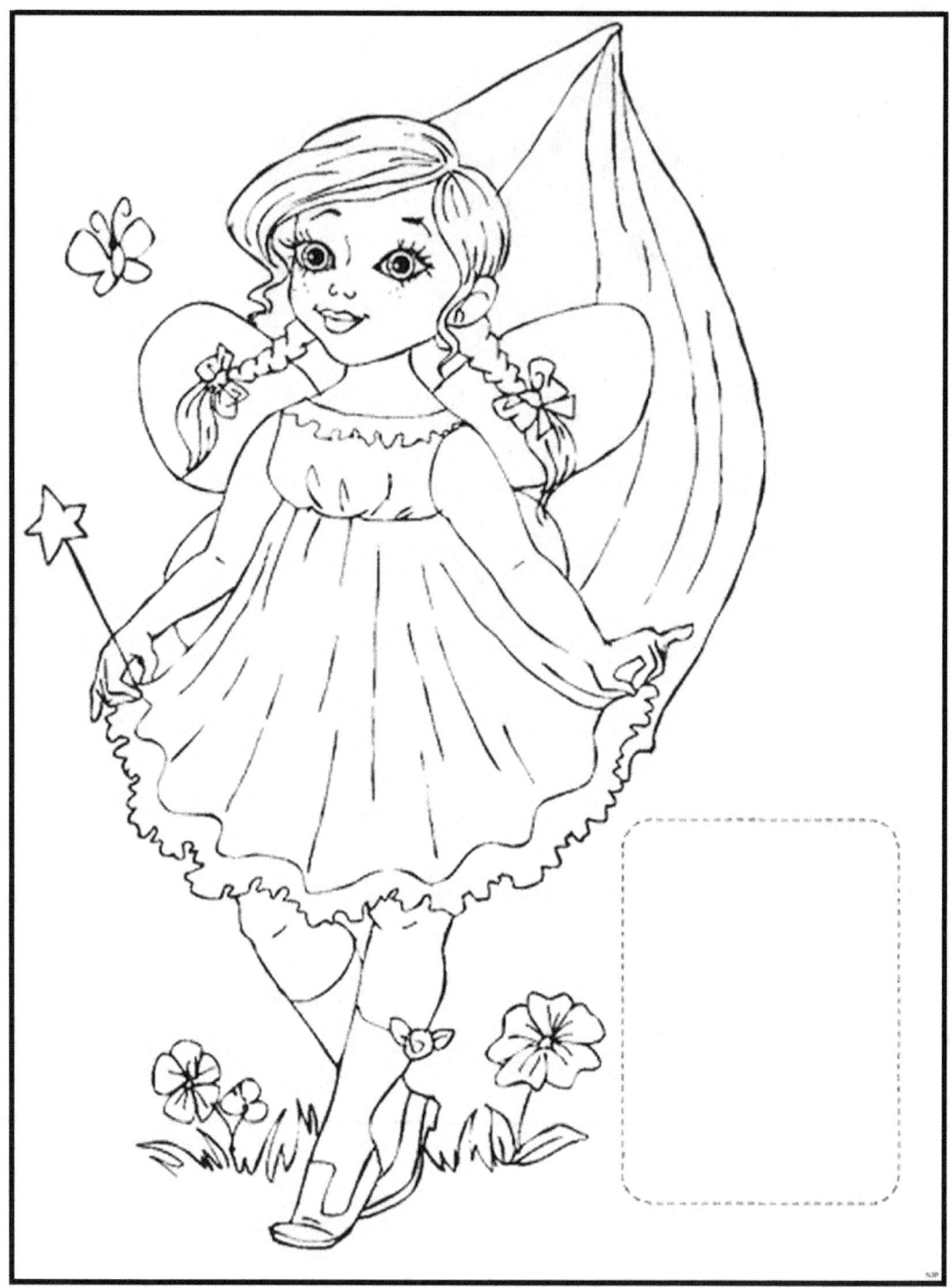

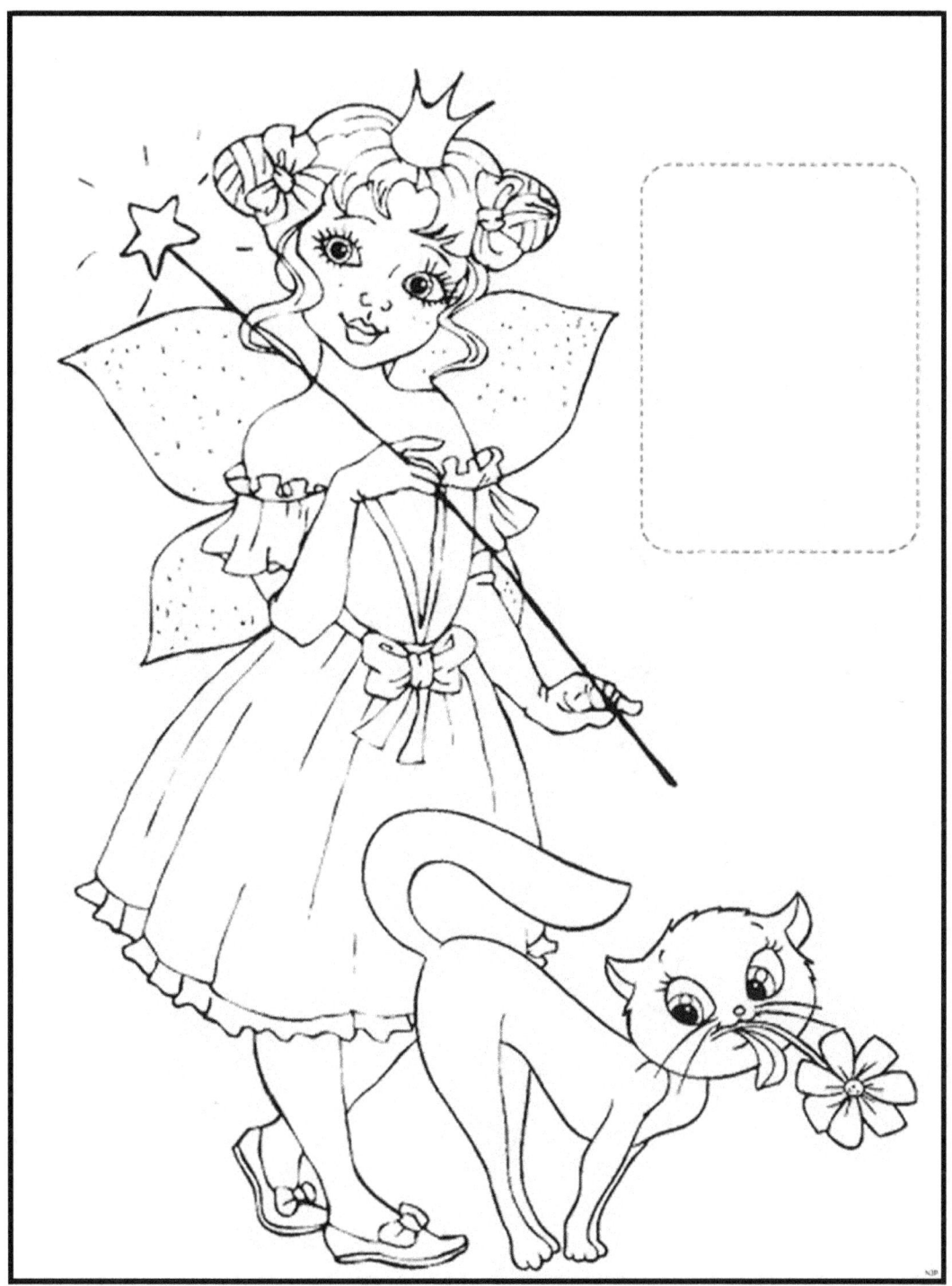

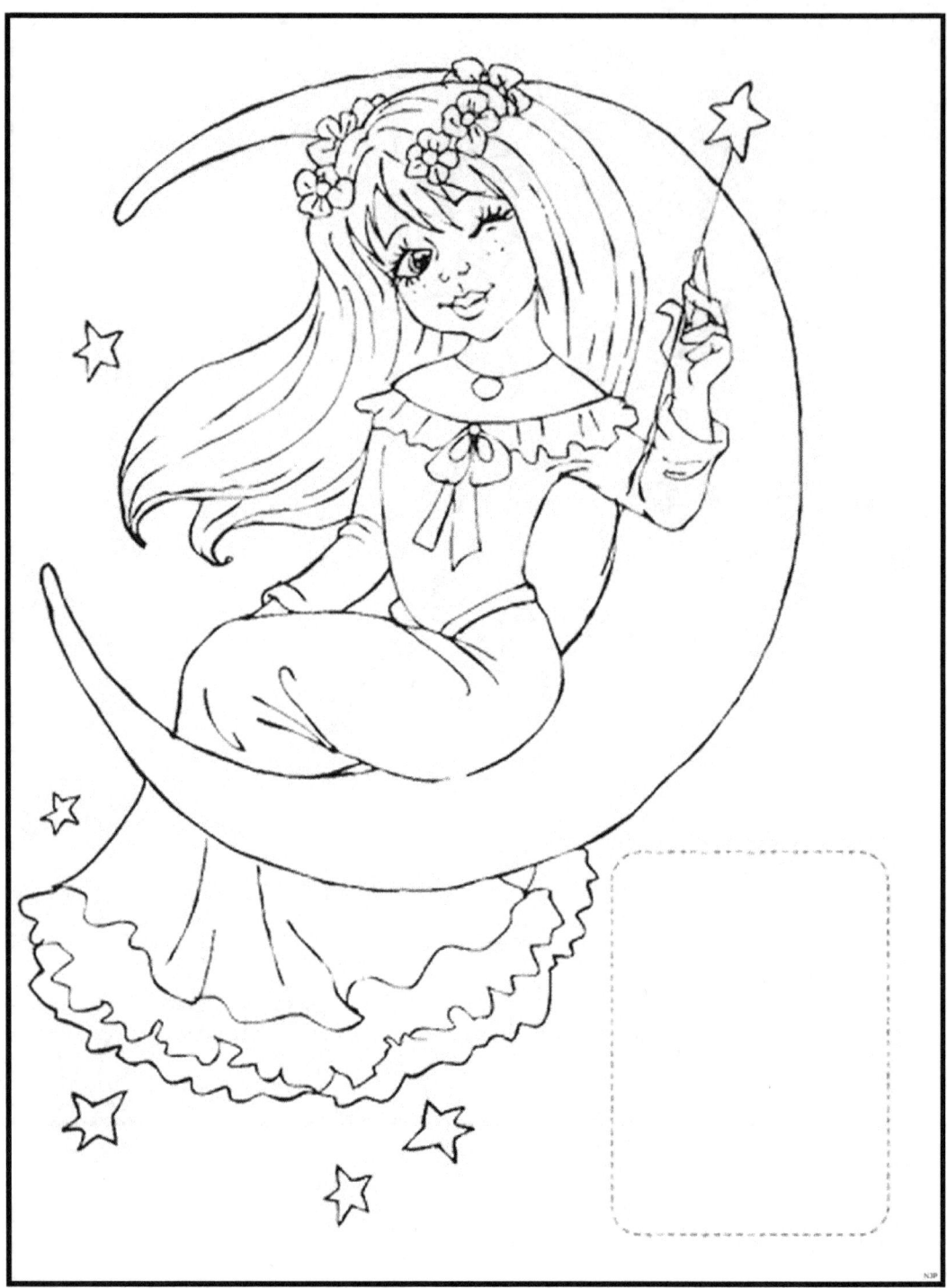

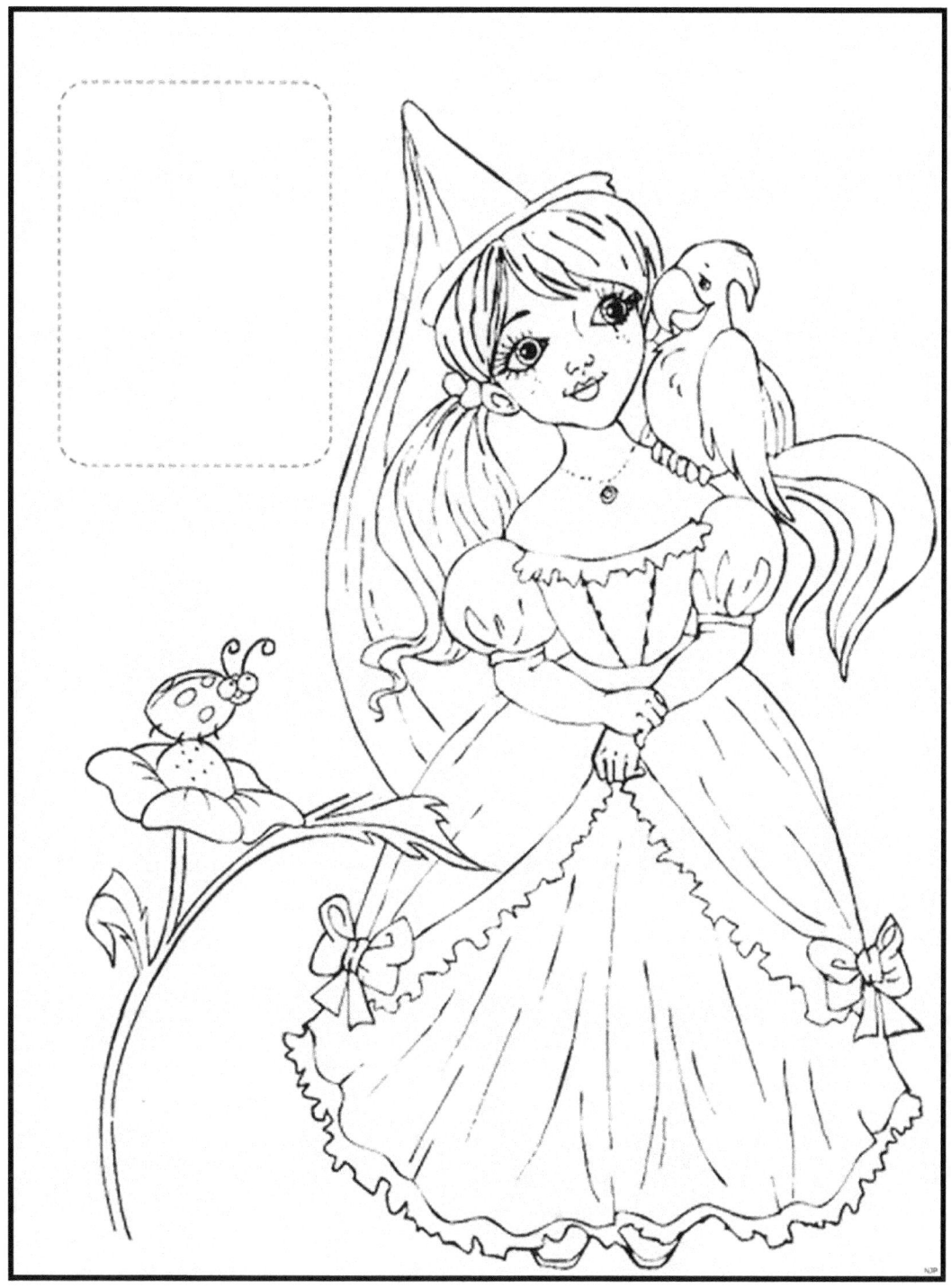

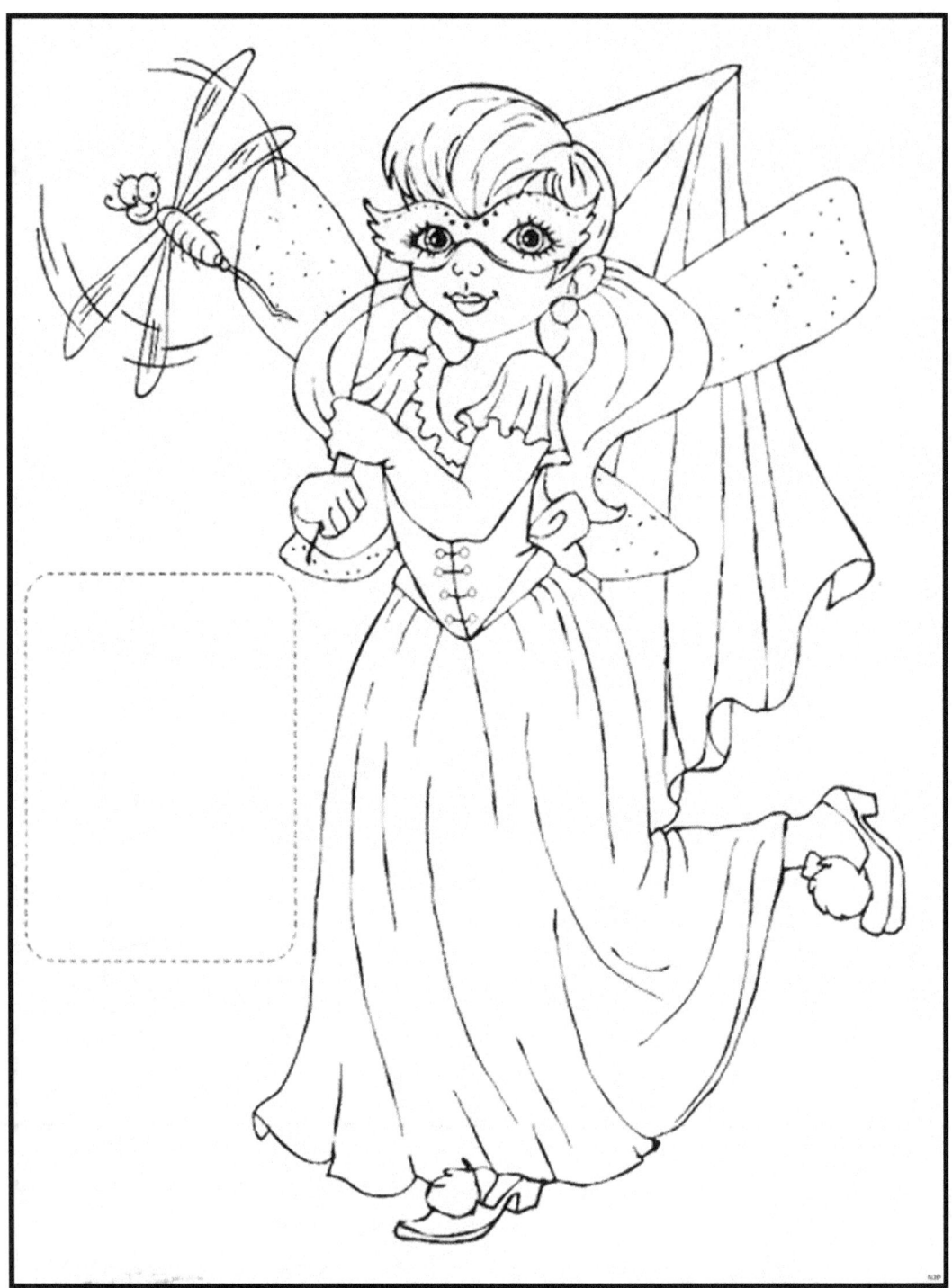

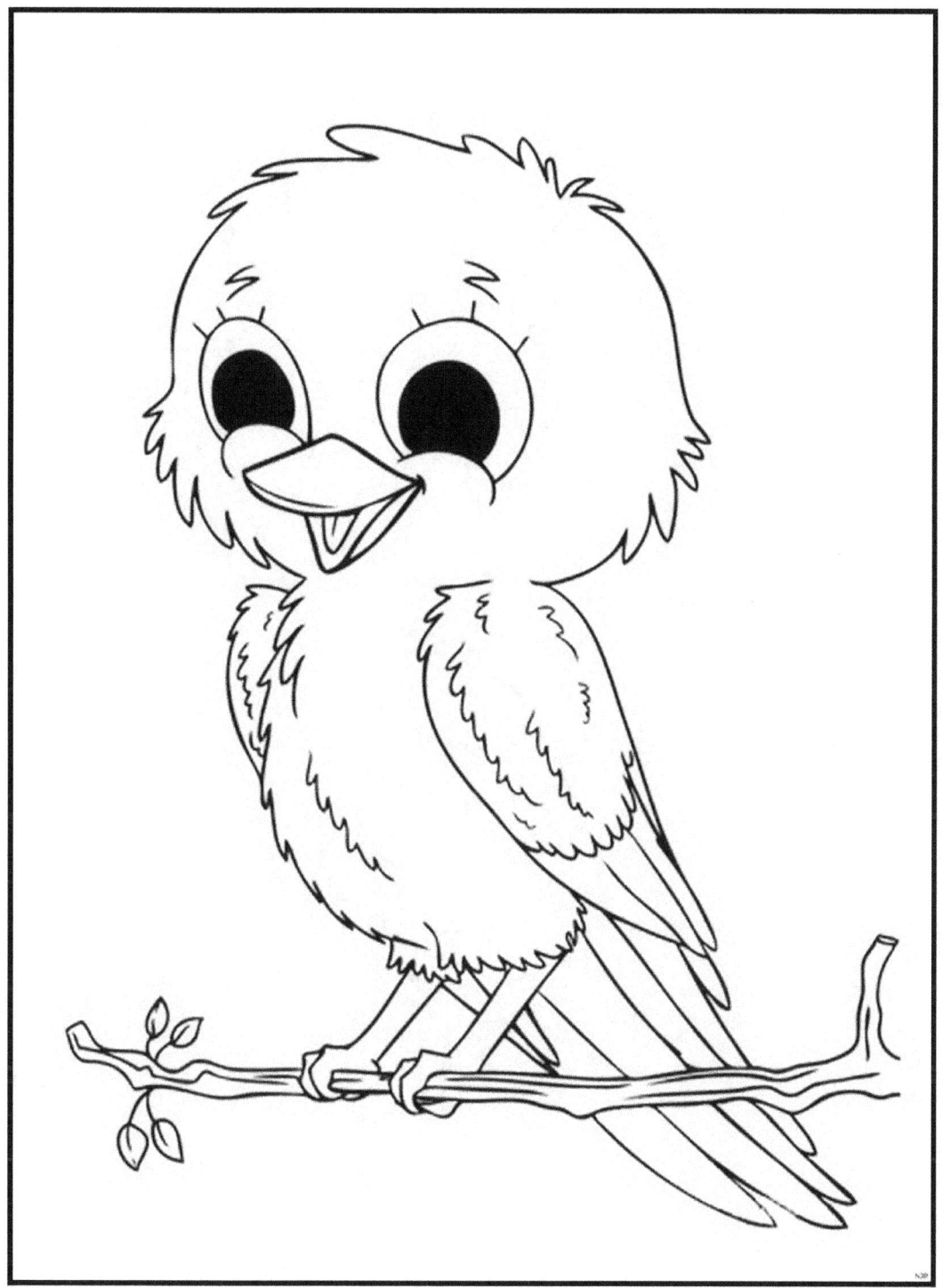

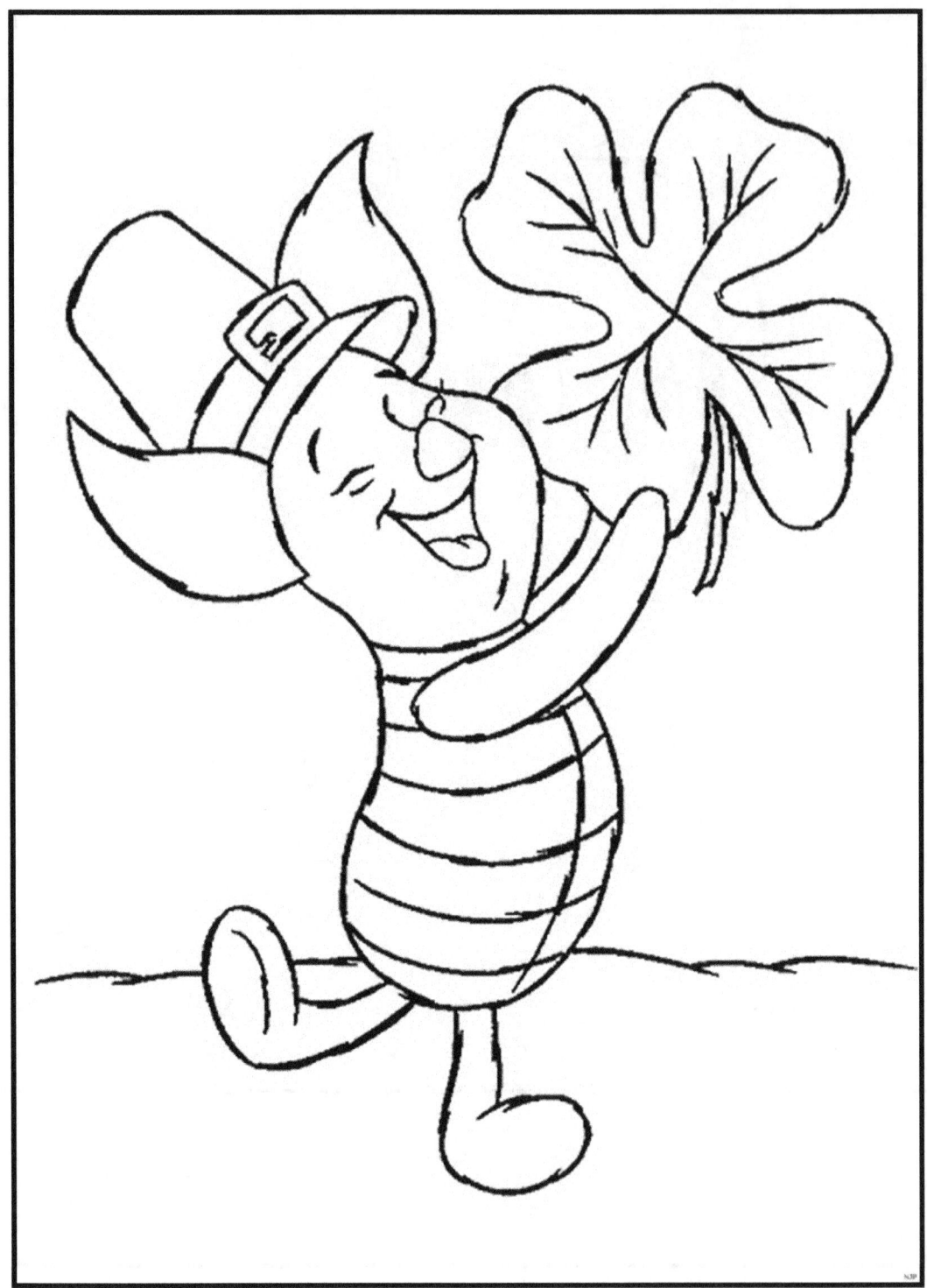

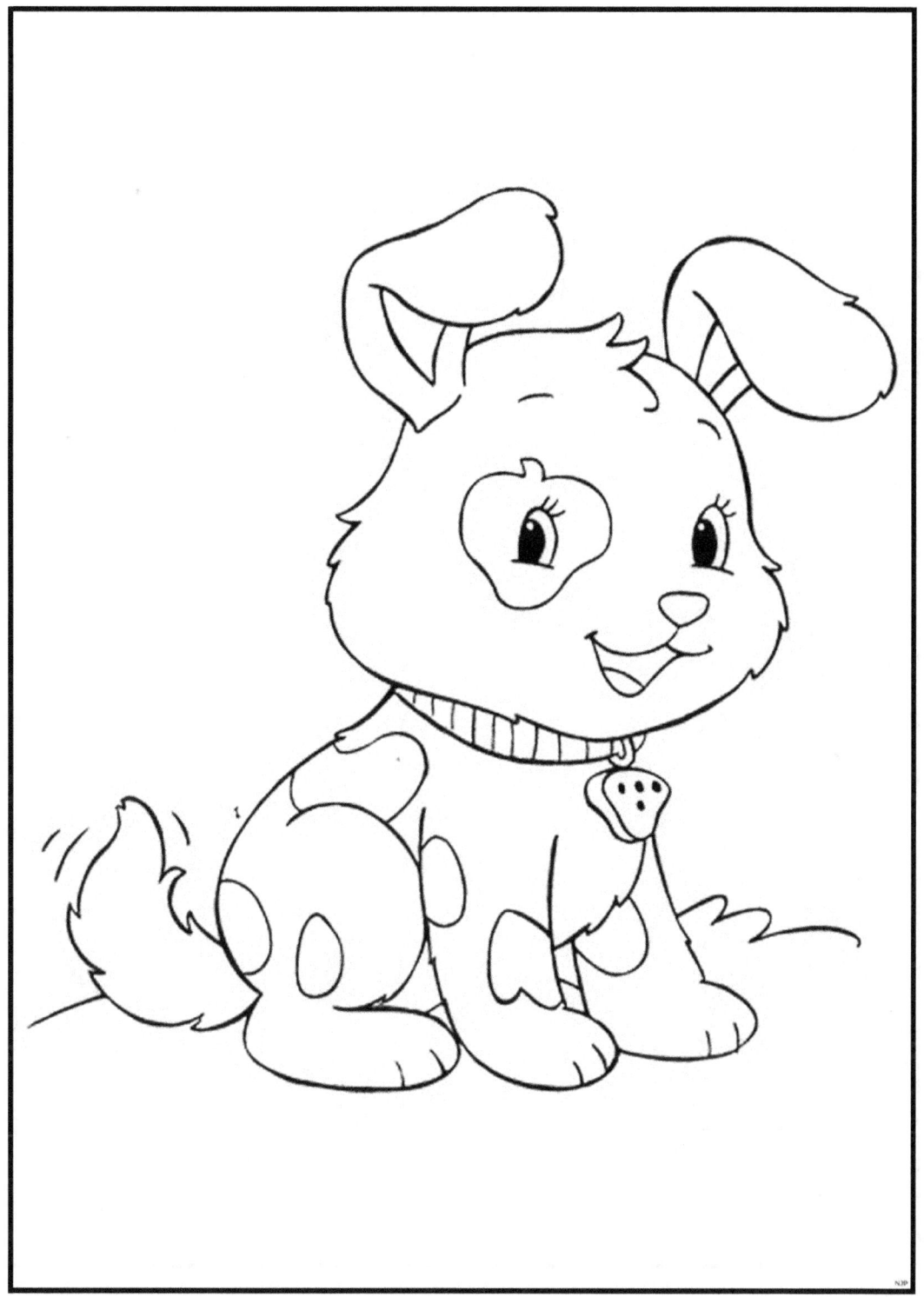

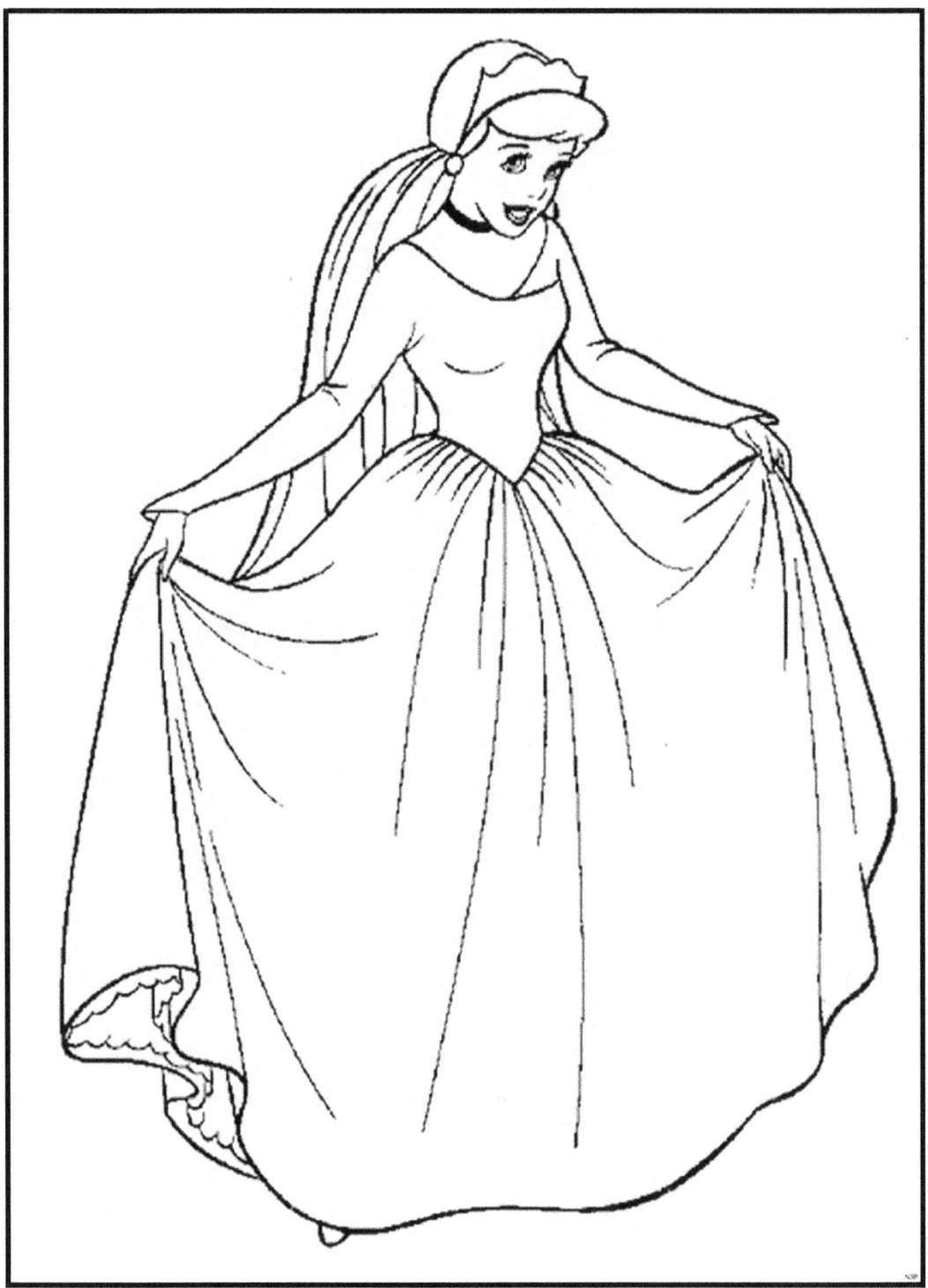

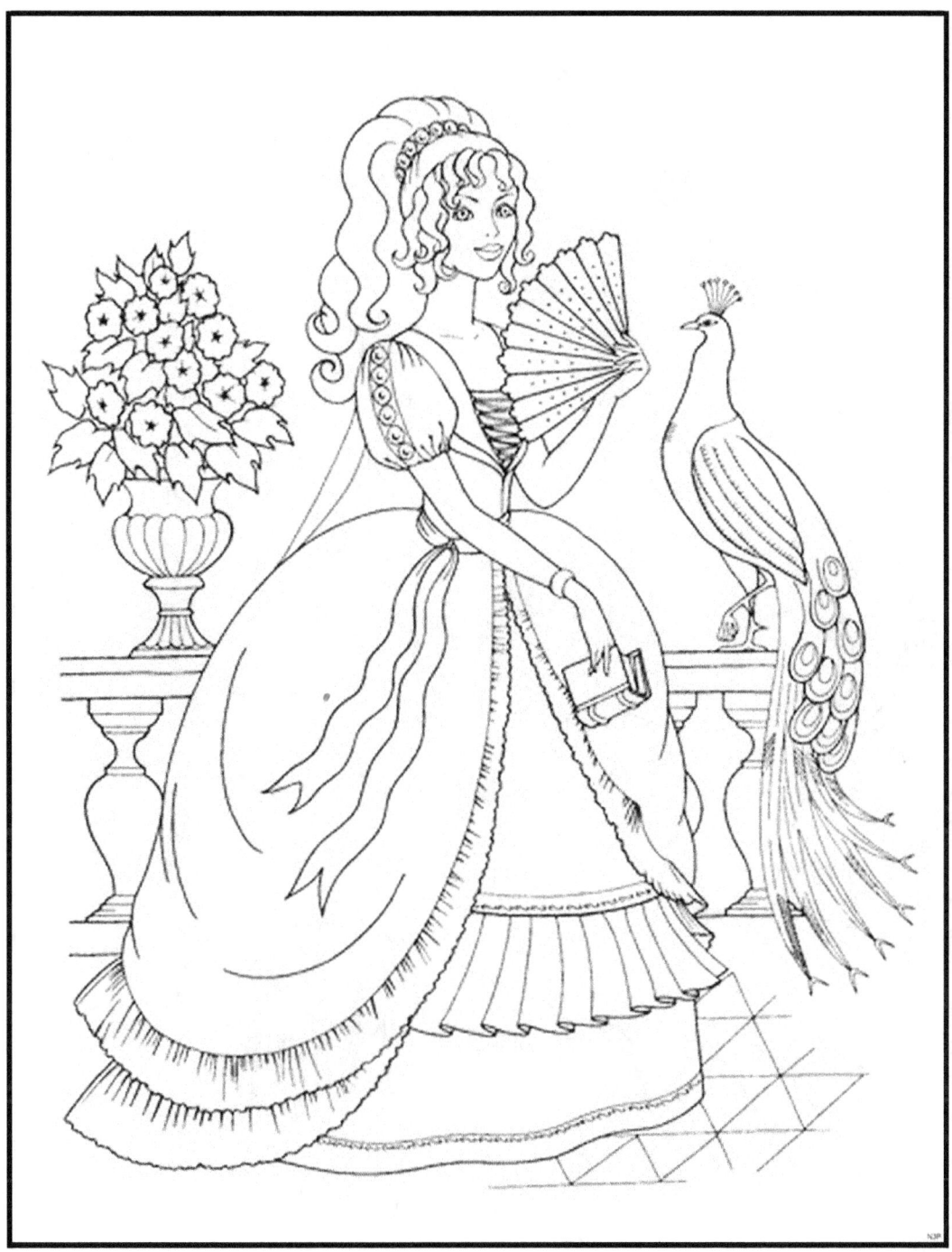

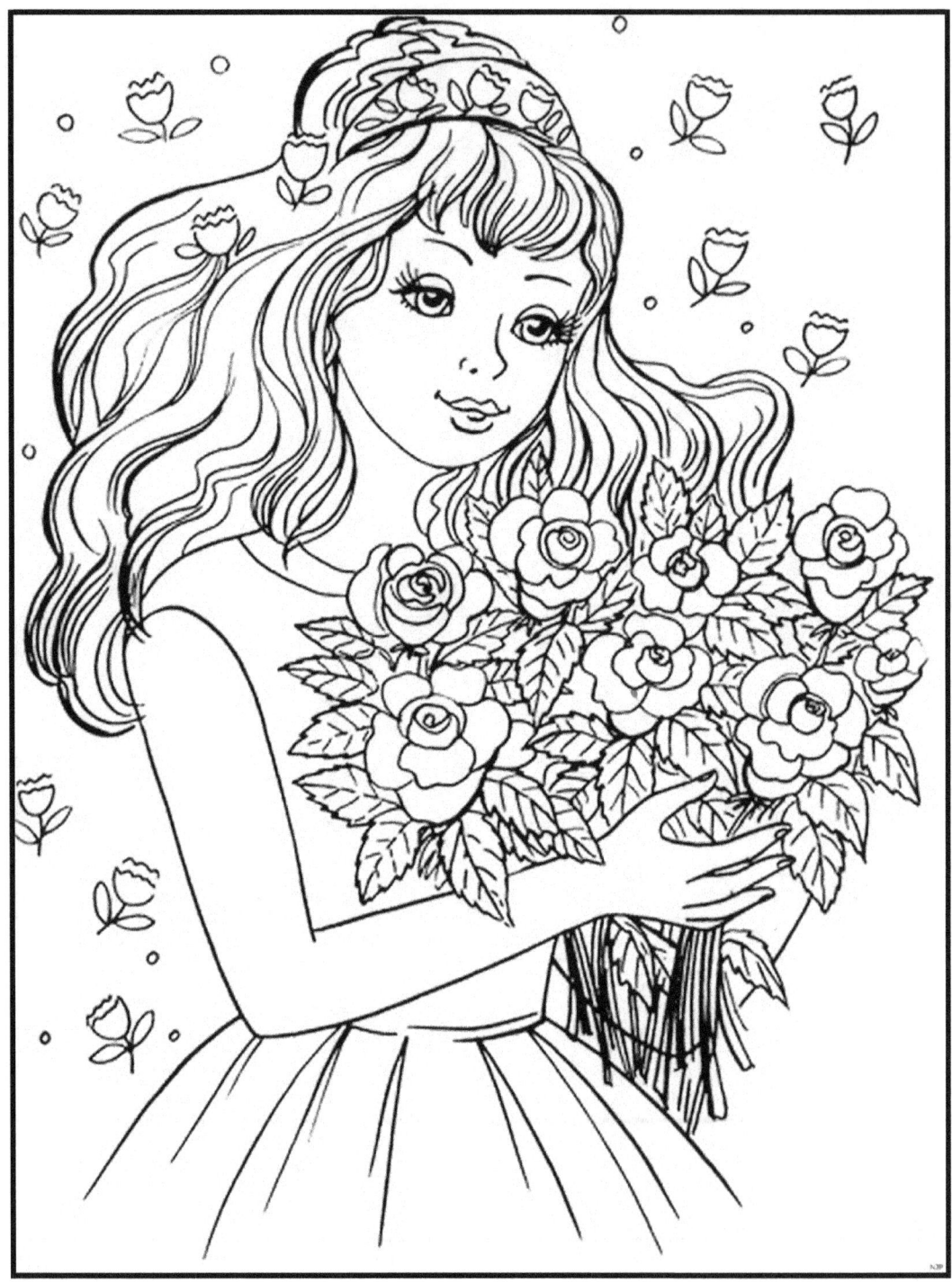

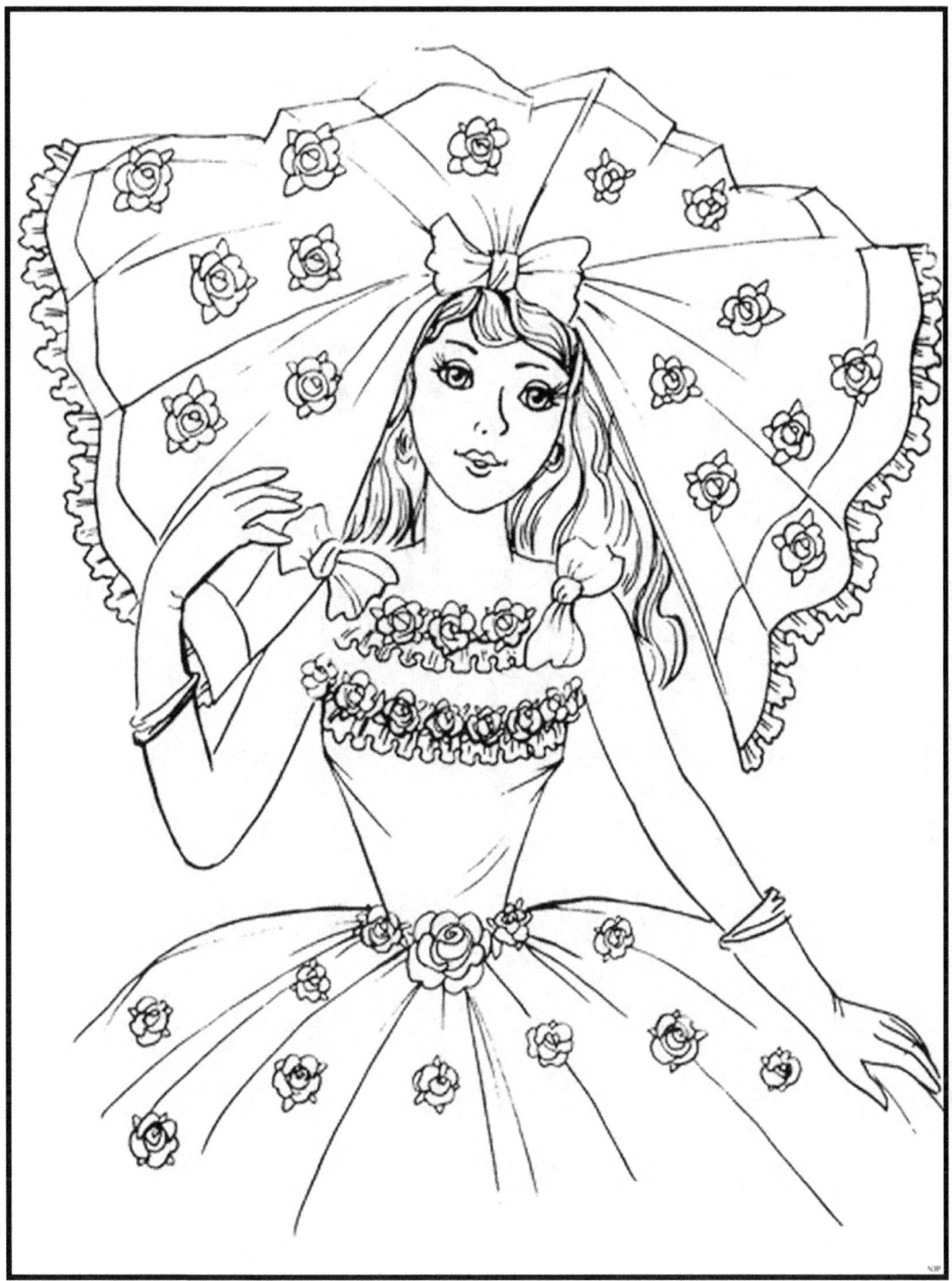

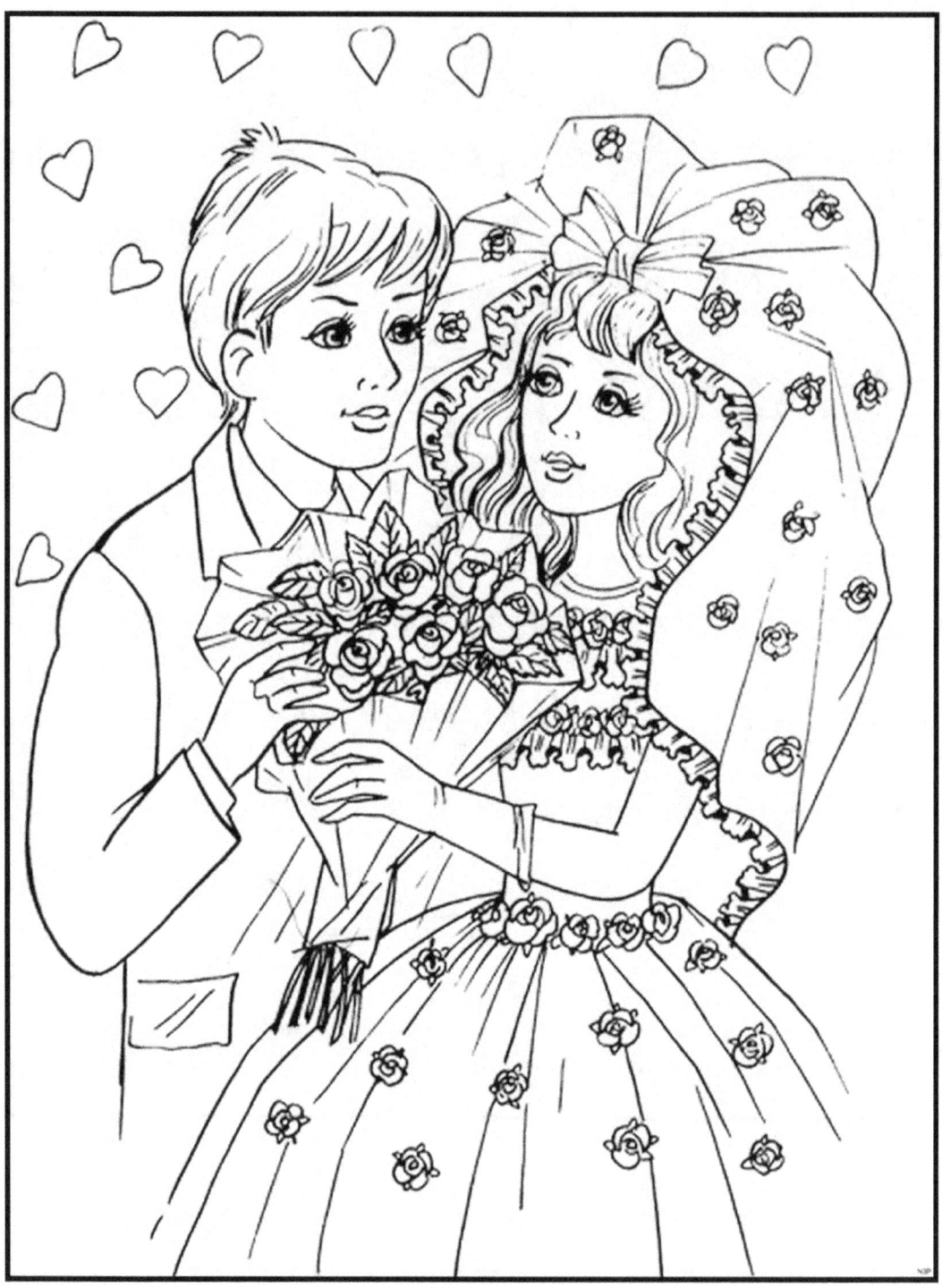

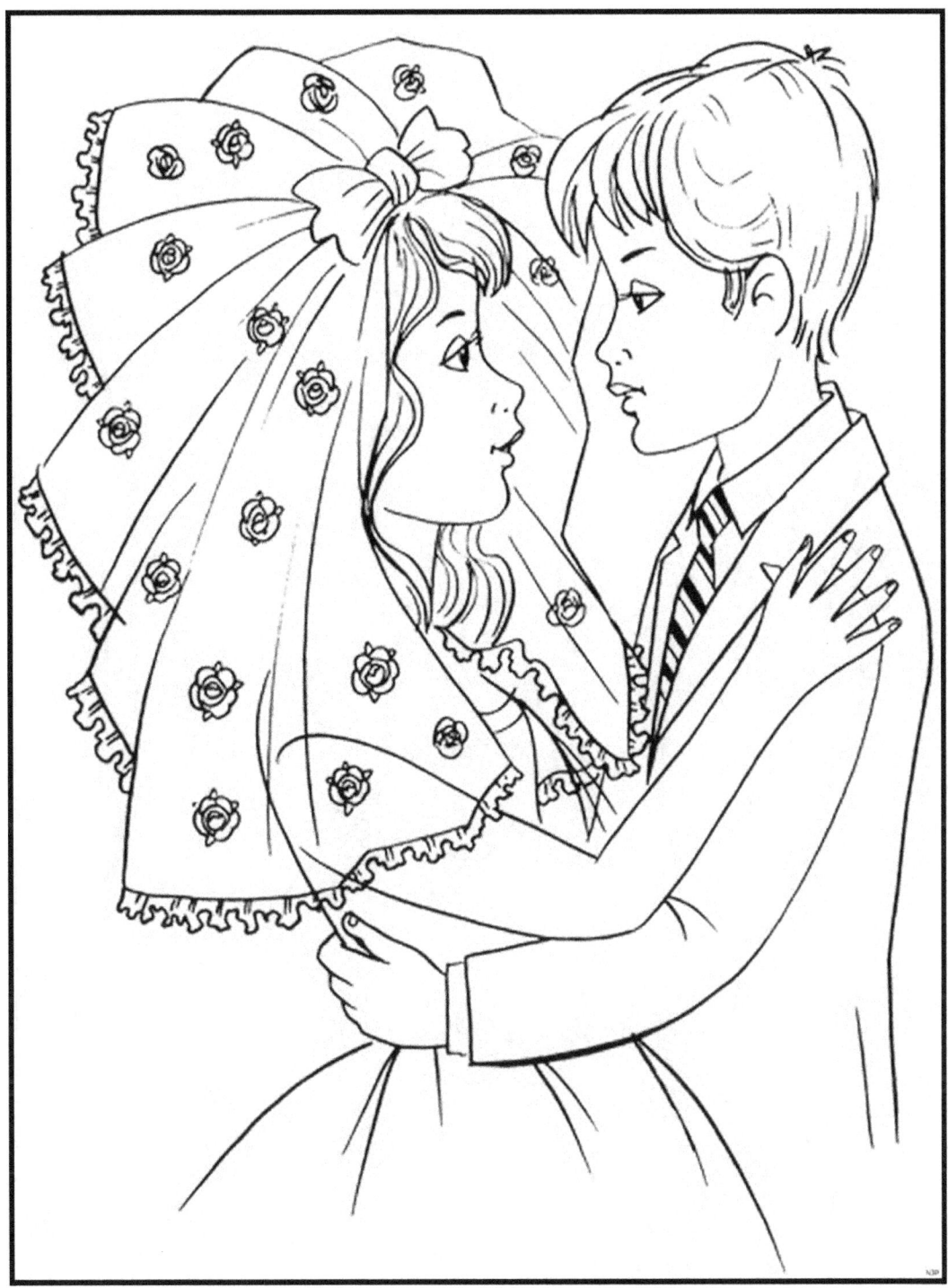

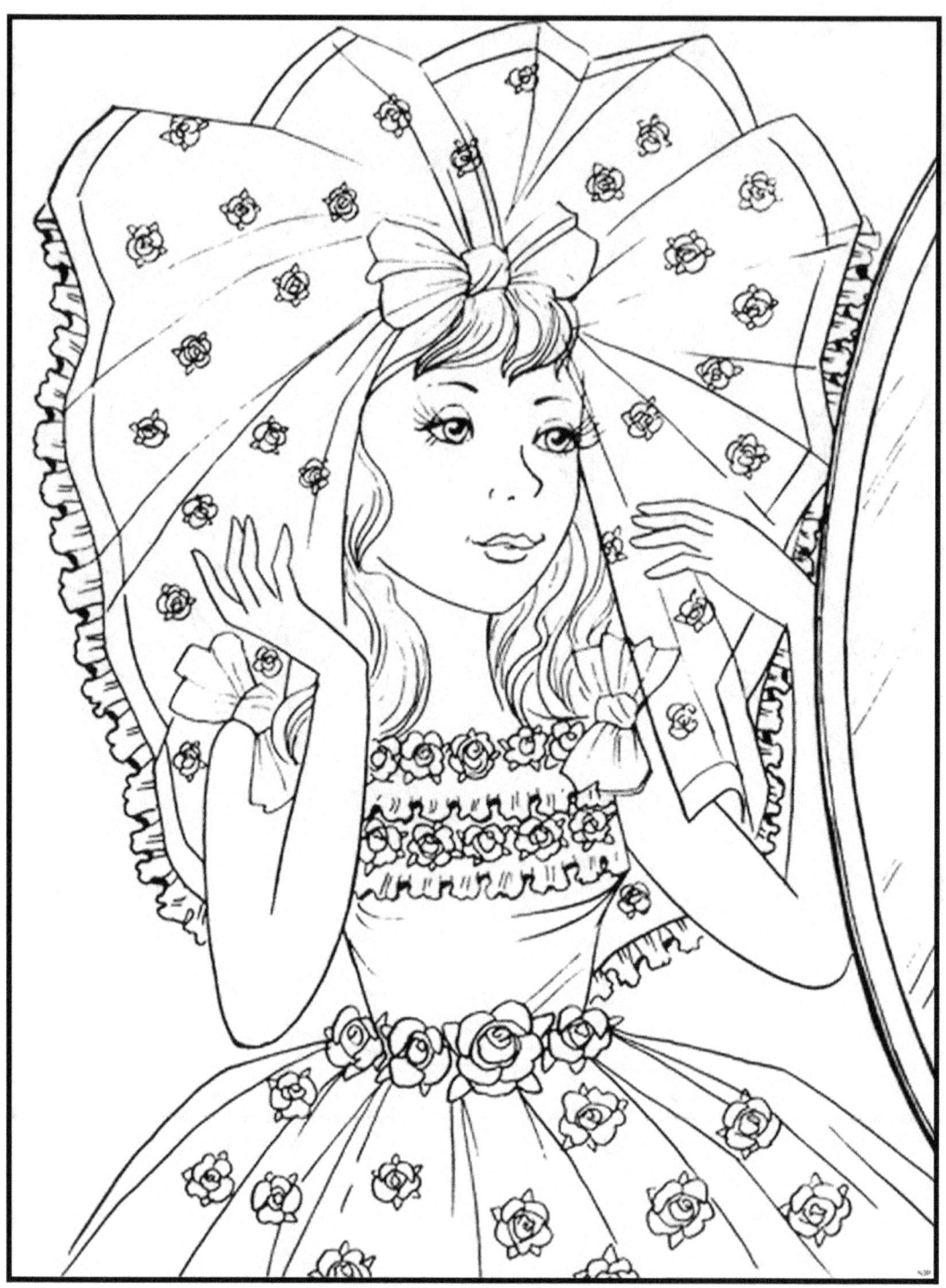

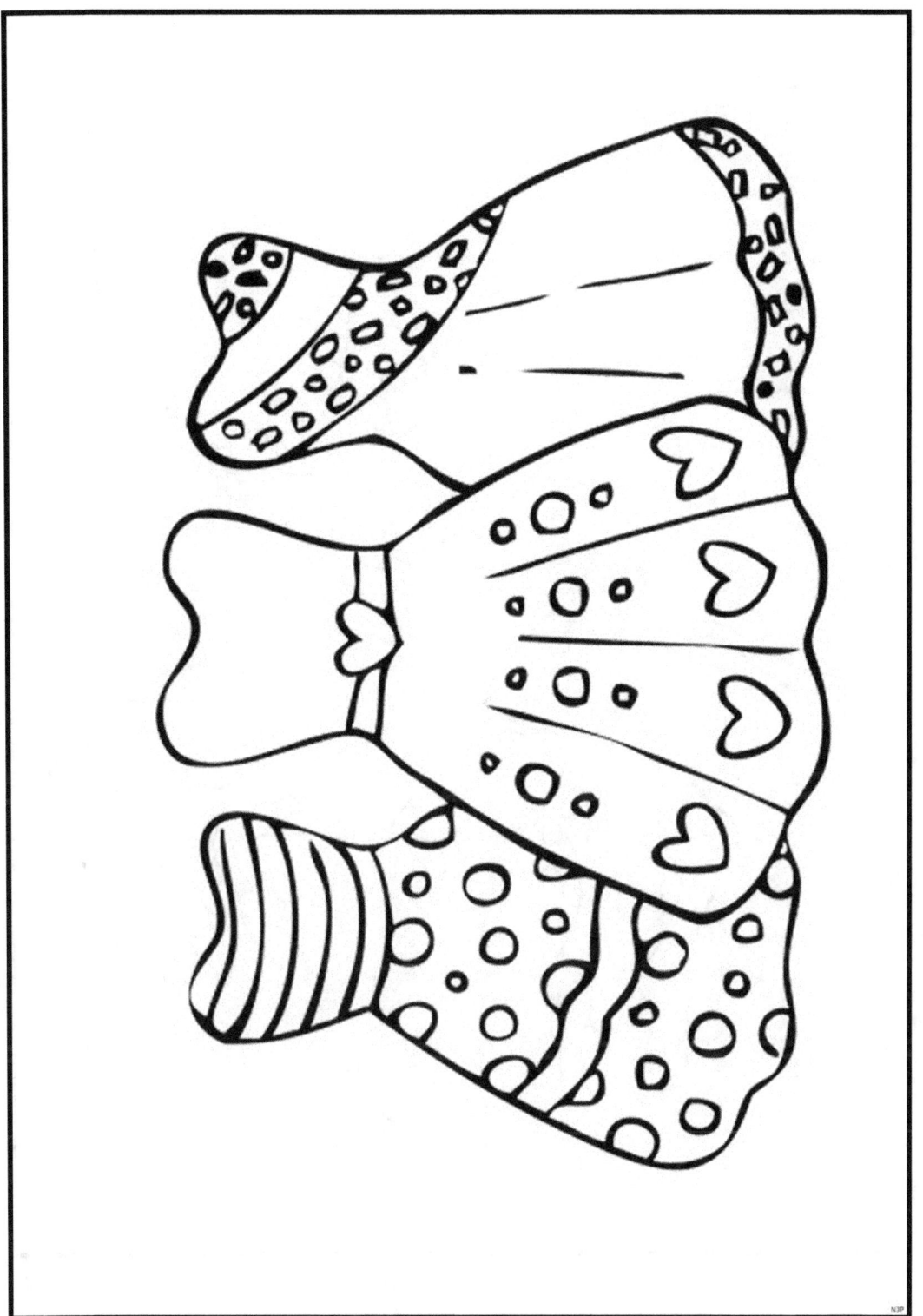

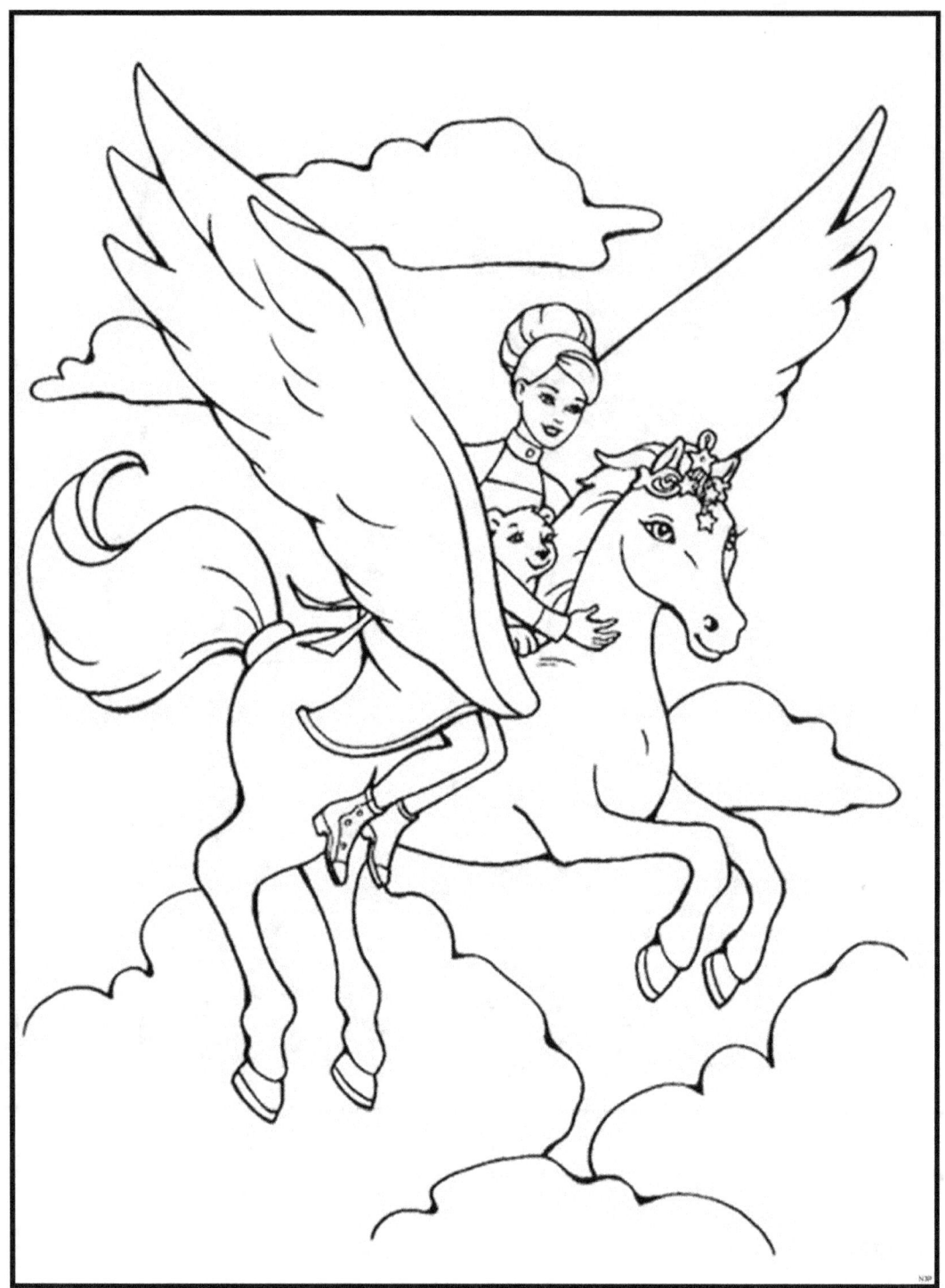

www.ingramcontent.com/pod-product-compliance
Lightning Source LLC
Chambersburg PA
CBHW080705190526
45169CB00006B/2247